WALKING THE WATERSHED

The Border to Cape Wrath along Scotland's Great Divide

by DAVE HEWITT

Illustrated by CHRIS TYLER

TACit Press

First published June 1994 by **TACit Press**:
House 48, 170 Sandiefield Road, Glasgow G5 0DL

ISBN 0 9522680 1 9

Printed and bound by Clydeside Press:
37 High Street, Glasgow

Thanks to
Mags, Grant,
Alan and Julia
for proofreading

for Warbeck
and for Mags

Now the geography was becoming clear, my knowledge becoming connected and I was seeing the relation of these mountains to each other...
With each new view, the pattern had grown inside me. Now the framework was there, and I would spend a lifetime filling in the gaps. These mountains would always be a part of my life.

Peter Boardman
Sacred Summits

The rivers in the distance
must be leading somewhere...

The Blue Nile
Heatwave

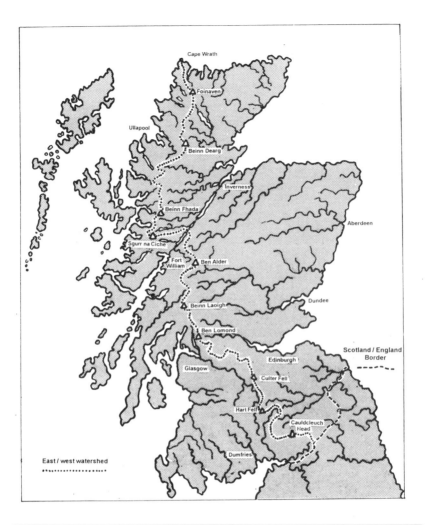

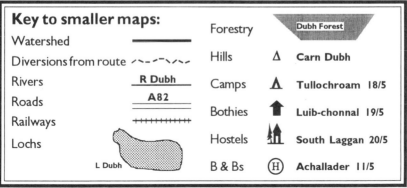

Key to smaller maps:

Watershed	———————	
Diversions from route	⌒~-⌒~⌒~	
Rivers	**R Dubh**	
Roads	**A82**	
Railways	++++++++++++	
Lochs		L Dubh

Forestry		**Dubh Forest**
Hills	△	**Carn Dubh**
Camps	▲	**Tullochroam 18/5**
Bothies	⬆	**Luib-chonnal 19/5**
Hostels	🏠	**South Laggan 20/5**
B & Bs	Ⓗ	**Achallader 11/5**

Cape Wrath

Foinaven

Ullapool

Beinn Dearg

Inverness

Beinn Fhada

Aberdeen

Sgurr na Ciche

Fort William · Ben Alder

Dundee

Beinn Laoigh

Ben Lomond

Scotland / England Border

Edinburgh

Glasgow

Culter Fell

Hart Fell

Cauldcleuch Head

East / west watershed

Dumfries

Acknowledgements

From first conceiving the idea to walk the watershed, to finally completing this manuscript, has taken seven-and-a-half years. It is therefore hardly surprising that large dollops of help and support need acknowledged.

Several people involved in the walk have hardly been seen or heard from since. A good few more who didn't know me when I had a rucksack on my back became firm friends in later years when a computer keyboard was rarely far from my fingertips. Many have been on hand throughout. Hopefully the following list will serve to reinforce the extent to which I was merely the front end of a very large operation.

But before rattling through the full supporting cast, special mention must be made of several star performers.

It was vital, both to safety and efficiency, that logistics were centralised - and Julia and John Bowditch operated a faultless base camp during the walk. No arrangements ever fell through, nothing ever went astray - plus of course they displayed utmost devotion by uncomplainingly washing my putrid socks.

If Julia and John undertook a marathon task, Sarah Craig and Michael Wright twice went the second mile. In donating, unprompted, a shiny new pair of lightweight leather boots, they prevented the walk from an early demise amid squelching bogs and blisters. Then, by offering long-term access to their house and computer, they smoothed the manuscript's transition from scribbled notebooks to hugely overwritten first draft.

Short sections of the book were written in two other locations. Chapter One started in a Sconser cottage rented by my sister Kath and her then fiancé, now husband, Geoff Snape. Most of Chapter Three was written in a cottage at Clochan, near Buckie, owned by Susan and Angus Turner, with beautiful, inspiring views across the Moray Firth to snowy Caithness peaks.

Especial thanks are of course due to Chris Tyler, whose illustrations and maps add so much to the basic text. And to Rachel and Craig Smillie - who, quite apart from managing to feature, one each, at either end of the walk, also wrote the two ceilidh tunes at the very end of this book.

And then there were...

Felix Aitken, Elspeth Alexander, Kevin Campbell, Mary Cox, Lucy Craig, Alan Dawson, Andy Dempster, Eildon Dyer, Michelle and Jerry Eve, Jim Faichney, Catriona and Angus Gray, Cwti Green, John Heaney, Betsy and

Derrik Hewitt, Maggie and John Hill, Irene and Calum Hind, Mags Hunter, Ray Kelly, Margaret and Stephen Lee, Fiona and Malcolm Lindsay, Frank McHugh, Lorraine McIntosh, Lynsey and John McIntosh, Psycho Jack McKibben, Rev David McLachlan and all at Gorbals Church, Little Dave McLaren, Duncan Merrilees, Davy Milligan, Ian Milligan, Eileen O'Donnell, Richard Perry, Linda Small, Janet Stewart, Kenny Symon, Bridget Tanner, Dr Brian Thomson, Marlyn and Ian Turbitt, Perkin Warbeck, Big Steve Young, Grolsch and Bert.

Thanks are also due to the following for important textual comments on the manuscript: Tom Atkinson, Hamish Brown, Livia Gollancz, Grant Hutchison, Elsie Luke and Andy Prospect Mayhew.

Acknowledgements to Hodder & Stoughton and International Music Publications, for permission to quote, respectively, from Peter Boardman's *Sacred Summits* and The Blue Nile's *Heatwave*.

The Aultguish Inn and the Oykel Bridge Hotel kindly retained parcels of food and clothes for collection during the walk. Thanks also to Tommy and all at Clydeside Press, and to the staff of the History and Topography Department of Glasgow's Mitchell Library.

After reading pp178-181, anyone interested in the Elizabeth Stenhouse Memorial (Scottish Charity No. SC 020328), should write to DVA, Kandahar House, 71 Meadowside, Dundee DD1 1EN.

A good many of this myriad throng make appearances in the pages which follow. I only hope that any helpers who do not, and who have similarly been omitted here, will forgive me. As they say in Glasgow, Thank youse all.

Foreword

by **Perkin Warbeck**, co-editor of *The Angry Corrie*, Scotland's first and finest hillwalking fanzine.

I had not seen the Figure for a few days. When we caught up again the gleam was in his eye. I had seen it before, the last time being the search for the three Us. He was convinced there was a point from which three of the big illuminated Us outside Glasgow's underground stations could be seen. As it turned out, no such point existed, at least not while standing on terra firma.

The gleam had also accompanied the cataloguing of all 1428 taxis in Glasgow and other projects of a topological/numerological bent to which the Figure's teeming brain was drawn.

— *I was up Meikle Bin at the weekend.*

— *All the water on one side flows to the Forth and all the water on the other to the Clyde.*

— *It's therefore a point on the east-west watershed. The locus of all such points would be a unique line from south to north dividing Scotland in two.*

(He didn't actually use these words, but it's a lot more concise than the rambling monologue on which he embarked. I can't now remember if the actual phrase Holy Grail was mentioned, but that's the gist. He reckoned the route had never been identified or walked before.)

— *And I'm going to walk it.*

— *Because it's the watershed you would never cross a river. It's the only route from south to north where you would keep your feet dry.*

(This particularly outrageous claim was later tested to the full and found to be slightly erroneous.)

— *You would get great views. And your pals would have to spend the next three months with no other thought than how to keep you fed, clothed and emotionally buoyed up.*

(He may not have said this either, and it's a pity; someone might have had the sense to dissuade him.)

It seemed no one had ever plotted The Watershed - it assumed capital status about this time. Probably because it squirmed all over the country like Bonnie Chairlie's wanderings. Which brings us to the book. This very book you are reading now. The Figure's guide to walking The Watershed and his thoughts on Life, the Universe, and why the answer is not 42 but 452.

Hillwalking books appear to be a commercial prospect if they are either written by someone already famous or if they detail epic new ways to conquer the Munros in less time or more precarious circumstances. The Figure was then an unknown sub-Joycean Giant without even the cult status he now enjoys as editor of *The Angry Corrie*. His walk derived from the natural topology of the land with Munros falling on or off The Watershed as they saw fit. His observations did not fit neatly into the *"Turn left at the bagpipe shop and remember to ask permission to camp. We are guests of the landowners"* genre. Who would publish such an eclectic work?

TACit Press, that's who. The *Rough Trade* of the hillwalking scene, waiting for The Smiths to come along. Virile as a stag, but contemplative as a capercaillie.

And thus you hold in your hands a guide of sorts to the country of Scotland. There will be few if any mentions of Bonnie Chairlie. No-one will get frostbite or crotch rot whatever that is. The scariest moment is when a sheep gets into his tent. What you will get is the thoughts of a man who has spent a year of his life in his tent, three months of which are the period of The Watershed. A man who cannot see a 499m spot height without thinking of Hanif Mohammed. A man for whom the words trail mix and Beanfeast became like the infamous albatross itself.

Read and enjoy, but remember - if you think of walking The Watershed yourself, you *will* get your feet wet.

Introduction

What follows is, if anything, an adventure story. Ostensibly the story of a long, long walk, it could also be filed under Autobiography, Geography, Topography, Survival Skills, Psychology, Asceticism, Meteorology and, at a pinch, Gastronomy. It is about a period of twelve weeks in the mid-1980s, about a country, Scotland, and a person, me. It is about the intertwining of these things, the weaving together of people, places and time in perhaps the simplest of all ways, that of putting one foot in front of the other: walking.

I say "adventure", but don't expect Indiana Jones or James Bond: it is not that exciting, there are no grapplings with monster snakes, no shootouts with hi-tech weaponry - and, sadly, no late-night wooings or softly-lit seductions. Neither should the reader anticipate high jinks at high altitude: no struggles to attain Himalayan summits in jetstream winds, no desperate descents from death-zone bivouacs with broken legs. Scotland is, despite occasional patriotic pomposity, a quiet, undemonstrative, subtle country, while your man here, for all that an idea can burn inside him, is a relatively humble soul. The two seem to go well together. Thus an adventure story, but a small-scale, modest adventure.

For starters, though, before whistling on the scene-shifters to prepare the main act, a little background must necessarily be painted in by way of personal detail and historical hard fact. After all, if you have taken a notion to spend twelve whole weeks in my company, you had better first come in for a cup of tea and a blether.

In the summer of 1986 I was 25 years old, single, unattached and unemployed except for various part-time and voluntary community work involvements. I was also, and had been for a number of years, an extremely keen, regular and reasonably fit hillwalker. In a nutshell, I was footloose and fancy-free.

Living in Scotland - for a number of years in Aberdeen, latterly in Glasgow - I had "grown up", in the hillwalking sense, in the great tradition of weekends and days spent in the Highlands as means of escape from nearby conurbations. Scotland is ready-made for this: for all that kailyarders and dewy-eyed romantics croon, the land boasts very little, if anything, in the way of the fabled One True Wilderness. Already I had come to recognise that even the most remote hills - Fisherfield, Ben Alder, innermost Cairngorms - could, in the course of long, near-perpetually-daylit summer's days, be climbed and returned from by anyone in possession of sturdy legs and strong lungs. Don't listen to the equipment manufacturers and guidebook Jeremiahs when they try, for the betterment of their bank accounts, to convince you otherwise. In the Scottish hills it is, as the footballers love to say, a case of win, lose or draw, you get home to your bed just the same.

Nor was I ignorant of the fact there never really had been any great wilderness. In days gone by, the glens now gleefully labelled "remote" - and consequently supposed to be somehow intrinsically attractive, virtuous even - were lived in, not just by one or two hermit-like weather-beaten ascetics, but by whole structured communities which were to be systematically and disgracefully wiped out during the 18th, 19th and 20th centuries. Thus the taken-as-read history of the Scottish Highlands comprises a large degree of myth - although a myth deeper and more tragic than that under which modern-day coffee-tables creak and groan. That these lands, particularly those north of the Highland Line, are relatively empty and barren compared to the richness and vitality further south has only come about because people made it that way.

Yet I was no historian, only a hillgoer, and the empirical knowledge borne out of hundreds upon hundreds of ascents had made me alert to the misapprehension that things could be all too easily oversimplified. Scotland is not a soft touch for walkers, not just a Lake District, High Peak or Snowdonia on a slightly bigger scale: the climate sees to that. For all that any hill can be day-climbed in the long summer months, so even the most puny of peaks can prove unattainable on a fierce winter's day when the winds blow, the snow sheets down and the few precious hours of daylight snap shut like a knife. Anyone spending any amount of time in the Scottish hills knows this: one has to in order to survive. Not survive so much in the literal, avoiding-death sense (although the casualty figures each winter are always worth more than a cautionary glance), but in terms of evading becoming downbeaten and disillusioned by the worst the weather can throw at you.

What else did I know? At a personal level I knew that I wanted to move beyond the day trip/weekending mentality of a hill here, a hill there, then back home to the city. I wanted, at least once in my life, to devote a considerable length of time to the one thing I relished above all else: the climbing of hills. Any walks - not just those confined to the hills - can, route-wise, be divided into three main categories. Firstly comes the straight there-and-back walk, from A to B and back to A again by the same route. Then there is the circular walk, again from A to B and back to A, but returning, like the Wise Men having met King Herod, by a different route. These two variants on a theme are, in the main, the domain of the car-based walker, who has no choice but to wend his or her way back to the dreaded box-on-wheels. But the third and intrinsically far more satisfying option, that of a linear walk, from A to B and so on to C, was what interested me. Throw off the shackles of the infernal internal combustion engine, forget about the need to return to a place labelled Home; no matter that my dream version of a linear walk was not just a matter of A-B-C, but so on to Z with half of every known alphabet in between. This was what I wanted, what I yearned for, what kept me awake at night: the sense of going somewhere.

Yet what, precisely, to do? Just as there was a long, egalitarian tradition of regular and committed hillgoing from across a wide swathe of the population, so there was also a notable history of what had come to be known as Long Walks. I wanted to do something original - not so much so to claim a "first", more to intrigue and motivate myself with the shock of the new. But most obvious Long Walks had already been successfully - and often very publicly - attempted. Sandy Cousins, the Ripley brothers and ultimately Hamish Brown with their Munros-in-one-go expeditions - followed by copy-cat variations by the Kathy Murgatroyds and George Keepings of this world. So that was out. Also off the slate was the mega-bag of Munros and Corbetts together: this had recently been achieved by Craig Caldwell. I was reasonably competent in winter conditions - as anyone who learned their trade in the Cairngorms had to be, lest they find themselves relegated to a mere four-months-per-year access to the bigger hills. But even here, Martin Moran had, only recently, swept away what appeared to be the main prize: that of all 270-odd Munros in a single winter season.

I could, of course, opt out of structured walks altogether and go for what the old-timers call a *stravaig*. Yet although two or three months of where-the-mood-took-me wandering sounded pleasurable enough, idyllic even, I feared the lack of a structure would, at best, make me lazy and slipshod, at worst see me losing touch with my motivations completely and quickly giving up. No, what was needed was a way of pushing myself to the limits of what I could do, and a relatively rigid framework was hence a necessary evil.

Quite how the idea finally arose I cannot now remember, just that one day I was still lost in a directionless mist, the next I had an entire itinerary well on the way to completion. From slouching in front of the TV watching the test match, my living room became a frantic flurry of maps and note-

13

covered scraps of paper. I suddenly knew what I wanted to do, and the idea came complete and unabridged, needing only to be transferred first to the world of maps, paper and planning, then to that of the hills themselves. The gestation period was brief.

It was the Munro idea that was wrong: why hadn't I perceived this earlier? My idea for a Long Walk would move away from the artificial structure of a *munro opus* towards what could be termed a more "natural" route. One which, no matter whether the heights of the hills were denoted in feet, metres or pieces of eight, would always stay the same. A route where size didn't come into it at all, having been completely written out of the equation at the outset. The name of such a route? The watershed.

Turning briefly to semantics, the word *watershed* has two connected, if subtly different, meanings. The first is that of a dividing-line between separate river systems - ie river systems which at no point intermingle. The second sees a watershed as the river basin itself: the catchment area demarcated by a line of hills. This latter interpretation occurs mainly in American English, where, for instance, the great north-south spine of the USA, the Rockies, is colloquially known as the Great Divide, with the drainage areas east and west of the high ridges regarded as the watersheds.

14

That this isn't the situation in Britain is evinced by taking note of the word's most common usage in the general ebb and flow of the language - as metaphor. Sportsmen and women speak of a watershed in careers, politicians of a watershed in negotiations, Mary Whitehouse of the 9 o'clock TV watershed; the image is of a dividing-line, a significant something needing to be crossed in progressing from A to B.

Nor is the comparison with America as facetious as it sounds. The Land of the Free is, like Britain, longitudinal in shape - ie with east and west coastlines predominant. Hence the main watershed runs, in a cartographical sense, vertically. The comparison can even be extended to the fact that both nations have their main watersheds disproportionately near the western seaboard. Just as water running east off the southern Rockies meanders tortuously towards the Mississippi Delta and the distant Atlantic, so water draining east from, say, Sgurr na Ciche in Knoydart takes a near eternity to find its way to the Inversnechtie Delta and the Moray Firth. Conversely, both American and British watersheds have, in places, astonishingly short western drainages - that from Sgurr na Ciche to Loch Nevis being scarcely three miles.

Beginning to get the idea? You will of course appreciate there are, within any piece of land, innumerable smaller watersheds: any glen, any valley will divide and rule its own localised water table, even if only for a short time. For example, the familiar watershed running through the Cairngorms, separating the major rivers of Dee and Spey, is in turn subdivided by smaller watersheds, keeping apart rivers such as Lui and Derry, Einich and Feshie, which only later feed into their parent flows. Hence whilst the summit ridge or plateau of any given hill is usually home to a simple two-way-split of a watershed - eg Ben Lomond walls off Clyde (in the shape of Loch Lomond) from Forth (via the Loch Ard feeders) - the overall picture for any given area is much more complicated, such that a map of Scotland showing each and every watershed, no matter how large or small, would resemble one of those gruesome diagrams in *Gray's Anatomy*: a body stripped of skin to reveal the blood supply, the *vena cava* branching into main veins supplying the extremities, with these in turn endlessly subdividing down to capillary level.

Were Scotland a more rounded shape of country - eg a Germany or a Spain - not only would we be much better at football, but our watershed map would have no clear shape to it, no feeling of direction, of thrust. But we are a linear land, with a consequently linear main watershed, and to someone such as myself, with an eye for map-reading and an urge to take up my bed and walk, that linearity, once perceived, was always going to prove irresistible.

The idea having come to me sometime in the summer of 1986, the first priority was for the route to be meticulously mapped. That this proved easier than expected was primarily down to the very hilly - and therefore well-defined - nature of the terrain itself. Only where the watershed crossed the Central Belt - the relatively low-lying ground between Glasgow and Edinburgh - was there any cartographical confusion, with trickles of burns and even artificially-cut drainage channels sometimes seeming to do the impossible by flowing both ways simultaneously. It was this kind of difficulty - thankfully short-lived and localised in Scotland - which finally disabused me of any lingering notion to walk not just the main watershed of Scotland, but that of Britain as a whole. This existed, at least in theory - England being every bit as linear as its northern neighbour. But while the dripping-and-tripe end of the English watershed would be well enough defined (a traipse along the Pennines, for instance), the thought of what awaited below Sheffield was enough to make even the most hardened walker blanch. Dodging bicycles on the campus of Keele University, meandering endlessly through the Acacia Avenues and Laburnum Crescents of Birmingham housing estates, being blown sky-high by land mines on Wiltshire firing ranges... Plus the fact of England being the least enlightened country in Europe when it came to freedom of access and wild camping. Plus the entire route being more than doubled in length. No thank you!

Mapping the Scottish watershed proved a learning experience in itself. As my 1:50000 OS maps steadily gained a squiggly red line which felt-tipped its way northward from the Border, I was quickly surprised to note just how many of the country's major hills were bang on the dividing-line. Cairngorms were too far east, of course, just as the Nevis-Leven-Coe complex occupied a western niche all of its own. But many of the main Borders hills straddled the route, as did Ben Lomond, Cruach Ardrain, Beinns Laoigh and Achallader, the entire Blackmount horseshoe, Ben Alder, the high tops immediately east of Creag Meagaidh, the Loch Lochy group, the eastern end of Knoydart's Rough Bounds, then a grand tour of much that was good in the big western glens: over half the South Cluanie Ridge, Beinn Fhada, Ceathreamhnan, Bidein a'Choire Sheasgaich, and on into the north via a whole batch of Fannaichs, some Deargs and Conival, before finishing with a final flourish: Foinaven to Cape Wrath.

Any lingering doubts as to the seriousness of what was being undertaken were dispelled by these maps. They were tangible reminders that I didn't want a stroll of a walk, and the watershed most certainly wasn't going to provide one. For all my Munrophobia, the route was to include almost fifty of the damn things, backed-up by twenty-five Corbetts and a whole host of lesser peaks.

16

Yet I wouldn't have had it any other way, and this mapping process was crucial in emphasising the eclectic nature of the watershed. The variation in the size of watershed hills - from 1100m giants such as Ben Alder right down to tiny 100m bumps unable even to boast a name on the map - simply didn't matter. There was something pleasingly egalitarian about it all, something integral. The little hills weren't meaningless distractions between the bigger ones, nor *vice versa*. And when the much-heralded Greenhouse Effect raises the sea-level a metre or two, a number of marginal Munros will necessarily be chalked off *that* list (including my own route's borderline three thousand footer, Sgurr nan Ceannaichean). But the sea-level could rise up to our necks and beyond for all that the watershed would remain unchanged. Only the heights of the hills would alter, not the line itself. The route was the route was the route. It was, to misquote Forster, a case of Only Connect.

The planning of these connections was to occupy much of my spare time during the winter of 1986/87 - although to view time devoted to the watershed as spare was becoming a bit of a joke: it was the rest of my life which felt dispensable, irrelevant. The watershed was what really mattered.

By breaking down the route into manageable portions - hill-bytes, perhaps? - I gradually gleaned that the whole shebang was to be some 800 miles in length, involving the best part of 80,000m of ascent and occupying roughly twelve weeks. I planned, in the main, to walk alone, but geared the logistics around rendezvous with friends and fellow walkers every weekend. This would allow for replenishment of supplies - both fresh food and clean clothes (long-distance walking is a smelly business) - and give something to look forward to. Three months is a long time, especially when spent mainly in self-imposed solitary confinement, and the need to keep morale high would be crucial. Recognising this in advance, I noted every third weekend conveniently brought a youth hostel, where several consecutive nights could be spent in relative comfort. Already - rightly as it transpired - I was doubting whether more than three weeks could be allowed to pass without some form of battery-recharging.

Once the route had been established, other factors could be firmed-up. What to do in terms of accommodation? was largely determined, not by the river flow of the watershed, but by the cash flow of my bank account. I was skint, overdrawn already, and must perforce use tents and bothies as much as possible. This, however, suited me fine, and was of course necessary given I would often as not be voluntarily benighted far from roads and houses. On the rare occasions when hostels or - luxury of luxuries - bed-and-breakfasts coincided with my route, they could just about be afforded. But I had already spent the best part of a year of my life "under canvas" (or whatever has become its pre-stretched nylon equivalent), and knew I would relish the freedom, mobility and privacy this allowed.

A corollary to this was the question of where exactly to spend my nights, location-wise. In attempting to explain the watershed to bemused friends, I had taken to using the neat description of it being the only route through Scotland not to involve crossing a river. Technically true (although various low-lying bogs *en route* were to prove little drier than rivers themselves, while there was at least one lochan which flowed both ways), this begged the important question of how to obtain water for drinking and cooking. Scotland might be one of the wettest lands under the all-too-rarely-seen sun, yet I was choosing the driest of all lines through it. Fortunately this merged neatly with another concern - the establishment of a routine not too dissimilar to that of standard hill days. I decided, unless the weather was so stunningly good as to justify camping high, to descend slightly off-route each night, thus resolving all these difficulties in a oner. That I was already learning to treat the walk as work was shown by this desire to clock-off and, however nominally, go home each night.

Having until now implied there to be no possible variation in the line of the watershed, it must be conceded I did have a couple of route-finding decisions to make in advance of setting off. Scotland is, as already suggested, primarily a country of two coastlines - so much so that the common perception of national character is itself split between garrulous westcoasters and more taciturn, gaunt types from the east. Yet Scotland also boasts a dim and distant north coast, and this comes into play at the top end of the watershed. I was forced to choose between one end of my walk being Cape Wrath at the northwestern tip, or Duncansby Head, its sibling in the far northeast. The split - a kind of geological Georgemas Junction - occurred so far up in Sutherland's Reay Forest, so near the northwestern end of things, that my choice was never really in doubt: the Caithness diversion would involve some fifty miles more. Not only that, while both variations reached the sea at suitably impressive sea cliffs, the Cape Wrath option kept up its hill-character all the way, whereas the John o' Groats branch not only ran the risk of encountering coachloads of camera-clicking tourists and tacky shops selling tea-towels and scottie-dog biscuit tins, it would also have taken me through the bogs and flatlands of the Flow Country. Fine though this would have been from a scenic and ornithological standpoint, the prospect of several days' bog-trotting through the domicile of the pied shankwarbler didn't exactly fill me with glee. Tom Weir I was not. The Capes of Wrath awaited.

Similarly, I had to decide whether to go north-south or south-north. This, a crucially important decision, vexed me somewhat. I quite fancied the idea of starting in relatively familiar country - and, ironically, had climbed a good deal more hills in the far north than the much more adjacent Borders. But common-sense eventually prevailed: for one thing, the rolling greenhills of Roxburghshire would provide a more palatable entrée to fitness than would grey Sutherland gneiss-heaps. For another, winter, like the trains, never ran on time these days, and the slightest delay could see me slogging up big, steep, northern hills with a fifty-pound sack through impossibly deep snows. Even before the turn of the year I had irreversibly opted to start my adventure in an obscure valley on the Union Boundary by the name of Hobb's Flow.

The question of what time of year to walk also needed finalised. This was, thankfully, less difficult. Winter was out of the question, for me at least. Summer was too moist and midgy, autumn ran the gauntlet of the stalking season and encountered the nemesis of ever-shortening days. Spring shouted out to be walked through: improving weather, beckoning daylight, the fresh vitality of all things new. Spring it would be.

The early months of 1987 flew past in a blur, tempus fugiting furiously. Lightweight equipment was bought, manufacturers sooked up to (almost invariably without success) for freebies or discounts, various horrible-tasting freeze-dried foods were weighed, both literally and gastronomically, against other horrible-tasting freeze-dried foods. All sorts of items were tested, modified, scrounged or borrowed. All manner of things were done which normally fill countless appendices of books such as these, but which will, for the sake of the reader's sanity, be skipped over here.

A brief diversion occurred in the form of panic on noticing a previously unread reference to the watershed in Moran's book The Munros in Winter. He cited some companion having mooted the possibilities of the all-Britain route, only to be discouraged, as had I, by the prospect of canal towpaths through the Potteries and the like. He never seemed to have considered the Scotland-only option, and a brief check elsewhere assured me the watershed was still virgin territory, the walker's equivalent of a first ascent. Not that I really minded: even had the route been trod a myriad times, it was still going to be uniquely different for each and every person making the attempt.

Simultaneous with the route-planning, discussions were taking place with various of Glasgow's charitable bodies, such that sponsorship forms were eventually drawn up to enable each mile of the watershed to raise a little

money for an Oxfam agricultural project in Nicaragua. I wasn't all that bothered about this, the walk being far too personal an experience to be sidetracked into serious fund-raising (or maybe I was just becoming too single-mindedly selfish), but it would scarcely impinge on the organisation of the thing to set up this one small sideshow. And anyway, the cause was good.

I was even more ambivalent about genuine publicity, only agreeing to the slightly melodramatic step of issuing a press release to raise awareness of the half-hearted fund-raising. Not that this achieved much in the end: the only things to appear in print were a snippet in *The Great Outdoors* and a brief photo-story in Glasgow's *Evening Times*. The latter was notable for the poor man's paparazzi insisting I be pictured wearing an enormous fleecy jacket which I wouldn't have dreamt of wearing on the walk itself, so that I "looked like a mountaineer". Weren't the beard and the boots enough?

Suddenly it was early April and almost time. Bidding temporary farewell to friends was, of course, the hardest part, although even here things were lightened by a late-in-the-day conversation with my parents. I had explained the whole concept to my mother - as unlikely a hillgoer as you could ever meet - earlier in the year, and had been somewhat surprised to hear no objections raised, no cautions expressed. Was this not the woman who once decreed I should never possess such a dangerous machine as a bicycle? Or who, in my schooldays, prevented me from captaining my school chess team one night on the grounds I had done enough gallivanting that week already? Yet now, on the eve of the biggest risk-taking venture of my entire life, silence. Strange.

The mystery was only resolved just before leaving, when in the midst of phonecall assurances that Yes, I would keep in touch, Yes, I would wrap up warm, she asked the question which had been ticking over in her mind since first hearing of the project: "There'll be a path all the way, won't there?" Yes, mother, yes.

I was ready to go.

1: Below the Belt
(Saturday 11th April - Wednesday 22nd April)

Seven o'clock. The alarm brings a day I both long for and fear. Watershed day: when the cluttered, untidy flat I know as home is to be forsaken for a bulging, heavy rucksack currently propped against the living-room wall. I'm about to cast off from friends and familiar places to fulfil a dream, to realise an idea, which suddenly seems absurd and impossible. In the instant of waking, doubts and fears rise in my mind, range upon range of them, stretching twelve weeks into the future, seemingly impassable: intangible mountains far more treacherous than any real rock-and-water hills on which I'm about to set foot. Perhaps it is these I'm really setting out to climb.

Such thoughts aren't allowed progress beyond the back-of-the-mind stage for fear of losing nerve and crawling back to bed. It is too late to be asking difficult questions, there are jobs needing done. Having slept on the living-room floor, I go through to the bedroom to wake my sister Margaret. She had come up from Derbyshire the previous day, clearly excited by events, and her presence gives confidence.

A glance out of the window to see a bright but unsettled morning. A rushed breakfast of muesli and water - I have been weaning myself onto this throughout the previous fortnight. A final check of the rucksack, not that anything omitted could now possibly be crammed in. Then the doorbell rings. Already it is eight o'clock, and Rachel is here to collect us. I wake flatmate Davy for a parting handshake, hand him my door keys, leave.

As we cross the Kingston Bridge, snowy peaks are seen away to the northwest under a threatening sky. A chill wind blows and even the lowly Campsies carry fresh snow. We swing away east, then south, speeding along the quiet Saturday morning motorway, soon escaping the concrete sprawl of the Lanarkshire steeltowns, passing close beneath Tinto's white cone. The excitement of breaking loose from the city fades as we drive through Abington and Crawford, small roadside hamlets on the long haul over Beattock. I realise within a week I will pass through these hills once more: on foot, heading north, alone. The thought briefly unnerves: I look away.

Tom Waits on tape helps ease the tension a little, as does a coffee-break in Lockerbie. Soon, though, as we drive east into less familiar territory, I'm again distracted and distant, not the best of company. If only the next hour or two could be lost in some instant timeslip and I was alone and walking. If only the first unfit week was complete, the rhythms of the walk having

23

slipped painlessly into order. If only I was standing at Cape Wrath, twelve weeks of walking stretched southward, behind me, a string through a labyrinth. *If only...* These are dangerous thoughts, and I stop them. The walk is to be experienced as a whole: enjoyed and endured. There are to be no short-cuts, no easy options.

Small roads through small hills down into the steep-sided town of Langholm. Conditions here lose the bright storminess of further north, become merely grey and damp. We pass beneath the square top of Tinnis Hill on the back road to Newcastleton: here I occupy myself in debating whether or not to take the ice-axe. Barely have I decided to do so than we reach the cottage at Dinlabyre where it is strapped onto the rucksack. A sign reads "Lewisburn via Bloody Bush". Perhaps it should read "Cape Wrath via Bloody Watershed".

Waterproofed against the dreich day, we set off up a forest road: no tops visible, just a vague line of cloud somewhere above the trees. Slopes north of here named Rain's Hill seem more apt than the Mountain View we pass. Two walkers are met, crossing from Kielder. They found the pass windy and unpleasant - and express disbelief when, on asking my destination, are told Cape Wrath. This, though, is hardly surprising: I'm heading due south at the time.

Higher up, more open forestry allows views back across bare hills west of Liddel Water, but the strong wind discourages halts and we keep moving. Above the treeline the track becomes a boggy path, gently rising to the shoulder of Hurklewinter Knowe and a difficult moment. Photographs are taken, hugs and kisses exchanged, then Margaret and Rachel turn back toward the forest. Seeing them disappear over the horizon is like watching the sun set. I find it hard not to cry.

As if by way of distraction, the weather suddenly deteriorates, forcing me to turn from sweeping rain which descends like a curtain on the scene. I stumble down to Hobb's Flow, a boggy corner of the forest fence marking the most southerly intersection of the Scotland/England border and Scotland's east/west watershed. A brief stop - not for a photo or a dram, but to unceremoniously pee over the dividing-line - then back into the storm.

Driving snow makes the short pull onto the Larriston Fells feel much harder than it ought. In cloud now, on a bearing, I put up grouse every few yards: they clatter noisily off into murk as I reach the clutter of summit cairns. The weather is too grim to go walkabout in search of the trig point: I make do with a tall thin cairn and keep moving.

Featureless terrain is soon relieved by a scrappy metal fence meandering through acres of bog. An anonymous Point 396m brings slight easing of the surrounding unpleasantness, plus a wide firebreak leading down toward the road. Already thinking about calling it a day, I relax while weaving through a curious green terraced area above some ruined crofts. Peel Fell, hidden across the valley under fresh snow, can wait until morning. Time to camp.

The late afternoon sky begins to brighten as I reach Deadwater Farm, where a friendly worker leads to a sheltered spot beside the burn. He tells of the previous night having been very wild: several sheep lost. I have chosen the right day to start the walk.

The tent takes an age to erect, delays compounded by annoyance at having forgotten to repair a torn-off peg-loop. This at least gives something to do while Beanfeast simmers on the tiny Epigas burner - newly bought in preference to a trusted but bulky Trangia. A lot of fuel seems wasted as wind catches the unshielded flame - and while carrying the apparatus across to a dyke for shelter, I knock over the saucepan, provoking the first loss of temper. This, however, is short-lived, the sun choosing precisely that moment to break through the clouds.

Time and again during the coming weeks I'm to discover how quickly a change in the weather can raise or lower morale. By the time I have eaten and strolled along the road to the Border, an evening fading into cloudlessness has me feeling relaxed and eager to face the days ahead.

Darkness falls, the temperature gains a cold edge, I hurry back to the tent for a satisfying night's sleep: the only one of the walk to be spent in England.

A cold night: I wake to find an inch of ice on pans left to soak. This at least allows use of the ice-axe, even if in unorthodox fashion! I pack and walk by eight-thirty - the morning crisp and white with frost - and follow a steadily rising forest track beside the Deadwater Burn. Although hoping wherever possible to keep strictly to the watershed, here, as in other parts of the Borders, blanket afforestation forces divergence. Having often battled through dense foliage, emerging covered in scratches, sweat and pine needles, I know from all too painful experience the foolishness of even contemplating a direct line. Vital to progress is the need to enjoy myself, especially at this early stage.

Roe deer and feral goats provide company before recent felling allows easy access to the snowy upper slopes of Peel Fell - or The Peel as it is known locally. The summit view sparkles: a jumble of rounded tops to the west, patched dark with forestry, reaches away toward the main Borders hills encircling the Tweed headwaters. Yet it is not these which draw the eye, for far in the southwest, rising white and clear across the Solway, are peaks of the northern Lake District. I pick out Blencathra and Skiddaw, clean and sharp under the blue sky: a mystery of distant hills adding excitement to an already invigorating morning.

Perhaps this sense of well-being distracts me, for on turning due north, away from the Border, I make a silly navigational error which costs time and energy. Leaving the gear at the rise for Hartshorn Pike, intending to contour round to a track on Wheelrig Head, I become confused by new, unmapped plantings and drop too far, toward the Peel Burn. The further contouring necessary to regain the route leads through ranks of ditch-divided young trees and has me cursing the heavy sack - which, having precipitated the error, now compounds it. A full hour is lost in working round to a track

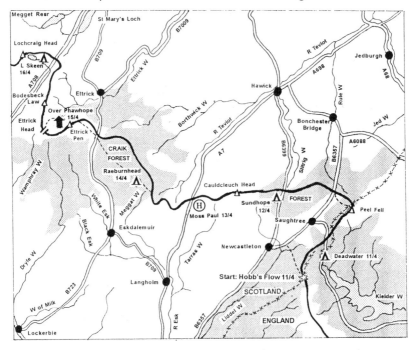

Border - Loch Skeen

26

on the Coomb Edge ridge. Later, looking again at the area on the map, the episode seems laughable - but at the time there is no such lightness of emotion: I merely rage against the inadequacies of the Ordnance Survey.

Badly needed lunch is eaten on a sunny bank beside the Newcastleton-Bonchester Bridge road, chatting to a biker who, like most folk thus far met, has "come over from Kielder". The good weather won't last, he says - and, indeed, high cloud already encroaches from the west. Although still early in the day, I decide not to make the big push for the A7 but to camp at the next road-crossing. I feel tired and unfit - as I have always tended to do on the second day of any walking trip, no matter how long. And again the early-walk caution: no point overdoing things this first week. The greater need is to think long-term: big days will come in due course.

A convenient firebreak allows unhindered progress up Dog Knowe before more new plantings again slow things on Wigg Knowe. The breeze having risen, I shelter in the lee of the summit radio station, listen to its low-frequency hum, gaze westward to a view now dominated, hillwise, by the Maiden Paps jutting north of Greatmoor Hill.

Very tired, I follow the ridge over Fanna Hill before dropping down. Plod plod plod past the white cottage of Windshielknowe, down under a disused railway bridge where the road buzzes with red cars. Rain is not far away now, but tired beyond hurrying, I stop several times before camping beside the Sundhope Burn. Utterly exhausted with the day's effort, I vomit after pitching, then drag myself inside and fall instantly asleep.

I wake at midnight, much refreshed, and lie in darkness listening to rain and wind on the flysheet, satisfied at the route beginning, albeit tortuously, to take shape. Away from Kielder and truly into Scottish waters, the Liddel-Teviot watershed has been reached. The first major river system, the Tweed, is starting to have its say.

On waking again the rain is heavier and cloud reaches down to the tent. First thoughts are to take a day off, to stay cocooned in the dry cosiness of the sleeping-bag, but it is important to reach the telephone at Moss Paul that evening. Jack has offered to drive down on Tuesday, and his visit will allow disposal of the ice-axe and heavy tweed trousers. The bringing of these was, I now see, a meteorologically pessimistic error: they weigh down the rucksack like ballast to a balloon. To be rid of them will, hopefully, have uplifting results. This, though, depends on specifying a meeting-place to Jack - it is too much to expect him to drive between three or four possible locations - and this need to make contact can only be fulfilled by moving on. Strangely, I never think it simply too early in the walk for a day off. Already the start seems very distant.

The previous evening's sickness has left residual weakness which an unsatisfactory breakfast of tuna and pitta bread does little to alleviate. The only cause for optimism comes in the form of a slight brightening through the cloud, on which I half-pack and crouch beneath the bare flysheet, awaiting further improvement. This comes at nine-thirty, when rain stops and cloud, having earlier filled every fold of the valley like a sailor asleep in a hammock, begins to prop itself on one elbow. A marked improvement. I set off.

The map indicates a path leaving the farm for Scaw'd Law and so on to Stobs Castle and Hawick, but on the ground this soon disappears amid long tussocky grass - which itself all but disappears as I climb into cloud. Short, tangled threads of sheep-track give some easier going, but mostly it is bog and thigh-deep grass - each blade tipped with silver beads of moisture attaching themselves to legs with the certainty of leeches.

When an already gentle slope eases to the horizontal, I stop to consult the map. With young, dark trees looming ahead and steeper ground beyond, I deduce I'm too far east and on Leap Hill - an intended omission even though it lies on the watershed. Forestry or no forestry, my sins have found me out! Navigation is easier now, as to follow the fence westward leads inevitably to the top of the pass.

Then, just before the final rise, a brief clearance shows the ridge ahead - and although cloud quickly rolls back in, the secret is out. I'm where I want to be, confidence restored. On reaching Scaw'd Law, the view along to the Maiden Paps clears completely. Greatmoor Hill is the planned lunch-break: here I sit in a circular shelter-cairn, waiting while the kettle hisses. The morning's lack of energy soon offset by soup and biscuits, I feel progressively better from here on.

Cauldcleuch Head next, the first classified hill: a Donald. (The designation covers Scottish hills over 2000ft to the south of the Highland line, of which there are 89, Cauldcleuch being the easternmost wholly in Scotland.) Although the flanks appear quite steep and grassy, the summit proves a large miry plateau where sheep and fences come and go. There is no cairn and nothing with which to build one: I'm fortunate the cloudbase has risen. Indeed, the day is clearly on the mend: patches of blue open up overhead. The view back Bonchester way repeatedly demands attention, filled with interesting green, conical hills including the volcanic plug of Rubers Law.

After cutting down slightly for water from Langtae Sike, I rejoin the ridge and lapse into a dwam - so much so the summit of Tudhope Hill is mistaken for the already-crossed Millstone Edge. It is thus a pleasant surprise to find a trig point on top!

Westward of here the hills steepen, today showing innumerable bright shades of green in late afternoon sunlight. Swayed by this, I follow the watershed down toward the Carlin Tooth before the glint of a burn, running through fields framed in drystane dykes, becomes too much to resist. The valley, alive with birdsong and newborn lambs, is a celebration of sunlight. It is difficult to believe this as the same day which started so dismally.

On past the neat white farmhouse at Linhope, back over the watershed, into the Moss Paul Hotel. Here the proprietor, Mrs Paterson, is welcome personified. I'm given a double room, the floor of which soon disappears under the contents of the rucksack, wall-to-wall, like a well-spread piece. A hot bath precedes a huge, too-much-to-finish meal: I'm fit for human company again.

Strangely, the hotel has no public phone - so contacting Jack involves a series of reverse-charge calls and left messages: he isn't at home. Later, he rings to let me know his ETA: exactly the back of eleven.

Later still, while drinking with three Yorkshiremen headed for Hawick, someone broaches the subject of the weather. Mrs Paterson's ingenuous response sends me to bed amused and justified: "We don't take any notice of forecasts here: we're on the watershed!"

The room is too stuffy for my liking - already the familiar draughts and noises of the tent are needed - so I rise early, before eight, to a mammoth breakfast. Cornflakes, eggs, bacon, Cumberland sausage, black pudding, tomatoes, fried bread, toast, buckets of tea: there seems no end to it. With no other guests (hence my eating for six?), Mrs Paterson chats before I stroll outside to check the continued feasibility of walking after such trenchery.

A gentle, soft-lit morning, calm only occasionally broken by the grinding roar of a juggernaut changing through the gears as it crests the pass. I sit on the bridge and watch several cars pull in for petrol before Jack, as expected, arrives within a minute of the bar's opening. I'm beaten two-one at pool, then we put unwanted equipment into his car, buy sandwiches, set off up Comb Hill shortly after midday.

The hill rises immediately behind the hotel, and we haven't gone far before the Paterson's twa dugs come chasing after. Initial efforts to repatriate - or repetriate? - them prove successful: they are deposited unceremoniously back over the fence. But respite is brief: 100m of climbing later they are with us again, having squeezed through a hole in the wire like escaped POWs. All attempts to collar them now fail, such that eventually, frustrated in attempts to corner them on open hillside and after much shouting, swearing, barking and a couple of near-bites, we decide to cut our losses and take them up the first hill. Lambing-time makes this quite a risk: although the dogs don't seem dangerous, any shepherd encountered won't be impressed. But the afternoon wears on, and I don't want Jack - who has driven a long way - denied even the one hill.

So the four of us climb Comb Hill together: dogs careering off in every direction, Jack and I as sheepish as the ewes themselves. High up we meet two local walkers greatly amused at our predicament: theirs is the humour of déjà-vu.

On reaching the col to the southwest, I do my best to hide behind a fencepost while Jack takes the mutts in tow. He later tells of no-one back at Moss Paul having noticed their absence in the slightest.

If he seems unperturbed by the foreshortening of his day, I take out my annoyance by storming over Wisp Hill: at least a lighter rucksack and fuller stomach now make sudden energy-bursts more viable. Momentum sustains for some time, until I stop for a look around on Pikethaw Hill. North and west are bright, Skelfhill Pen prominent among the smooth green hills flanking Teviotdale.

Then, as I lie in warm sun gazing to distant Eildons, the day unexpectedly lifts from mediocrity to be placed firmly in the top drawer of memorabilia. Silently, completely oblivious of being seen, a fox trots past not twenty metres away. To see sunlight on golden-brown fur delights, as does the way it freezes, front paw half-cocked, my presence suddenly detected. We stay motionless, eyeing each other, fully fifteen seconds. I then surreptitiously reach for the camera... and break the spell. No longer a lifeless object worthy of curiosity, I'm something to be feared. The fox moves noiselessly away downhill, out of sight, gone.

Tension vanishes with it: I wander the few remaining metres up Pikethaw Hill feeling happy and refreshed. The cairn, like that of Wisp Hill, sits on a small grassy mound from where the Solway glistens silver to the south, its brightness emphasised by storm clouds hiding Lakeland beyond. To the west, broader, hag-strewn hills lead toward Craik Forest, their names more interesting than the tops themselves: Rashiegrain Height, Causeway Grain Head, Haggis Side. I follow the fence, aware of bad weather to the southwest nearing with every glance. Ettrick Pen, the main objective tomorrow, darkens to the colour of the huge forest it dominates.

Hurrying now, anxious to avoid a soaking, I begin to feel a chafing to my heels, the result of heavy boots saturated by miles of heavy going. This worsens as the day wears on. I enter the forest at four-thirty, by a track west of Dod Fell. Considerable thought having been given to the best line through, I opt for a route via Corlaw, Raeburnhead and Aberlosk - thus staying reasonably close to the watershed while avoiding unnecessary climbs.

The map portrays the area as uniformly green, yet these southeastern reaches hold a spacious atmosphere: mature trees divided by angular stretches of open hillside. The high, undulating line of the dirt road allows frequent glimpses of roe deer, white rumps betraying their presence in clearings below. Gradually the forest closes in: views south to the Esk replaced by a slit of sky overhead. This green-walled corridor numbs my mind, ensuring little will be recalled of these miles other than the growing soreness to heels and a general eeriness as treetop mists swirl. Light fades and a second fox crosses in front of me. Then an owl, gliding low in search of food.

A more open section brings Raeburnhead: a pair of deserted cottages beside the forest road equivalent of Spaghetti Junction. Finding a campsite here proves awkward: too much long grass and rubble of fallen dykes. I finally pitch to the rear of the first cottage, a site which entails lying diagonally between bumps. Carrying a two-person tent does have benefits!

31

The sky darkens prematurely and mist moving in the trees scares a little - although this is soon eased by the satisfaction of progress made. Already, Moss Paul seems a long way back: come morning I will enter the great swathe of high ground stretching the width of the Border country.

Weariness catches me that night. I sleep deeply, despite waking to hear a mouse nibbling a high-energy bar inadvertently left in the bell of the flysheet. Then a Range Rover roars past in darkness, headlights raking across trees like sun through the slats of a garden fence. It is as well sleep refreshes me, for the day to come will long be remembered as one of suffering and unhappiness. Communing with nature, as the poets have it, isn't always amicable: today we are to fall out.

Sore heels are the problem: even as I pull on boots they feel tender, and I know it won't be long before socks are again saturated, rubbing skin raw. Never before having been troubled by blisters, it is strange and worrying to lower feet into boots as though gingerly stepping into a too-hot bath. There is, however, nothing to be done except face the discomfort ahead. Like bad weather, it will, hopefully, pass - with any progress made seeming doubly valuable in retrospect.

The threatened rains have come to nothing more than a dampening of the air, although cloud still reaches down to tree-level. I immediately take a wrong turning amid the plethora of paths, then correct the mistake and strike out across Craik Muir. Traversing open ground again, albeit briefly, is a relief after miles of green claustrophobia - but this clear eye in the maelstrom of trees soon passes: I'm back in forest by Aberlosk.

Passing several dead frogs and a mouse, I climb beside the Fingland Burn. Ettrick Pen can be seen ahead, its snowpatched summit only three miles across the valley. The watershed has little time for flying crows however, taking a circuitous route around the headwaters of the Esk, more than twice the direct distance. Esk, from the Gaelic *uisge,* water, is a name common among British rivers. Two can be found in Angus, one in Lothian, another in the English Lakes.

Rounding a corner brings a caravan containing an elderly couple devouring an extensive breakfast. Not having the neck to invite myself in for tea and toast, I merely enquire as to the forecast. Not bad, they say, spreading marmalade on another slice.

I press hungrily on, finally escaping the twelve miles of forest walking via a road leading down to Scotland's only seismological station, Eskdalemuir. Hopes of approaching feet causing tremors come to nothing - and another possible cuppa fails to materialise.

Soon after starting up the public road to rejoin the watershed, a woman stops to offer a lift. She is a little put out at my polite refusal, as am I at having to proffer one, raw heels having now slowed progress to a shuffling limp. Even placenames offer scant encouragement: a farm called Foulbog doesn't exactly bode well for the hills to come.

The road rises to over 350m at the regional boundary, where I leave it to climb Cross Hill. The top, a corner in the deer fence, is just in cloud. Ditto Blue Cairn Hill beyond. I hobble through young plantings over Ewe Rig before lunching below the conspicuous steepening of Dobs Craig.

This is to prove the brightest part of the day: cloudbase up to 600m, fragmentary blue sky overhead. I take advantage of temporary dryness to haul off boots and inspect the damage. My feet are, literally, a bloody mess. There is little point applying plasters - they would fall off within minutes - so I simply change socks, stuff lavvy roll down the back of boots, then hope - and hop - for the best.

The next climb is steeper, and pain eases until the gradient does likewise beyond Mitchell Hill. Heels are hell now, provoking a stop every couple of minutes to adjust the amateurish padding. Eventually, reaching a state of despair only previously thought causable by midges, I try walking without

33

boots at all, in socks only. Feet become immediately cold and wet of course, but the rubbing stops and the novelty of a new discomfort briefly makes progress bearable. Then a foul bog beneath the summit slopes of Ettrick Pen forces a return to sodden footwear. These feel like displaced thumbscrews.

Eventually I arrive at the cairn, grinning with pain, way behind estimated timings. Never has a hill given so little enjoyment. Thankfully there is no-one around to see my condition: when suffering is neither fatal nor lasting, it is perhaps sometimes better to suffer alone.

A faint view of my destination, Over Phawhope beside the Ettrick Water, vanishes: I continue over Hopetoun Craig and Wind Fell in heavy rain. When the fence splits, I follow one branch down to Ettrick Head - a significant place. My south-north route here crosses a major west-east one: the 212-mile Southern Upland Way. Ettrick Head must have been one of the first places inked-in for inclusion, not only very fine scenically but also the most definite of all Borders watershed passes. Notwithstanding the condition of my feet, I feel excitement at having reached here, along with eagerness for all that lies ahead.

The promised land must wait however. First, a night of rest and recuperation. I follow waymarkers into trees and onto a forest road, descending with the river. Feet now reach a threshold of pain, beyond which there is no noticeable worsening: I'm able to attain an approximation to rhythmical movement at last. Even so, the mile down to the bothy takes close on an hour.

What a relief to push open the door, let the rucksack fall, collapse onto the plank bed! The building, roomy and dry, is later explored barefoot, but shows no sign of fellow-sojourners. A brown, shapeless meal of stewed meat and herbs does little to lift morale. I lie amid scattered equipment, internally debating options for the coming few days.

If the weather stays wet, the most inviting - and sensible - plan is to take a rest day here, then cross to the Selkirk-Moffat road on Friday and hitch into the latter for Saturday's supply drop. Alternatively, I face the music tomorrow and earn a two-day break in Moffat. Finally, and ideally, I walk both Thursday and Friday, thus reaching the Devil's Beef Tub by the weekend. This, though, seems most unlikely as feet are slid into sleeping-bag with the same care required in the old fairground game involving a metal loop passed along a twisted electric wire. One slight tremor and alarm-bells ring.

From darkness into light. Chill air tells of a change in the weather even before eyes open to see blue sky through the window. An immediate resolve comes over me: to cross the hills today whatever the state of my feet. Better pain in the sun than pain in the rain.

I have slept late - nearly till nine - yet potter about, making breakfast, sweeping the bothy, before moving out into sunlight for pedicure. Ancient bandages unearthed from the rucksack allow a cats-cradle of crêpe to be rigged for each foot, and walking becomes tolerable once more. The main problem today is to be bruised toes caused by excessive padding!

The number of lambs beside the track seems to have increased: overnight births, or simply the freshness of morning playing tricks? Certainly awareness and appreciation of my surroundings increases a hundredfold. Whereas the previous day had, like me, dragged its feet, today is already running and leaping, enlivening with every step.

I gain the pass in twenty-five minutes, the same time required for Capel Fell - at 678m the day's highest hill. It gives a fine panorama, both nearby - low morning light emphasising gullies on Croft Head - and slightly further afield, with Hart Fell and White Coomb, north of the Moffat Water, snow-edged and incised deeply by a series of classical U-shaped glacial trenches. All day this view reminds of the Cairngorms: steep-sided glens shoring up extensive areas of plateau.

These are tomorrow's hills however: for now I turn northeastward, following a dyke to a boggy col where the path from Bodesbeck crosses. I meet an old-timer *en route* to visit a friend down the Ettrick, having already reversed much of my own day's trek - but who claims to be too old for walking!

Bodesbeck Law - first cairned top of the day - proves another fine viewpoint, the wooded side of Carrifran Gans rising abruptly across the deep defile to the north. East of here the ridge straightens, each top shielding from sight the ones beyond. The sun is warm enough to warrant a T-shirt. Shorts would be comfortable too, but I decide against disturbing the intricate webbing around my feet: if it ain't broke, don't mend it.

After Andrewhinney Hill and Herman Law, the ridge broadens and leaves the 600m contour for good. Whereas the Southern Upland Way sneaks through hereabouts prior to St Mary's Loch and the Tweed at Traquair, my route jack-knifes back westward, descending grassy slopes beside a small gorge to reach the road at Birkhill.

Time was when this cottage doubled as an inn - providing, as did Moss Paul, hard-earned refreshment for travellers crossing what could, in adverse conditions, seem quite a high pass. Although traversing this particular watershed the wrong way, so to speak, I also stop for food and drink - albeit only water and a bran bar. Such has been the interest provided by clear conditions, I have eaten nothing but raisins since leaving the bothy.

The pre-walk plan was to camp just below here, near the road. Now I sit for a rethink. Only four in the afternoon, weather ideal, feet recovering remarkably from the screaming pain of yesterday, fitness beginning to seep into legs. I decide to climb again, to make Loch Skeen home for the night.

Forty-five minutes bring Watch Knowe, named for the Covenanters who stood lookout for armies trooping up the long glens below. A skirmish in the 1680s resulted in four Covenanters being shot by Claverhouse's men near here. As my own presence isn't a matter of life or death, I'm able to study the landscape nearer to hand - a landscape dominated by Loch Skeen, backed by the broken east face of 822m White Coomb. The name is an outcrop of old Gaelic - a corruption of *sgine*, or knife, as in the better-known Sgurr na Sgine in Glen Shiel - and presumably derives from the shape of the loch. The whole area now comes under the aegis of the National Trust for Scotland, with a well-worn path leading to the loch from the Grey Mare's Tail car park.

Even so, I'm surprised to run into a large group of youths resting by the shore. From Motherwell, on a Duke of Edinburgh, they are exhausted but happy. Soon after leaving them I find a great campsite: small and gently sloping, but with a burn only yards away, screes plunging across the loch and hardly a ripple to break the surface of the water itself. I lie outside the tent, unwrap the feet, cook a leisurely meal. Happiness is.

The first week is nearly over. A crisis has been dealt with and I will reach Moffat next evening with time in hand. I feel for the first time to really be coming to terms with what I'm attempting. The walk is no longer something to be held at arm's length, to be objectively pondered over: rather, it is now close to me, close as the clothes I wear and starting to feel every bit as comfortable. Each day's rhythmical moving-on gradually impresses its steady, subconscious beat, such that night-stops, relaxation, looking ahead to new ground and back to that already covered, these are all as much part of the walk as the steady progression from A to B to C. Perhaps more than ever before, I feel profoundly satisfied with what I'm doing.

I wake in darkness as though shaken by an impatient hand. Instinctively I know the reason, and poke my head out to gaze up and around. Stars everywhere, the sky thick with stars. Well-known constellations familiar to city dwellers lost in the vast network of shapes, the sweeping arc of the Milky Way casting enough light for surrounding hillsides to be clearly visible. This clarity adds a crystalline quality: pinpoints of light sparkle as though turning in slow unison, reflecting brightness from a still greater source. From the depths of my mind a phrase from Joyce rises to the occasion: *The heaventree of stars hung with humid nightblue fruit.*

The return to sleep takes a long time: I'm too aware of the enormity outside reaching down to the minuteness of my tent. The prospect of access to such sights for the coming ten weeks brings unquantifiable excitement. Mine is a rewarding insomnia.

❑❑❑❑❑

The tent downslopes a little too much for comfort: sleep comes only fitfully through the remainder of the night. Dozing finally abandoned, I emerge to find stars faded, gulls and oystercatchers screeching with the dawn. Vaporous mist rises off the loch, disperses into cloudless blue overhead. It is going to be a scorcher.

Strapping feet takes longer than before, delaying departure until eight-thirty. Half-an-hour later I'm on top of 800m Lochcraig Head having climbed steeply amid small crags and scree to hit the plateau right beside the cairn. Views back along Loch Skeen are already hazy with heat: I'm glad of both the high camp and the early start.

The weather may have opted for a slow, lazy day, but I still have a fair distance to cover, coupled with the highest hills thus far. Annoying, then, to feel a heavy lethargy settle over me on the climb to Firthybrig Head - due, no doubt, to need of a good feed. Supplies, especially of the snack variety, are running low.

Fence leads to dyke, where I dump the sack, munch the last of the raisins, set off at a tangent for White Coomb. Not quite a watershed hill, it is nevertheless the highest of the group, rising impressively from the road in broad wooded bluffs. After tinkering with the camera's self-timer and peering over the snow-rimmed corrie which names the hill, I hurry back, slightly guilty at mixing tiredness with extra exertion.

Off Sheet 79 at last! Toes feel the steep descent to well-named Rotten Bottom, gained by a series of long traverses, first one way, then the other, as though on some invisible stalker's path. In a prelude to high summer, late snowpatches melt to reveal flattened grass, small birds swoop and swerve low above the heather, insects emerge from winter incubation to whirr and hum in the heat - which takes the form of thick haze all but obscuring the sharp notch of Saddle Yoke half-a-mile to the south. Northward even horizons are lost, blurred between smoke-blue sky and a desert of straw-yellow hillsides. A hint of Fruid Reservoir can be seen - until even this fades to leave a scene transferred from a pointilliste canvas.

Noticing a fellrunner haring off Hartfell Rig, I contour round to intercept halfway as he does likewise. In training for Yorkshire's Three Peaks race the following weekend, he tells of relishing the peace and freedom of these Borders hills. We agree too many folk speed along the A74, bound for the Lakes or the Highlands, neglecting this vast area accessible both to northern England and central Scotland. True, there are few great crags here and the landscape rolls rather than rocks, but the solitude quotient is high. How different things would be were a handful of Munros scattered through the region!

38

We part, and suddenly I'm conscious just how few people have crossed my path this first week. While the Borders valleys bustle with villages and towns, their tops are unfrequented enough to make meeting another walker both pleasant and unexpected. Although not truly a wilderness, in hill-terms at least I will need to wait until beyond the Shiel-Cluanie divide before encountering such lonely country again.

That said, the fellrunner reported the D of E crowd on top of Hart Fell. Forty-five minutes later they are still there, laughing, joking in the sun, revelling in their break from less inspiring surroundings. I stay with them for lunch before continuing westward. They descend to Moffat more directly, via Swatte Fell.

The fence gives out and I resort to compasswork through the dense heat. All day there has been no sign of Thursday's hills, and even traffic-noise, clearly heard before, is muffled and faint. A sore-footed descent precedes Whitehope Heights, lacking both name and height on the OS map. The green, twin-topped ridge is also shapelier than on paper: a worthwhile viewpoint on a clear day? As it is, I can scarcely discern the flamboyantly-named Crown of Scotland a little to the northwest - a craggy knoll perhaps deriving its title from proximity to three great river-systems: Tweed, to which the hill lends its water, and the tributaries of which I have been skirting for almost a week now; Annan, falling south with gravitational directness from the nearby Devil's Beef Tub; Clyde, soon to be reached and followed on its broadening route to urban decay. These hills may be small and infrequently visited, but they give rise to great things.

A twisting ridge showing exposures of rock leads to the rim of the Beef Tub with its startling 200m drop. The sides are not vertical, merely holding grass at an angle rarely seen. Far below are pastures where the Johnstones of yore hid stolen cattle from which the name derives. The river slips away almost surreptitiously - as though overawed by its surroundings - through a neck as tight as a Cornish cove. The Beef Tub may not be the Annan's most remote source - Hart Fell lays claim to that - but is certainly the most impressive. It is doubtful whether any other river in the land has a birthplace quite so womb-like.

From Great Hill, the Edinburgh-Moffat road can be seen, precariously ringing the far hillside. I'm soon on its tarmac, glancing across to check the feasibility of the next batch of forestry, then thumbing from a layby. After thirty minutes the lift comes, oddly, from the wrong direction: a roadpainter's lorry turning before heading home.

Moffat is, as they say in Derbyshire, thronged. I have completely forgotten this is Good Friday. Indeed, Holy Week has slipped past without so much as a nod, wink or prayer. Thoughts, however, soon turn to what currently seem more pressing concerns: food and accommodation - with the former assuaged by a double fish supper eaten beneath the sheep statue in the town square. The latter requires more thought. I had planned another bed-and-breakfast, but the balmy evening, combined with high morale, suggests a camp.

The site is easily found: a vast green lawn of such whitewashed neatness as to evoke images of well-kept cemeteries - the kind populated by slow-moving limousines in American movies. This morbid thought fails to deter: I'm soon making good use of all available facilities.

A stroll into town for necessary phonecalls precedes the eating of lasagne in the Star Hotel. The evening only cools as darkness falls - when I sit in the main street watching the excited holiday bustle slowly quieten as the bars empty. Thoughts drift back to childhood Easter outings - remembered as always hot, always spent at Cromford Black Rocks. These thoughts gradually merge with those of the coming day, the first rest day. The holiday feeling is deeply instilled, and surely earned: almost a hundred miles covered, the back of the Borders broken, more familiar hills drawing near. Michelle and Janet will soon arrive, bringing food, clean clothes, dry boots - and, most important of all, enthusiasm and support.

I return to the tent as a distant train clatters through the warm night. If I do have an Easter prayer, it is one of thanksgiving.

I'm woken not by the anticipated heat of sun creeping across the campsite, but by light rain needling the flysheet. From no discernible direction, propelled by no noticeable wind, cloud has drifted in to embrace the hillsides around the town. The holiday spirit thus dampened, I retreat to bed before persistently noisy cows in an adjacent field force me into town to forage for food.

The morning passes slowly, the expectation of friends failing to offset a listlessness clinging to me as the cloud clings to fields and hills. This combination of indolence and impatience - to recur with each succeeding rest day - is something with which I will never fully come to terms throughout the walk.

Janet and Michelle arrive at one, bearing Easter eggs and mail along with more obvious necessities. The tent is bundled into the car boot, plimsolls replace still-saturated hill boots, more lasagne is eaten. Fellow diners must be bemused at our chattering, hyperactive conversation: there is so much to tell.

The remainder of the afternoon slips away in folk museums, craftshops, tearooms - the latter all apparently owned by northern English exiles. Then a return visit to the Beef Tub from the normal, touristy side. Too soon, though, the hours together have gone: the women prepare to set off back to Glasgow. Thus begins another recurrent supply day theme: time, having started so slowly, races away like a train gathering pace from a station. Despite dozens of things still to say, experiences to relate, news of home to hear, I'm dropped beside the A701, the last moments bad-temperedly wasted on a frantic equipment check. Sights are already too set on the next oasis to fully appreciate this one.

I pitch on a grassy track in the forest north of Tweedshaws, only yards from the road yet completely hidden. Within minutes the rain, having relented for much of the afternoon, returns with more serious intent. I dive for cover, then doze as tent wall drumming settles into a metronomic beat. Non-campers rarely realise the amount of noise generated by rain on a nylon tent. Even a light fall can disrupt sleep, and to this day I'm occasionally conned into wrapping-up completely before emerging to nothing more than drops caught in the wind.

Now, though, it isn't the rain wakening me, but dogs barking deep in the forest. In the nebulous territory between sleep and wakefulness, I feel scared - a fear countered by forcing myself awake to study maps for the coming week. Yet even this proves problematic. The newly-delivered Sheets 72 and 65 aren't my originals showing the watershed in red ink, but unmarked spares lent as backup by a friend. Fortunately I can recall much of the route from memory, leaving only a few gaps, easily pieced together.

Another minor logistical nuance needs sorted. Two more Glaswegian chums, Eildon and Ian, are offering to come out on Monday, but meeting them entails reaching either Coulter or Biggar by tomorrow night: a long walk if the weather stays bad. I have sent word to hang fire and await further instructions.

These things are all pondered as I lie in darkness, letting my mind move ahead over the coming week as the one just completed recedes from interest. I eat some of the mountainous food filling the tent - *how am I ever going to carry all this stuff?* - then sleep as rain, dogs and cars join chorus against the night.

The sense of unease remains in the grey morning light. Wind and dogs had continued to howl through the darkness: I'm glad to move. The sleeping-bag stuffsac having inadvertently vanished back to Glasgow means the resultant fibre-pile bundle reduces rucksack space even more. Strenucus effort crams everything in - bar a ready-cooked chicken left to dangle, bizarrely, from a strap. Fortunately the dogs fail to get wind of this as I pass Tweedshaws, thus avoiding a reprise of the Moss Paul farce enacted all the way to Biggar.

Tweed's Well, official source of southern Scotland's longest river, bubbles up hereabouts. There will be no suitably long-distance views today however: clouds bank all around. I carefully connect with Friday's clocking-off point, then follow an aisle-like firebreak onto Bog Hill. Inevitably, with a name like that, badly-drained ground squelches underfoot.

By nine-thirty I'm atop Clyde Law: a significant landmark. Just as Annan succeeded Esk, so it too is left behind as my route swings onto a north-south axis. The Clyde, in various manifestations, will stay with me, like a dog at heel, until the onset of the Highlands more than two weeks hence. I give an internal whoop of delight: the physical watershed crosses a mental one.

I press on, desolate glens to my left, dense forestry to my right. Although the latter proves a useful bolt-hole from the fierce wind, mostly I'm content to be bowled along by gusts pushing square against my back. The hills steadily increase in height from south to north, like a line of Russian dolls - each summit visible over the shoulder of its predecessor. This telescopic effect urges me on, such that Coomb Dod comes by ten-thirty, without a break. A shepherd in a Land Rover can be seen one bump further along, dogs chasing ahead, but drops westward toward Crawford long before I catch up.

Taken thus, these hills merge: only short descents separate the gently swelling tops. One such rise finally brings a sight as longed-for as the Clyde itself: Tinto, its dark, cloudcapped cone a sign of welcome to familiar places. I'm now in Lanarkshire - by no means a favourite county, but one which can, reassuringly, be mentally pictured without recourse to a map. I think back to my first ascent of Tinto - arduous through waist-deep snow, the whole country dazzling in the sun, today's hills lost in wave upon wave of a white sea to the south.

Conditions differ greatly now: sunlight breaks through fast-moving clouds to briefly highlight rich patches of colour - a green field, water suddenly blue - before moving on elsewhere, a spotlight on a stage.

Reservoirs are seen on both sides - Fruid, Talla, Camps, Culter - all compressed into narrow valleys, easing identification of the confusion of hills above.

Glenwhappen Rig: the day's first hill to give real pleasure from its own shape, shallow corries harbouring old snow and a long, high limb reaching away out above the Kingledoors Burn. Northward comes the low pass of Holm Nick: here I pause for lunch of Easter eggs, jelly tots and coke!

The weather has been closing for some time, and rain catches me on the rush up Culter Fell. This is the first hill on which I have set foot previously: a recent winter trip when Michelle and I, knowing a return to be in the offing, hid 10p under a rock at the summit. Arrival today coincides with the storm being cranked up to maximum intensity: horizontal rain abetted by staggering (in both senses) gusts, paying scant respect to waterproofs as it pours through. Unsurprisingly, attempts to recoup the dosh last approximately five seconds - so if anyone is ever short of change for the phone...

Culter Fell proves expensive all round, as during the frantic, dripping descent I decide to blow the bed-and-breakfast money saved from Moffat. As downpour abates to torrential drizzle over King Bank Head, Coulter becomes the target once Scawdman's Hill has rounded off the day. But even this plan abruptly aborts at the foot of the normally inconsequential 100m climb: the fiercest of many gusts leaves me gripping the fence like a sailor clinging to a masthead. Like it or not, my subconscious yells common-sense: *Get down!*

After a tortuous descent to Nisbet, black, tangled heather and the funnelling gale relent as I reach the relief of open farmland in the valley floor. Just as a narrow reach of river flows more swiftly than a broad one, so wind spreads its energies once free of a tight valley.

With Coulter showing no sign of bed-and-breakfast signs, I traipse the two miles into Biggar. Here I'm soon luxuriating in the hot bath of a guest house allied to a French restaurant next door. Having put in a twenty mile day, I'm now ahead of schedule and able to take Monday off. Hopefully the break will allow the weather to settle again. Otherwise, all is well. Toes and heels are recovering fast, due mainly to a snug pair of lightweight Trionics. Kindly bought by friends and originally intended merely as backup, these are now to be worn all the way to Cape Wrath with only one short break. For once, feet are the only part of me to have remained dry!

A breakfast only slightly less substantial than that at Moss Paul should still be filed under compliment rather than complaint. Mme Herault (or Mrs Herault? - I forget to ascertain the correct form, just as I omit to enquire whether there is any connection with the stately home of Chatelherault near Hamilton), generously pushes a pound back into my hand as sponsor money when I pay the bill.

I wander the town searching without success for commemoration of Hugh MacDiarmid (the poet settled in Biggar in 1951), then try to find a good spot for photographing Tinto, which looms large down the main street. A rucksack-on-legs *en route* from Glen Coe to Galloway disgorges from a bus, incongruously armed with ice-tools, grumbling about mild conditions.

The wind hasn't really relented, but it is a dry, bright morning: clouds scud across only the highest tops. I retreat to the Crown Hotel and televised snooker before Eildon - named for the Melrose hills - and Ian arrive shortly before midday, weans in tow. After lunch, we drive to New Lanark, Robert Owen's progressive eighteenth-century mill village below the Falls of Clyde.

Back in Coulter, the afternoon improving all the while, I shoulder the sack as we wave mutual goodbyes. The walk back up the Nisbet Burn still feels windy, but having it dry means I continue past several tempting low-level swards to pitch just over the watershed itself: a high-but-sheltered site giving distant views of sharp Pentlands.

Fabric repairs to the tent precede a late evening stroll round Cardon and Chapelgill Hills in a breezy hour. Tinto, as ever, catches the last of the sunlight. My own next hills are jumbled amid farmland and backroads to the north. There is to be no more ground over 600m before Ben Lomond.

Two precedents are set today, to be adhered to with remarkable consistency over the coming weeks. First: any high camp, no matter how settled the conditions on pitching, will always be struck in cloud and rain. Second: in any given week, Tuesday will always be the longest, most tiring day.

Thus I wake to swirling whiteness, the tent doused every few minutes as a shower comes through the pass above like a squeezed sponge. During one interlude I venture onto Scawdman's Hill only to receive the inevitable drenching at half-height. Obviously a hill I'm destined never to have dry!

On a northern top - Black Hill - I emerge from cloud just high enough to see the aptness of the name compared with White Hill beyond. The contrast between heather and grass is striking. I descend March Brae on a good path of small white stones, carefully built but for no clear reason. A ruin stands beside the track leading from Cow Castle to Kilbucho Church - although there is no sign of the map-marked settlement on White Hill above, only scores of rabbits racing between gorses as I reach the road and stop to change films. With the day rapidly brightening, the pull onto Goseland Hill comes easily. From the summit, Biggar appears neatly laid-out: quiet outpost of the Central Belt.

Following yesterday's delivery-run, I'm at last armed with correct maps. These show not only the route, but have each road-crossing numbered for ease of reference when phoning base. Now, between roads nine and ten, comes an awkward obstacle - one anticipated despite all the pre-walk blurb

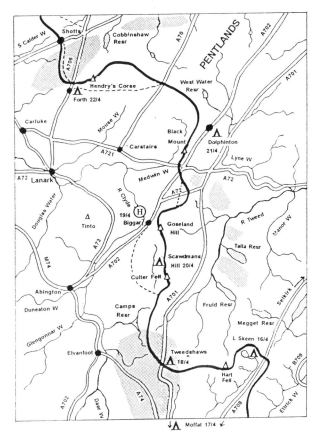

L Skeen
- Shotts

45

about never having to cross a river. The wide strath connecting Clyde and Tweed, seven miles in length, contains a daunting irrigation ditch: sluggish and deep, steep muddy banks dropping to dark, reedy water giving no hint of a bottom. A medieval moat could scarcely have formed a more effective barrier. I'm content to diverge a mile west, utilising a bridge on one of the abandoned railway lines which once wove together the Tweeddale towns.

Finally across, I sit trying to work out the exact line of the watershed before giving up none the wiser. So flat is this stretch of land between the two great rivers that times of exceptional flood see the Clyde burst its banks and spill into the Tweed - technically creating an island of Scotland north of here.

Seconds after setting off, I'm again offered a lift. Considering the hours of my life wasted at roadsides, arm stuck out like an old-fashioned railway-signal while BMWs and Range Rovers flashed past, it is now laughably ironic to be offered two untakable lifts within six days without having to so much as remove hands from pockets.

The afternoon brings several tiny green hills, the type Gaelic nomenclature would probably prefix *cnoc*. I'm about to climb the first of these, an unnamed mound above Skirling, when a farm Land Rover appears, checking on lambs. This provokes a snap policy decision not to trespass on farmland if at all possible: farmers surely find it hard enough administering crops without errant walkers wandering about. Thus a track past South Mains is followed to the footpath linking Broughton and Skirling, scattered wood pigeon feathers hinting at a local fox. Gallow Law stands above the fresh-painted village, giving fine open views back to Broad Law and Culter Fell: bigger hills seen from Biggar Hills.

En route to the next bump, a shepherd roars over on an ancient motorbike, dog close at tyres. I fear a lecture on the privacy of farmland, but he is of course merely across to pass the time of day. Weather set fair, he says, then tells of a pub due to open in nearby Dolphinton during May: I'm just too early! He races away to his sheep while I, with Broomy Law being worked, descend more sedately to Candy Mill, from where farm tracks cut a corner leading to the big road junction at Melbourne.

A much needed rest and some raisins are called for. Any thought of pushing on to West Linton for the night has faded: legs possess only enough energy for one more hill, not two. Wearily I climb 516m Black Mount, wading thick heather, using the fence as banister when the slope steepens. The summit view contrasts the high sprawl of Broughton Heights with flatlands now only a day's walk away. Everything slips into soft focus as the weather settles.

A wood glows rich green in low evening light: to stroll between broad, well-spaced trees is a joy. Rabbits hurtle across fields as I wander down to Kirkhouse Farm to be met by two small boys who excitedly lead to their father in the kitchen. Yes, of course I can camp - and use the shower too! The kindness shown by total strangers is again and again a source of uplift and encouragement.

I pitch in the lower wood, pheasants and horses nearby, with a view down across the Dolphinton streetlights. The end of a section is also nearby, almost a complete walk in itself. Even were I to break an ankle tomorrow, I would at least have traversed the Southern Uplands, from an historical border to a geological one. The morning will mark the leaving of the Tweed, my knowledge of which has grown from a quiet trickle to a broad, flowing affinity. I will return to these hills with renewed eagerness, but also with a naïvety now lost forever. Somehow I feel both happy and sad.

Birdsong and blue sky mark the beginning of another warm day. After waving goodbye to the farmer - already busy in his tractor - I wander down to the houses of Dolphinton: a village unique in being split almost equally between two regions, Strathclyde and Borders. This must cause more than a few administrative problems. Is refuse collected on same day? Do residents pay the same taxes? Do children go to different schools? Dolphinton is a true watershed village!

I'm hailed by an elderly bespectacled man out walking his dog. "Are you the walker I met yesterday?" "No, sorry..." "Well come in for breakfast anyway!". With the face of AJP Taylor and the voice of Ivor Cutler, he proves a fascinating character. Founder member of the SYHA - in the days when not even cyclists were allowed entry, only walkers and climbers - he tells of arriving at Balquhidder hostel, sadly no more, and being led out to the barn to gather straw for his bed. How different today, when finding a parking space is most hostellers' first consideration, while the buildings themselves more and more resemble intercontinental hotels rather than cheap accommodation for the hard-up but enthusiastic. My new friend serves up stories of wartime Egypt along with a bacon-and-egg breakfast, as well as expressing interest in my own doings. After a lengthy stay, much revived, I reluctantly press on - although the whole day could have been whiled away in conversation.

Feeling both full and fully fit, Mendick Hill quickly comes and goes with only one pause - to inspect a newly-dead fox. The distinctive stepped flank of Dunsyre Hill looks well from the top - breezy enough to discourage thoughts of changing into shorts. Strange conditions: cloud and wind, but oppressive heat nevertheless.

The Pentlands. At last a group of hills clearly definable, instantly recognisable by name. Others climbed during the past days possess names linking them with their neighbours - Ettrick, Moffat, etc - but none are installed quite so firmly in the mind of the populace. The reason is obvious: while the Pentlands are no more notable than these other groups, the presence of nearby conurbations breeds familiarity and affection. To hundreds of thousands living in Edinburgh, their northern reaches are in countless everyday views: seen beyond the end of city streets, from parks and office windows, always available as an instant weather forecast and clearly marking the limit of city suburbs. They represent that which can be escaped to, whether from work or unemployment. The soon-to-be-reached Campsies, above Glasgow, play the same role - and as a result become much loved, even by those who would not dream of setting foot on their slopes.

My route merely passes through the outskirts of the Pentlands them-selves, like an indoor athlete's kick off the banking before the long flat straight to come. There is an exciting, urban feel to the land: traffic thrives on the roads, distant chimneys smoke, windows glint and every hollow seems to cradle a reservoir - water dragged and diverted against gravity into countless homes. I'm creeping up on the blindside of the city.

Crossing North Muir onto Catstone, one such reservoir, West Water, glistens below, its surface broken only by an angler in a rowing-boat. Deep heather - itself as heavy as pulling an oar - causes many a stop. The moorland over Fadden creaks and croaks with grouse before burnt heather eases progress up Craigengar - a lonely hill and westernmost Pentland of any note. Here I look back to the waters of Tweed for the last time prior to embarking on my circuit of the Forth. This initially takes the form of Linhouse Water - which merges with the Almond before entering the Firth at Cramond.

The day having settled into haze once more, I check the compass for the long, aimless descent westward. Over an hour passes before the paradoxi-cal Dry Burn brings the road near Tarbrax. Here an appropriately large hoarding - both Americanized and Americansized - advertises the "Lazy Y Western Bar and Lounge."

My No Trespass policy means taking to red-tarred roads wending away into the heat through farmland and old mineworkings. I set the mental alarm-clock for three hours' time, memorise the necessary junctions, let nine-tenths of my mind drift off to sleep, start plodding.

Shortly before Auchengray, this peripatetic siesta receives rude interruption in the form of a sharp shower which materialises from nowhere, drops its payload of water, dissipates into the haze again. Surely summer has arrived!

These are desolate roads winding through arid country. Only two cars pass despite the supposed rush-hour. A wry west-of-Scotland name for these parts is Darkest Lanarkshire - reference both to the grimness of towns and villages and to the prevalent religious bigotry. The phrase applies well on the backroads: a lone walker breaking an ankle here stands less chance of encountering help, be it from Samaritan, priest, Levite or Orangeman, than on numerous hills which spring to mind. All this, set alongside the natural beauty of the country just crossed, makes Lanarkshire very much a game of two halves.

Mind you, footsore and hungry, the drab grey council houses of Forth are as welcome a sight as the shimmering spires of Venice - well, almost! With nowhere designated for camping (Forth isn't exactly a holiday town), I turn to the usual last resort: the recreation park. For one night's rest this is usually a safe bet. Rarely does anyone object - apart from in those parts of England where the law seems specifically designed around abusing wayfarers - and even then the effort and co-operation necessary to enforce eviction would most likely take more than an evening to organise.

Not that this is ever likely here. As so often the case, the friendliness of locals belies their unappealing environs. Forth has high unemployment and not a little poverty, yet I experience a warmer, more genuine welcome than in more affluent communities where privately-owned mansions stand aloof in leafy streets. I have no qualms whatever about leaving the tent unguarded for a couple of hours to visit the Talisker Arms - where Dundee United are to be seen thrashing mighty Borussia Mönchengladbach two-nil amid scenes of jubilation both on- and off-screen.

As in Moffat, it feels strange lying in bed to hear dogs barking, cars revving, people shouting and laughing: the ordinary sounds of a town settling for the night. The great, previously unknown expanse of the Southern Uplands now lies behind, while familiar territory waits ahead: the Central Lowlands followed by small, domesticated hills carrying the watershed round the north side of Glasgow. The football result matches my mood perfectly. Having survived the crucial away leg without too much of a drubbing, I now hope to progress to the next round in front of my home crowd.

2: Homeland heatwave
(Thursday 23rd April - Thursday 30th April)

To speak of the lowlands of Scotland is to speak in relative terms. Only when seen amid the proliferation of high ground furrowing the country does the phrase have even occasional relevance. The flow country of Caithness is perhaps describable as low - although such roughness of moor and bog demands redefinition of the word. The same cannot be said, however, for its northeastern sibling, the shoulder jutting into the North Sea nowadays known as Grampian Region. This, along with several other areas designated by tourist brochures as *lowland,* is jam-packed with a jumble of small hills which would, if sited south of the Border, be the cause of considerable excitement, the inspiration for innumerable coffee-table books, and quickly be ring-fenced into a National Park. Only intermingled farmland and distance from higher hills provide a sense of a gentler, more habitable land.

One part of Scotland can genuinely claim to fit the lowland bill however, and it was in this I now woke to a warm, windless morning. I was in the long, narrow strip of land between the Southern Upland Fault and the Campsie-Ochil-Lomond barrier to the north, corked at both ends by big cities: the Central Belt. For the coming few days the mantle of hillwalker would, like an ill-fitting rucksack, rest uneasily on my shoulders. Backroads and farm tracks would link together to allow quiet passage through the busiest part of the country, while simultaneously laying me open to a host of curious glances and nudged remarks. As my surroundings levelled to become less threatening, so, paradoxically, would I become more vulnerable in my own self-awareness. To be away from the shelter of hills was to be as exposed as a lone tree in a lightning storm.

The morning was vague and featureless, much like the landscape itself. I read a newspaper over breakfast, then wandered the streets of grey pebbledashed houses comprising virtually all of Forth's accommodation. The name probably stems from *ford* - as in the English suffix to Stafford, Salford, Bradford etc - but an inebriated inhabitant offered an alternative, more whimsical derivation. He reasoned this to be the fourth Calder, after West, East and Mid, until nineteenth century boundary changes left the young Lanarkshire mining community cut off from its West Lothian neighbours. The name remained nonetheless, only with Calder dropped and the spelling adjusted to that of the distant river.

A second curiosity came to light when another local remarked on my height. Being six feet eight, having to endure such comment was common enough - only this time I merely served to spark mention of two Forth brothers, George and Hugh Gracie: both over seven feet tall and the former the tallest man in Scotland. I was definitely in the lowlands compared with these high tops.

Michelle arrived at midday, when we sorted supplies in a strange little waiting-room: half bus shelter, half glasshouse, one wall lined with photographs of jockeys and old long-shorted football teams. I left out a fair amount of food: this would be readily available throughout the coming week. We arranged to meet again in two days' time, leaving the location open. I was to phone on Friday evening.

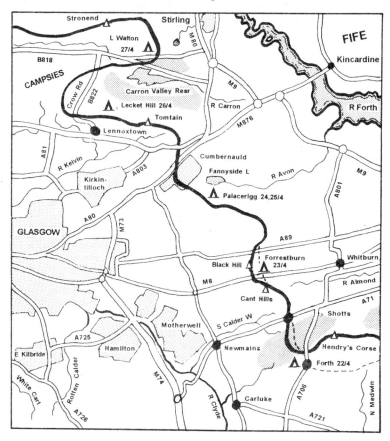

Shotts - Stronend

Then, having no desire to end both this walk and all walks by plummeting down an open mineshaft, I stuck to the roads for the long afternoon trudge to Shotts. Stuck in more ways than one, the tarmac tacky with heat and every slight rise carrying its black mirage of water. Lorries leaving the Headlesscross opencast site fumed past as though in some gargantuan grand prix, each recycling the cloud of dust raised by its predecessor. Horses stood immobile in a field, black as their backdrop of coal bings forming the area's only high ground: vast tumuli, burial-mounds for generations of hard labour.

Once across the busy A71, I soon entered the shapeless amalgam of villages forming Shotts. Positively sophisticated compared with Forth, the town was originally named Bertram-Shotts after a local landowner of mammoth physical proportions who could reputedly deal with a dozen ordinary men at one go. The Gracie brothers, Bertram, myself. Truly there were giants in the land.

Into the library for a flick through Poucher's *Scottish Peaks* - his walking routes drawn onto photographs in thick white roadpainter's lines - before pressing on northward past a grassed-over reservoir where a trig point sat behind bars like some caged zoo animal. I crossed the railway again: the meandering, lived-in backline between Edinburgh and Glasgow. This linked the cities in a slack bowstring compared with the taut, tensioned directness of the M8 - the sound of which now rose like heat from a cutting ahead.

The motorway had become the day's main objective, a broad blue river stretching across the map, and I crossed to the north bank near Hirst, leaning over the parapet to mindlessly watch the flow of traffic beneath. Lazily deciding to swerve Black Hill and its television mast, I camped beside nearby Forrestburn Reservoir.

Slotting the tent between reeds and roots proved a test of dexterity, but to have found such a secret, peaceful campsite was an unexpected bonus. Across the water two fishermen cast unerringly to the centre of ripples. A flotilla of ducks was anchored close by, every now and then frantically splashing their wings. A tractor to-ed and fro-ed across fields like a shuttle on a loom.

Humidity gradually faded with the evening - remembered as one of watercolour-blue sky above small green boulder-strewn hills. The lights on the TV mast brightened against imperceptibly gathering darkness, while the distant whoosh of the motorway sounded, in the confusion of thoughts prior to sleeping, like the roar of some giant blowtorch.

The heatwave which began as I crossed the Pentlands today approached its zenith. I was lucky not to have hills to sweat over, but to stroll through the day in shady confinement of farm tracks and abandoned railway lines.

A low morning sun silvered the reservoir as I took the track through Baads farm - named as if transported from the Transvaal by some mysterious agricultural telekinesis. Cows jostled and shoved between tubular steel railings, wild-eyed, lurching in response to bullying, wordless shouts from farmhands.

A brief diversion onto the railway preceded a track leading up past Bedlormie towards Drumbeg. Here an insignificant notice giving the standard warning, *Beware of the dog,* proved scant preparation for the highly significant Alsatian bounding from behind a Range Rover to growl and snarl. I suddenly wished Bertram still frequented these parts and would now stride jauntily round the corner, crop in hand, to the rescue of a fellow giant. No joy: I had to be content having the brute called off by a non-giantess sporting tweed cap, yellow gumboots and RP accent, who enquired as to my literacy. At least her bark was preferable to the guard dog's bite!

More barking at Drumbeg kennels - thankfully from inside wire pens - hurried me on past the quietly preserved National Nature Reserve of Blawhorn Moss. A path overgrown with brambles, accessed by a stile overgrown with barbed wire, led to Easter Whin: here it was belligerent sheep defending the farmyard. I cut across country toward Black Loch, nestling high on the surrounding land and one of the few natural lochs in the area - albeit much enlarged last century to create a reservoir for the Monklands Canal. Southern approaches having been newly corrugated by forestry plantings, I was sweating and thirsty on reaching High Limerigg with its sunblind of tall pines.

The afternoon was now very warm, yet for some reason I omitted changing into shorts - a mistake paid for on leaving the shade of the village: moorland gave off heat like a griddle. On top of this, at Drumbow farm, another fearsome dog gave vent to its feelings from the end of an equally fearsome chain. I edged nervously past, musing that the proliferation of Cerberean offspring in these parts paralleled that of local penal institutions, and the two might be connected. The human lock-ups at Longriggend, Shotts and Polmont, all well within escapee range, perhaps provoked the more wary locals into acquiring a second line of defence.

If so, the sight of a fugitive hillwalker must have aroused suspicions as I avoided roads and villages, dodging behind houses on disused railways and old brickpaths to work my way off Sheet 65. This was the least inspiring, topographically, of all watershed maps, yet all afternoon there was a curious sensation of being on high ground despite a reality of scarcely 200m above sea-level. Haze and the lack of running water contributed to this, along with the desolate, forlorn atmosphere of an almost-dead mining area. The once-rich seams beneath here were some of the earliest in Britain to be worked, such that in 1890 Longriggend boasted forty pits in full production. The 1920s saw this reduced to six. Now there were none.

The houses of Caldercruix, another old mining village, were briefly seen before they too dissolved into haze. This, rather than the spurious Forth, could lay claim to be the real fourth Calder did not the North Calder Water, the crooks or windings of which gave the village its name, flow westward to join the Clyde near Calderpark Zoo. The river system uniting the three Lothian communities flowed the opposite way, to the Firth of Forth.

A crossword puzzle of paths led to a squalid dump where I lounged in a torn armchair to watch a girl canter past on a white horse. This jumble of wrecked furniture and rusting, graffitied cars was no place to linger, yet showed more signs of recent human interest than did the deserted hanger-like mine buildings above Greengairs - passed on descent to the public road. Part of the track had flooded into a large pond, home to a variety of aquatic birdlife. Not sharing their willingness to plunge in and cool off, I made do with the deep pool of shade offered by Greengairs community centre. The village - strung along one main street like still-dirty clothes on a washing line - had a semi-tautological name: *gair* denoting a strip of green grass in a barren place.

Ever since leaving Forth I had been pondering the problem of where to spend this coming night. Thoughts centred on an idea of Michelle's: to camp at Palacerigg Country Park, where the staff, she surmised, would happily grant such a request. Initially I dismissed this out of hand on the pretext of being seen as an unwelcome intrusion. Besides, I soon needed to fit in a rest day, and the park manager, amenable as he or she might be, would surely be less than eager to take someone on board for a full weekend. But now, nearing decision time, I sensed my negativity hinged not so much on this defensive smokescreen as on my own unwillingness to make the request: I was simply too embarrassed to ask! This was daft: my internal pessimism with regard to human nature lagged well behind the empirical evidence of the past fortnight - and anyway, not only were the park rangers there to provide assistance, it might just make someone's day were a long-distance walker to arrive in search of a place to camp.

Having thus come to terms with my insecurities, it wasn't long before I passed through the wrought iron gateway and timidly chapped the door of Dr Brian Thomson, park manager. Sure enough, he was delighted to help, scribbling directions on a map to help me find somewhere quiet and close to clean water. As long as I watched the fire danger I could make myself at home. Leaving his office brought a feeling of relief, of a greater weight being taken from my shoulders than that of the rucksack now unpacked in a field some ten minutes' walk from the visitor centre. Odd how simple things can seem so difficult at times.

Food preceded use of the phone in the nearby golf course clubhouse, where a dinner-dance made for difficult conversation. I persevered, taking advantage of being within cheap rate range of home for the first time. Numerous calls were made: some to plan ahead, some merely for a blether. A minibus-load of friends was coming to Rowardennan for Ben Lomond the following Sunday, and I confirmed my intention of hanging back for them despite now being a whole day ahead of schedule.

The tie, jacket and stiletto brigade's inevitable progress to the Slosh signalled it was time to escape back to the warm stillness of my campsite, through golfers chatting as they completed their rounds, past animals retreating to corners of pens for the night, across long strips of sunlight broken only by silhouetted trees and highlighting early spring lushness in the grass. I slept within earshot of the human wildlife park known as Cumbernauld, knowing the following night would be spent in exactly the same place. Not only did the tent feel like home, it now felt almost as secure and firmly rooted as the sprawl of housing beyond the last of the trees.

This sense of permanence stayed throughout the coming day. As I wrote up my log late Saturday evening, a big red sun sinking behind the tower blocks of the New Town, I was able to look back on the most refreshing, relaxing break thus far. Indeed, these had been the only truly restful twenty-four hours of the whole fortnight. Moffat and Biggar were merely frantic stops to refuel: now the car had been parked in the garage overnight, the engine given a chance to cool down.

Not that the above is an appropriate metaphor with the heatwave having continued unabated. Little in the way of actual cooling down was done: only at the start of the day did the sun show any restraint. I had woken to a morning of fragile, translucent mist, sunlight filtered as through a net curtain. Dew lay heavy on the grass and a line of leafless, almost lifeless trees seemed bent and frail, unprepared for the heat to come. The early morning held an unreal, ephemeral feel of seasons changing, of spring emerging from its winter chrysalis to dry wings before taking to the air.

Careful not to repeat Friday's mistake, I dressed in shorts immediately, then embarked on an exploration of the park. Covering 700 acres previously under farmland, Palacerigg was designated a country park in 1969 and started taking visitors three years later. Extensive planting saw one fifth of the land given over to a quarter of a million trees - an ideal habitat for the wide variety of woodland animals and birdlife. Additional to this was a fine collection of Scottish and other northern animals: wildcat, wolf, arctic fox, northern lynx and a very smelly polecat. All were presenting themselves, eagerly expectant of feeding time - while a neighbouring enclosure saw a ranger feed a noisy commotion of goats, sheep, ducks and floppy-eared rabbits, aided and abetted by a gaggle of young boys.

Mist began to disperse into pale blue brightness as I wandered further afield, in search of Shetland ponies and Soay sheep. That the latter were never reached was the result of chancing on the most commonplace, yet most wonderful of all miracles: birth. The mare was less than a hundred metres away and well advanced in labour when first seen. Gradually a tiny foal emerged, shiny as the dew still covering the grass, to be gently licked dry by other ponies gathered round in support and encouragement. The mother then broke free by simply standing and walking away. Within ten minutes the foal was also trying to stand, on spindly, disjointed legs, until after a half-dozen chaotic, Bambi-like failures it was suddenly aloft, as uncertainly stable as a Giacometti figurine. I had been the sole human witness to the peaceful start of a new life.

Once Michelle arrived we strolled back to the tent with supplies - notable among which was a container of vitamin supplement, an unappealing mish-mash of beans and greens, much like coleslaw only minus the mayonnaise and bearing the Alice-in-Wonderland message: *Eat this, or else!* This came from Marlyn Turbitt, who had been in charge of base camp up to that point. Her administrative duties now passed to Julia and John Bowditch, newly back from holiday and to be my main contact for the rest of the walk.

The day drifted lazily on in the heat. We returned to the animal pens, but their inhabitants now sought patches of shade, hiding from sun, from clicking cameras and pointing children. Full of tales of the ponies, I insisted on a return visit and was glad to see the newborn firmly established on its feet. A game of putting marked the end of our exertions. The remainder of the afternoon slipped sleepily away watching windsurfers on Fannyside Loch.

Later, we drove into Cumbernauld in search of a curry house. The only one to be found was posh and pricey, but what the hell! The cost of the meal was nothing compared to that of allowing morale to descend from its present high plateau.

Michelle stayed late, before vacating the stage - apart from a cameo appearance on Ben Lomond - until Cape Wrath itself. But as a final bow, she left the most eagerly awaited of all supplies so far. In the dark clutter of the tent, like treasure in an attic, lay the first maps of the Highlands.

Maps or no maps, treasure or no treasure, the Highlands were still several days' walk away. I had enough time in hand to be sure of a two day rest at Rowardennan youth hostel, but three small ranges of hills still needed crossed before I could lie back on the well-made bed of progress. Through the first of these, the Campsies, my route was to follow a boomerang course. It was the outward arm of this I hoped to complete today.

The morning broke clear of mist earlier than had its predecessor, and the effort of trying to cram everything into the rucksack brought on the first of many sweats. Eventually I set off along a wooded track leading to an industrial estate, glad to be moving again if somewhat unenthused by the immediate prospect of having to cross the largest centre of population on the entire watershed. Many walkers tell of navigational difficulties in poor weather conditions on the hill. This is understandable, yet whilst occasionally sharing their view, or lack of it (before the week was out I would do so again), I often experienced greater disorientation in towns and cities. So it was that two miles of concrete Legoland filled me with a certain trepidation.

Cumbernauld was the third of Scotland's postwar New Towns - after East Kilbride and Glenrothes, before Livingston and Irvine - and formed a complex rat-run of cold-shouldered (or should it be hard-shouldered?) unfriendliness. Bypasses, roundabouts, flyovers... A maze of grey too faceless to present anything other than a blank stare of welcome.

I couldn't be bothered trying to follow the watershed exactly, preferring the line of least resistance through the layered roads. High wire-mesh fences repeatedly barred pedestrian walkways, and the resultant road-walking saw me periodically buzzed by high-speed cars. But fortunately it was Sunday, the day of rest for juggernauts, so I was only occasionally forced to scuttle sideways into the gutter in avoidance of being hedgehogged into tarmac.

By Wardpark the worst was past, with trees and fields being seen again. By Banknock, having crossed the nadir of the Central Belt - where Antonine Wall, Forth and Clyde Canal, A80 and Glasgow-Edinburgh main line all squeezed through like wires into a plug - I was back in hill country at last. After four days away, the feeling was one of homecoming.

The village was Sunday-quiet apart from a few women scurrying to kirk, clutching their Bibles like handbags. Soon the houses fell behind: woodland tracks giving out onto a green slope of short grass, evidently well cropped by sheep which dotted the hillside like boulders. In celebration of returning to a lush, live landscape, I lay in the sun a long while, listening to water gurgling along a burn, trying to make out details of Strathkelvin below. Normally the urban tentacles trailing Glasgow's bulbous head would be in full view, but everything was now as fuzzy as a badly-tuned TV picture. Even the nearby reservoir at Kilsyth was difficult to distinguish.

The return to a three-dimensional landscape brought with it, inevitably, a return to thoughts meteorological. Apart from the wayward straggler of a shower at Auchengray, five days had now passed since the last scrappy remnants of cloud dispersed into the prevailing seamless blue. Yet the very fact of the weather being so settled was, paradoxically, beginning to have a curiously unsettling effect on my thinking: surely there must soon be rain, and plenty - it was only April after all.

Although in planning the walk I had eagerly anticipated two or three long spells of warm, dry weather - Scotland in springtime being rarely as wet as its popular image - I could almost have done without this present drought. In many ways it had come at exactly the wrong time: the past few days could have been walked in any conditions, whereas the long-overdue deluge would now catch me in less generous surroundings. Absurdly, this analysis led briefly to hope that the stratonimbular sluice-gates would open here and now, on the Kilsyth Fells and on me, thus draining the system before the harder going further north.

I was well aware of this being a ridiculous conclusion to draw, yet it stayed with me as I moved across the southern edge of Denny Muir through dense-as-ever heat. I eventually came to realise my only control over the weather took the form of time-in-hand: to maintain the present good progress would allow the option of sitting out storms when they finally arrived.

Lunch was eaten at the old Takmadoon road linking Kilsyth and Carron Bridge, where a man sat on the roof of his Mini to call-up, in the cryptic jargon of the Citizen's Band, colleagues doubtless similarly perched in Cumbernauld, Croy and Hamilton. A spongy path then accompanied the forest fence over Tomtain - which reared so abruptly in the distorting haze to have had me earlier mistaking it for the higher Meikle Bin. The summit was busy, people arriving from several directions. Concern over weather revived on the strength of the first breeze to blow in days, and on enquiring of the forecast to be told it was "shite".

Various minor bumps led westward, gradually withdrawing from the fringe of small, loose crags draped almost continuously along the southern flank. The sudden steepness of these slopes forms an attractive backdrop to much of Glasgow, especially when the crags are stencilled dark against the pure whiteness of fresh snow. But contrary to the impression given from the city, the tops are plateaux, not ridges, more conducive to ski-touring than walking. The latter tends to be largely confined to several distinctive knolls such as Tomtain - or, more commonly, the bitten-off chunk of Dumgoyne above wooded Strath Blane.

Exactly where the Kilsyth Fells merge into the Campsies is more a question of nomenclature than geography. Indeed, the latter are often colloquially extended to include the whole eastern arm reaching down to Denny. I was only sure of having crossed this invisible boundary once beyond Birkenburn Reservoir and beneath the Meikle Bin - looming massively, way above its true height of only 570m, slightly off-route to the north. I considered a diversionary ascent, but without the big view there seemed little point. Instead, I stumbled over wet moorland toward Lecket Hill, where a couple of fences needed crossed before reaching the tiny cairn. An easy descent then brought the glen draining the hill's southern slopes, and a green, tent-sized square of grass spotted from on high. This proved an ideal Campsie campsite: within earshot of a sizeable waterfall, still half-a-mile upstream of a busy layby on the Crow Road. A huge meal was cooked - and, along with the orange afterglow of the evening, savoured. I went to my bed content in the knowledge that Marlyn's enforced nutriment had, like the now completed crossing of the Central Belt, transpired to be much more palatable than anticipated.

It was merely the forecast which proved shite, not the weather itself. The flawlessly hot conditions were, though, far from ideal for hillwalking: I was thus woken early by my internal alarm to clock-on for an eight a.m. shift with extended teabreaks. Departure was delayed only by the need to evict a colony of earwigs which had taken up overnight residence in various neuks and niches of the tent. Once these were sent on their way - having painfully lived up to their alternative name of forkie-tails - the descent beside the Alnwick Burn was sheer pleasure: low, sharp light catching the froth and sparkle of countless small waterfalls.

No traffic passed during the mile-long pull onto the summit of the Crow Road, abandoned just before the cottage at Muir Toll. Easy-angled slopes - remarkably well-drained compared to the previous day's morass - led to the fence and trig point on Holehead. Here I turned north to begin the long loop around Endrick Water, which meandered westward through farmland to enter Loch Lomond via a marshy estuary, rich in birdlife, lovingly written of by Tom Weir. Initially this meant picking a way down the sawn-off edge of Dunbrach into sparse forest below, where a lochan moated an island like a quoit tossed over a stick. I was soon down the craggy nose of Dungoil and resting at the Crow Road once more - not in the least envious of a red-faced cyclist who puffed and blew past with half of his own long hot climb still to come.

Ever since mid-morning, the idea of an early curtailment had gnawed quietly at plans to cross the Gargunnock Hills that afternoon. The half-hour after my arrival at the next top, 321m Gartcarron Hill, now provided this parasitic thought with sustenance enough to effectively sap morale and achieve acquiescence. The western reaches of Carron Valley Forest barred access to the loose end of a Land Rover track seen probing into trees less than two hundred metres from, and slightly above, where I now stood. I took a deep breath and plunged in, to immediately flounder in a sea of undergrowth, glad to grasp the lifeline of a firebreak as a means of escape.

Unwilling to take No for an answer, I tried twice more, only to be snared each time by webs of branches and to emerge wearing pine needles like a camel-hair coat. Well beaten, resigned to wading the Endrick and skirting the forest via the road, I suddenly discovered another firebreak snaking into green darkness, apparently contouring the hill. This was almost rejected out of hand as another blind alley, but equally blind faith was, for once, rewarded. Apart from the odd fallen tree and a few moss-covered dykes, I was allowed uninterrupted progress to an area of felling, from where a track wound down to Gartcarron.

Enough was enough, though. After an extensive body search to remove pine needles - the arboreal equivalent of nitpicking - any thoughts of further struggles over Cairnoch Hill were rejected without debate. I would have a lazy afternoon.

But where to camp? Farmland filled every corner of the valley in a farewell fling of cultivation, severely restricting options. The shores of Carron Valley Reservoir were available if necessary, but the map suggested little Loch Walton as a more attractive venue. I turned west rather than east and, as at Palacerigg, set about muddling together enough confidence to ask permission. Hopes plunged on reading *Private loch* and seeing the BMW of an angling club member parked outside the keeper's cottage, but I chapped the door and cast the crucial question all the same. "Sorry", came the reply, "it's more than my job's worth to let you camp by the loch..." - I began to reel in my hopes, hook dangling empty - "...but you can use the garden if you like". I had landed a whopper!

The tent was soon pitched on the tiny lawn amid attention from two young children and a dog. John and Maggie Hill were genuinely kind and welcoming, offering mugs of beer along with access to the kettle in the caravan they were using while renovating the cottage. Their hospitality was all the more appreciated given they had good reason to be wary of unexpected arrivals: the exclusive thirty-member club kept the loch well stocked with brown trout, and two night-time visitors had been caught poaching earlier that month.

After dozing, I cobbled together enough energy and enthusiasm to walk the four hot miles into Fintry. Here postcards and provisions were bought from a low-timbered shop. Then, lying under the wide shade of a riverside tree to read the paper, I was suddenly made to realise, for the first time, how I was gradually slipping into a world of my own, distant from outside events. The press had pounced on the word *glasnost* to describe the new spirit of Soviet openness under Gorbachev. Glasnost appeared in headlines, articles, editorials, on the letters page, the arts page, the sports page and in cartoons. Hardly a column inch was read which failed to make hay while the Russian sun shone. Yet despite this gleeful saturation coverage, I could only guess as to the meaning of the word: nowhere was it defined! In the four days since I last clapped eyes on a paper, the media's tidal wave of information had swept across the country, leaving me becalmed in a quiet backwater of ignorance. It was to be several days more before my guesswork was enlightened.

A bar supper in the Clachan Hotel, followed by the requisite phonecall, successfully delayed the return walk to Loch Walton until the cool of the evening, the sunset an orange-red banner emblazoned across the well named Double Craigs. John and I sat up late, drinking beer and talking hills. The coincidence of our both having been brought up in Derbyshire before spending time in Aberdeen meant there was much of mutual interest. For the first time since leaving Glasgow, I was still awake at the start of the new day.

Waking at eight, I stepped outside to immediately be handed a mug of tea: John must have heard my rummaging. The night had been sticky, uncomfortable with heat, and the inner tent remained damp with condensation as it was crammed into the stuffsac. Hard to believe a similarly cloudless morning only sixteen days earlier had been white with frost.

Farewells were said, and by nine-fifteen I was away on the short roadwalk to Carron Valley Reservoir. Carron, like Esk, is a name common on Scottish maps, the word deriving from the Gaelic for a winding river, *car abhuinn,* and occurring elsewhere in Nithsdale, Kincardineshire and twice in Ross-shire. This Stirlingshire version was one of only two places - the head of Loch Quoich being the other - where the watershed had been humanly tampered with. In 1939 the valley was dammed slightly on the Endrick side, thus creating the strange situation of an already strong Endrick Water flowing to within touching distance of the dam, only to jink away westward like a mischievous child playing chickie-mellie, then running full-speed to evade capture.

At the dam wall I was faced with another sitka-spruce dilemma. Cairnoch Hill rose ahead, cloaked to its neck in a green cape of trees, giving no indication of an upright-walking route to its summit. Common sense suggested its omission: a hands-in-pockets stroll along the road would rejoin the watershed in fifteen scratch-free minutes. Yet some basic internal instinct argued otherwise: that the satisfaction to be derived from not cutting the corner would outweigh any discomfort involved. Thus it was that these undoubtedly mundane slopes suddenly took on the lure of some inaccessible rock peak in Skye.

A clamber over the debris of recent felling led to a Toblerone of stacked logs, from where a firebreak tunnelled into the interior. Once this petered out, I imitated a Cossack dancer: crouching low, arms folded across face as protection from the sabre-lash of branches. I shoved onward and struggled upward, navigating solely by the angle of the slope until the lattice of leaves lightened to give notice of younger trees ringing the bald summit of the hill. Here I rested, relishing the fruits of irrationality, wondering when last anyone visited this spot.

Northward, the Gargunnock Hills stretched a soft horizon, to be gained by rapid descent of runnels and firebreaks followed by the trudgery of a long, gently-sloping moor. The huge radio mast on Earl's Hill thinned to a hairline crack in the haze as I crossed miles of bog and burnt heather, imperceptibly nearing the tall cairn and prominent tumulus of Carleatheran - a prehistoric-sounding hill linking with Stronend to form a high escarpment above the Forth floodplain. Spin the Campsies through one-eighty degrees, with Fintry as axis, and you have the Gargunnock Hills: rotational summitry!

Faint paths and tyremarks crisscrossed westward over Lees Hill, where the blue flash of a lizard darted for cover in the instant of being seen. I made for shelter too - if somewhat slower - in the steep shade of the Spout of Ballochleam: normally a booming, water-filled gully, today merely a damp-rocked dribble with scarcely enough water even for the much-needed wash. I scrabbled around in search of a pool - then, through a bead curtain of dripping hair, received the shock of a ten mile view. There, suddenly, were the woods and white houses of Kippen, the dazzling wink of a windscreen in Thornhill, even the vague mauve outline of Highland hills beyond. It was as though the water had cleansed and refreshed the atmosphere as it had cleansed and refreshed me. Why visibility should have improved so dramatically without any other noticeable change in conditions was a mystery - and one destined to remain unsolved as all evidence was quickly hidden away. Just as a bather who accidentally drops a towel while changing hastily covers their embarrassment in hope of not having been seen, so the haze had been pulled up and wrapped round even tighter by the time I reached the summit of Stronend. Any further revelations were left to the imagination.

Bemused and distracted by this, I was glad of prior knowledge taking me straight to a break in the crags of the north face. Recall was far from total however: I had forgotten the scree-filled bowl beneath was guarded by an electric fence. Hence my blithe straddling of the wire only to yelp backwards as hand was almost welded to metal and legs went into momentary spasm. Similar obstacles had previously been encountered in the Borders - the Forestry Commission had quite a variety on display - but the present culprit was far stronger than the standard mild tingling, coming as a shock in more ways than one. Goodness knows what constituted the legal voltage, but this must have been cranked up to at least twice the permitted level. After sitting for several minutes to recover, I stepped gingerly over on tiptoe, fearful of involuntarily sterilisation, for once glad of my height. Walkers, be warned!

Mind still humming - imagining a line of farmers dangling upside-down like poisoned moles on a fence - I reached the tree-lined, rusty-gated road and a track through to Gribloch. Here a youth cranked up the rheostat even higher, so to speak, by unhelpfully refusing my request to camp while volunteering the disinformation that there was nowhere suitable within miles. To some extent, though, this *was* true: once Loch Laggan had been seen to be both private and keeperless, there was nothing for it but to trudge into Kippen. Here, as at Forth, I headed for the football park.

Arrival coincided with the start of a cup game between Kippen and Blanefield, so I pitched just beyond the corner flag to cook and watch simultaneously. Various of the players' children wandered over out of curiosity, then repeatedly tried using the stove to set handfuls of grass on fire each time my back was turned. Sadly, their efforts proved more successful than those of their fathers: the visitors won eight-nil, with spectatorial comments slowly veering, goal-by-goal, from cautiously optimistic support to wholehearted derision.

The result was also the main topic of discussion later in the Cross Keys (built 1703), where I sat drinking Greenmantle and pondering my attempt to book into Rowardennan by phone. Repeated calls had been answered by a child's high-pitched yelling, backed by sounds of total pandemonium. Initially assuming this merely to be a hopelessly crossed line, I became more concerned on noticing the hostel wasn't marked on the new edition of Ordnance Survey Sheet 56. Had the place been quietly bulldozed? Or commandeered by the MOD? Or converted into timeshare chalets? I would have to wait and see.

◻◻◻◻◻

The early morning ritual of removing twigs from socks was today conducted inside the tent. For the first time since Dolphinton there was a chill in the air, long strands of high cloud telling of an impending change in the weather as surely as the stretched-out frontrunners in a road race are a sign the main pack won't be long in pounding behind. Ironically, I changed out of running gear back into more orthodox cords!

The return along the road seemed shorter than yesterday despite now being slightly uphill: I was soon taking a forestry track onto Balgair Muir. Although many of the trees hereabouts were merely shrub-height, they extended well beyond the regular outline shown on the map. This caused slight disorientation, as did the continuing atmospheric myopia. The first movements of a breeze might be brushing against branches in murmurs of discontent, but the heatwave was in no hurry to relinquish its hold over the land.

Waterfowl - by definition the least likely of watershed birds - rocketed from beneath boots as I left the plantation, contoured the swell of Buchlyvie Muir (where I amused myself by punning with Buachaille Etive Mor), and returned to the road through Edinbellie farm. Here, calves being herded

uphill forced me as tight against a wall as a commuter in the underground rush-hour. I shouted a greeting across the beasts' backs to a flat-capped farmhand, who replied by echoing my concern for the weather: a gathering wind was excitedly whipping away the dust-sheets which had covered the landscape for so long.

Lunch was a bar meal eaten in Balfron, largest of the half-dozen villages scattered like handfuls of seed along the Endrick's fertile banks. The name was *Baile-bhroin,* town of mourning, from a tradition that one particularly dark day in the Dark Ages, a pack of wolves attacked and killed all the local children. One Balfronian who, being born in the nineteenth century, luckily avoided this fate was Alexander "Greek" Thomson, much of whose pillared (and, occasionally, pilloried) architecture is to be found in Glasgow. Ignorant of all this history at the time, I noted only the slightly less momentous milestones of this being my second consecutive meal eaten to the sound of a Eurythmics tape and that I had bought the first Mars Bar of the walk!

The curiously-named Indians Road led to Balfron Station, where I crossed the dismantled railway line - a continuation of that now carrying the great train of West Highland Waywalkers puffing slowly out of Milngavie. The Way was the obvious route through this final belt of farmland, so I followed the main road westward, past widespread carnage of hedgehogs and rabbits, to join the thistled waymarkers in Garadhban Forest. Twelve days had elapsed since leaving their lookalikes on the Southern Upland Way. The WHW and I were both heading to Rowardennan, but whereas any low-level walkers would push for the hostel that evening, I planned a camp before crossing the hills on Thursday.

A late burst of sunlight slanted through pines as the clean-cut call of a cuckoo announced my arrival at Muir Park Reservoir, last of the pre-Highland night-stops. Reedbeds squelching up the hillside meant it took time to find a high-and-dry spot, then pitch in the flailing, flapping wind. Even collecting water proved time-consuming, the burn little more than a trickle deep-set between heathery banks. After ten consecutive nights in the tent, I was ready for the relative comforts of the hostel.

Eventually all was well. Macaroni cheese and the *Glasgow Herald* occupied me until the sky darkened, when a slackening breeze drew me out onto a small crag to look around. The night was clear and almost calm, carrying the engine-noise and laughter of bikers from two miles away in Drymen. Southward, the outline of the Campsies dipped to the cone of Dumgoyne, dark against the fading colours of a diffuse sunset. Further west, the sodium glow of streetlamps showed the Vale of Leven.

There was an almost sublime completeness to the scene, doubtless enhanced in my mind by the satisfaction of having walked from the Border to now sit reverentially at the feet of the Highlands. Things were going smoothly. I had gathered fitness and maintained health. Problems had vanished as from a sheet falling out of crease overnight.

The only clouds on the horizon were real ones: far to the west was a darkness deeper than the soft coverings of late, perhaps already rolling its rain in over Kintyre and Arran, Argyll and the Firth of Clyde. Of all the new rhythms and requirements embraced over the past three weeks, one which had settled easily, naturally into place was a new-found ability to sense the approach and realise the importance of weather changes such as this. Rain, sun, wind... No longer were these mere conversational starting points: they had become the core of the argument, the hub on which everything else centred. Thus my night-time thoughts focused on one simple question, the only one seeming to matter at all - a question asked with the earnestness and concern of prayerful supplication. Could the rain hold off just one day more?

The answer was No. A grey, clinging layer of cloud greeted my emergence from the tent by instantly coating clothes and hair with a silvering of dampness. The wind was no stronger than before, but the depression had nevertheless moved in overnight with the smoothness of a roller-blind covering a skylight. I retreated into warmth and dryness for a rethink.

The major worry - and the basis for the previous evening's anxiety - was Beinn Bhreac: central of the three hills barring the showers, stoves and sheets of Rowardennan, and a notorious conglomeration of knobbles and peaklets, sprouting from its summit like acne from an adolescent chin. The prospect of navigating over this in nil visibility was far from enticing - but then so was an eleventh night in the tent, and the momentary thought of staying put, of using up one of the rest days by wandering into Drymen for a pint, was given short shrift. If I had been granted foresight to know this wasn't to be one of my better days, the alcoholic alternative might well have been chosen.

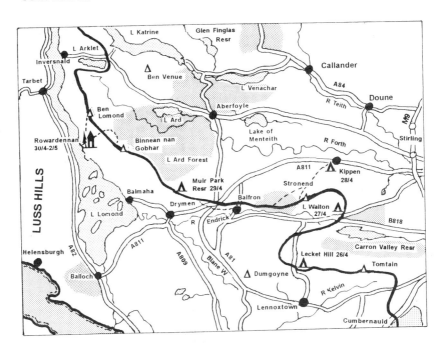

Cumbernauld - Loch Arklet

69

On even the sunniest of mornings the long, imperceptible rise of Moor Park would give a poor start to a walk. Today, with the cloudbase down around 400m, the two miles of deep heather and dayglo green bog seemed interminable. The forthcoming hills weren't forthcoming, so to speak, with only the miniature geological showpiece of Conic Hill above Balmaha managing to duck under the grey limbo-pole of cloud. Loch Lomond made an inauspicious first appearance: a few shades lighter than the sky and apparently tilted at a considerable angle.

The Highland Boundary Fault slanted its long diagonal through these hills *en route* from Stonehaven to Helensburgh before continuing across the Clyde, straight as an underwater pipeline, to bisect Arran. It wasn't merely a geological divide however: linguistically the change was just as apparent. I was immediately treading Gaelic ground: Gualann, Stob a'Choin Duibh, Binnean nan Gobhar. The old language may have died amongst the people here, but will never lose its footing in the hills. Conditions played the wet blanket at the great moment of crossing, as they had at the very start of the walk, defiantly worsening as if in intimidation - or, more worryingly, in intimation - of what was to come. Either way, the triumphal entry march was to the beat of rain drumming on goretex.

Iron fenceposts leading to the sharply defined top of Gualann raised hopes the day might not be too frustrating after all - especially when they grew into a three-metre-high deer fence shielding the forest. Good progress was made onto the broadening slopes of dreaded Beinn Bhreac - compounding its natural awkwardness by membership of the elite group of hills carrying a trig point on a top other than the summit (others included Ben Venue and The Saddle). Needless to say, the finding of the concrete pillar proved well beyond me, but was more than compensated for when a tall cairn looming out of the mizzle was identified, from the amount of rubbish crammed into its cracks, as the true summit. So far so good.

Things then began to go wrong immediately on leaving the cairn, when I was literally sidetracked into following a prominent path. This gradually drifted from the required bearing before disappearing downhill into the gloom. Getting back on course necessitated a cross-bearing, but after half-an-hour of steady contouring descent, there was sign of neither the col for Beinn Uird nor the forest fence last seen dropping away eastward halfway up Beinn Bhreac.

In an area where grassy hummocks and contorted peat-hags confounded all attempts at navigation, I cursed my negligence in having failed to reconnoitre these hills before the walk - especially since a whole evening had once been spent gazing out over their rugged profile from Loch Ard youth hostel. Two red deer, the first seen, materialised from mist to hurry across the hill. They knew where they were going. I didn't, and sat on the wheel of a crashed aircraft to chew over both an orange and my thoughts.

There were two options. One was to continue this hybrid game: blind man's buff meets timeless test match. The other was to admit defeat, cut my losses, bale out through Rowardennan Forest to the road. The return of the rain decided the issue and I took a bearing due west - only to then make an embarrassingly silly mistake, the kind of thing done by other people, never oneself. If my meanderings up until this point could be blamed on the weather, from now on it was definitely *mea culpa*.

The beginnings of a burn oozed from peat banks, seemingly heading in exactly the right direction. Foolishly, I shoved compass into pocket, started whistling *By yon bonny banks,* headed downhill. The deer fence came on schedule: I relaxed into thoughts of imminent dry clothes and cups of tea. It took another 200m of descent before the thoughts and whistling abruptly broke off as I realised something was badly amiss. The forest was no longer a continuously steep flank falling straight into the loch, having eased to a moderately-angled glen winding through patches of bare hillside. Slowly it dawned I had somehow descended the wrong side of the hill and was now in Gleann Meadhonach, in Loch Ard Forest. *Shit.*

I sat on the rucksack to try and fathom what had happened. The only feasible explanation was the burn having risen on the rough northern side of Beinn Bhreac, before swinging west-north-east while my compass lay pocketed and impotent. I felt very humble and stupid, and sat for a while not quite knowing what to do. I was too involved, too fixated by the walk to objectively see the situation for what it was: a minor blip at the end of a week of good progress. Instead, depression settled like an extra layer of cloud, my mental in-tray suddenly filling with a seemingly insurmountable backlog of weariness. The rucksack felt heavier, my stomach emptier, the hostel even further away than at the start of the day. Calculations showed I had effectively covered a mere six miles in as many hours.

Further down in the forest, beside Duchray Water, was a waymarked trail linking Kinlochard to Rowardennan. I had used this the previous Easter and now, as it seemed the surest, most sensible way of correcting the error, decided to do so again. But once my continued descent broke through the cloudbase near the rocky knoll of Dun Dhamh, it was only to find the glen narrowing to a gorge. Here, after several minutes spent tarzaning from trees, patience finally snapped. I turned *volte-face,* picked out a firebreak, stormed bad-temperedly back up the hill.

This proved my best move all day. Extra reserves of energy welled from hot springs of annoyance, and a breathless hour saw me round the shoulder of Beinn Uird onto Moin Eich, *the horses' moss*. Belatedly - but as if in sympathy - the cloud doubled its height to give an earlier-than-expected view of the great loch: smooth silver against rough-cut greens and browns. *By yon bonny banks* was for real now - and sung, not whistled.

On reaching the bottom section of the Ben Lomond tourist path I first-footed a hill which, extraordinarily, I had yet to see. It is doubtful whether the miles from Culter Fell could ever be repeated without even one glimpse of this most distinctive of beacon hills beckoning from the north. These thoughts, along with the relief of being home and wet if not quite home and dry, caused me to forget completely the earlier worries as to the hostel's continued existence. Of course the old white-gabled mansion still stood, firm as ever, on its lochside lawn. I arrived just as the doors opened, only two hours since sitting disconsolately in Gleann Meadhonach - but two hours which had taught a lot about the dangers of over-casualness and, more significantly, about the ephemerality of depression.

I booked in for three nights, then headed straight for the showers, dodging herds of school kids. All but two of the other seventy-two residents comprised a party from Cramond High, and while this begged obvious questions about the SYHA's block-booking system (other folk were turned away that night), their shouts and laughter came as a pleasant shock after the quietness of the hills. Foodstocks were low, so it was good to receive the message that Jack planned to come out mid-evening with fresh supplies. But there was no sign of him after an hour's damp wait at the tourist car park - made tolerable by a beer donated by a cabin-cruiser over from Inverbeg - so I retreated indoors for a pile of cheese toasties.

I didn't really mind. The real feast was the company all around and the deep-seated satisfaction of having made it this far. It felt good to have completed so much of the walk, good that everything south of the Highlands was over and done with. (Everything, that was, apart from a horrible shapeless worm which crawled from my cheese wrapper to be hastily picked up and thrown out before the warden did likewise to me.)

Things were about to change. The daily mileage would drop - already almost one third of the eight-hundred-odd miles had been covered - while the amount of ascent would climb steeply. Enjoyable though the Lowlands had been, they were never going to be more than kindling to the Highland fire.

72

3: Into May, into the Highlands
(Friday 1st May - Sunday 10th May)

*M*ayday mayday mayday. White-flecked waves cream the blue width of the loch in the rejuvenated light of May Day morning. Gone is the grey misery of yesterday's cloud-soaked hills, gone the preceding week's featureless expanse of heat. The light is alive again: sharp and hard-edged as the gleam of polished metal, resolving into fine detail loch-bleached pebbles and branches glistening with buds of dew, refracting through white wave-crests of metal-blue water. On the far shore, cloud-shadows like magic lantern silhouettes race across the steep heather and screes of the Glen Douglas hills, blown by a wind which has veered overnight to a bright northwesterly. The morning is a revelation: the new month brings with it a new beginning.

This sudden spaciousness of light is mirrored in the long-awaited spaciousness of time. Two blank days stretch ahead, lacking the routine structure of packing-up and moving-on, yet just as vital to progress as any eight-hour push northward. This type of extended break has been planned for the end of each three-week section, using hostels each time, the hope being not only to rebuild strength and stamina, but to counter loneliness, restore enthusiasm for the hills.

As yet, the walk is still too much of a novelty for these latter concerns to be of consequence, but I'm certainly glad of a physical respite. The previous evening's late tide of energy which carried me to the lochside was, I knew, a totally unreliable pointer to the true state of things: more end-of-week blow-out than sign of latent reserves of fitness. The latter are quietly accumulating all the while, but unless every available breathing space is well used in eating and resting, the result of the walk will, to use a political analogy, be marginal.

But how to rest? This was something to which I gave not a moment's consideration before setting off, assuming it the least of my worries. Now, with the question relevant, pressing even, it is asked as though in a foreign language, one I once knew, only to forget through lack of use. Sitting at breakfast, trying to decide how to organise the day so as not to feel bored and impatient with inactivity, I gaze wistfully out across the loch, yearning for the temporarily forbidden pleasure of pressing on in bright morning sunlight. I know there is no way, either logically or logistically, to move on - yet the desire refuses to be quieted until internal arbitration finally settles on a lazy morning followed by an afternoon stroll along the shore.

73

Meanwhile, the anarchic hubbub of the school party gains forced entry to the senses, making me feel, after the days of solitude and silence, bemused and slightly intimidated - like a cyclist emerging from a peaceful backstreet onto a hustling, jostling, noisy dual carriageway. In comparison to their charges, the teachers look jaded - an already hectic week rounded off by need to attend to a boy who somehow broke a bone through the night. The school have been here, canoeing and walking, all week. Now lunches are rowdily packed, stacked rucksacks shouldered and a long straggle of twos and threes set off down the single-track road to walk, it seems, to Balmaha - or perhaps, if the teachers are particularly vindictive, all the way back to Edinburgh.

I follow them out, unable to resist the lure of the morning - although in doing so almost miss Jack, who has quickly dropped off a food parcel and is driving away when spied just in time to be thanked. As he leaves for a Canadian holiday next morning and has thus far been even less diligent over packing than had the school kids, his sixty-mile round trip to keep me fed and watered is doubly appreciated. By now, though, the hostel doors have slammed shut, incarcerating both the box of goodies in the depths of the warden's office and a voracious appetite in similar nether regions of my stomach.

Little needs written of the remaining daylight hours. Letter-writing in the wind-shelter of an old shieling precedes a bowl of soup in the hotel (money is locked-up along with the food, preventing anything more substantial than a one course lunch); then comes an amble northward along the West Highland Way toward Rowchoish. The 95-mile Milngavie-to-Fort William footpath will never be far from the watershed during the coming fortnight, and the nearby section displays a split personality: easy Land Rover track 100m above the loch or slithery mud-scramble down along the shore itself via a path rising and falling like a heavy swell to avoid tree roots and small outcrops. I take the high road going out and the low one coming back, constantly distracted into gazing across blue water to the fantastic cracked-eggshell skyline of the Cobbler - beside which the other Arrochar hills appear shapeless and bulky, minders clustered round a celebrity. The tourist boat, Maid of the Loch, slips into view, trawling its white swallow-tail wake from pier to pier in long spirograph loops.

Back at the ranch, I sit on the step until the doors swing open promptly at five, then avidly set about the contents of the parcel: stirring saucepans with one hand, holding letters to read in the other. Later, heavy showers turn the half-mile stroll to the bar into a carefully timed sprint. Being Friday night, the place is noisy with crowds of young folk dressed in designer sweatshirts, up from Bearsden in their XR3s and GTis. I sit alone in a corner, pint and thoughts my sole company, aware the high jinks and jukebox camaraderie are beginning to make me feel low. The Spirit of the Weekend far from me, I decide on an early night.

Outside, rain buckets down, bubbling the road surface like boiling broth. Trainers, trousers, cagoule: all soaked within seconds. And who is this idiot driver honking and light-flashing? *You can easy get past without all that Close Encounters stuff - I am on the pavement after all. Come on hurry up I'm wet enough as it is. What do you want me to do? Lay my cagoule across the puddles for you to drive over like Sir Walter bloody Raleigh? What the hell are you still honking for?... hey hang on a minute... I know who...* Peering from behind the manic thrashing of wipers, through the dark blur of the windscreen, are familiar faces. I have chanced to leave the hotel at precisely the moment Kenny Symon and Elspeth arrive to search me out!

Together we splash back to the bar, laughing and joking now every bit as much as the rich kids next door. This impromptu arrival of friends changes the whole mood of the evening: whereas the previous hour dawdled past, this one races away like rain into the gutters. Gossip and stories could be swapped all night and all the next day!

Too soon, though, comes the pulse-quickening pothole-splashing rally-drive back up the track to the hostel, arriving with a minute to spare (years of practice having brought the calculations necessary to maximise drinking time into the realm of intuition). But horror of horrors: the doors are already bolted shut! I stand and hammer on a window while rain hammers down on me, fearing the degradation of a night in the public lavvies. Only after several minutes of panic - during which I see other hostellers petitioning the warden on my behalf - is the door reluctantly swung open to let me inside. I feel like an escaped prisoner demanding to be let back into Barlinnie prison.

The warden gives a long, bad look, but a check on other watches confirms suspicions of the doors having been locked early. Furious with this injustice in a system which strikes me as too legalistic in the first place, I keep mum for fear of being cast into outer darkness once more. Instead, the excitement of seeing friends suddenly tarnished, I shamble, dripping, to my bunk - slightly pissed, more than slightly pissed off.

I'm still annoyed on waking next morning - at least until the view from the window takes both breath and anger away. The rain has moved on in darkness, leaving a replica of the previous morning only now with fresh snow down to 300m. Waves ruffle the loch - almost always choppier here than on its more sheltered western shore - while skies are a washed-out, pale-but-bright blue. While Highland weather can scarcely be described as predictable, certain patterns recur with reasonable regularity year after year. One such sees the first week of May held tightly in a last snap of winter's jaws - a tradition adhered to perfectly this time round. A few crunching steps on the gravel outside are enough to tell two things: the temperature has dropped drastically overnight, and I want to climb Ben Lomond today.

Scaling a 974m peak may seem a strange way to go about resting, but with the hostel closed from ten till five it makes sense to structure my day. Besides, on the several previous occasions I have reached the summit of the same hill on consecutive days, the achievement always brought a singular, curiously existential sensation - as if an objective view of oneself twice within the same frame of reference allows increased awareness of time. And anyway, it had been love at first sight with this particular hill: a strong bond formed not only on some marvellous earlier ascents, but from having lived a year in a high Glasgow tenement where the Ben's bold, clean shape greeted me every clear morning as living proof of the name, Beacon Hill.

Tent, stove, clothes are bundled into boxes before being shoved under the bunk. Then I'm away, first out of the hostel, shouldering a daysack for the first time in weeks. The tourist track is out of the question: masochism doesn't extend to ascending that twice in two days. (Such routes invariably take the gentlest way uphill - and, with the exception of those on Sgurr nan Gillean and Lochnagar, rarely improve beyond purgatorial plods.) Instead, I use the alternative path onto the parallel ridge of Ptarmigan, joyous simply to be out in the windswept air of the first really sharp day since Peel Fell.

The northern and western sides of the Ben (only Nevis, Rinnes and Ledi are similarly hailed on first name terms), are much more broken than suggested by low-level lochside views. Today, blurred by a snow shower swooping in as I turn from a tiny half-frozen lochan to the final steep cone, the array of crags make this most southerly Munro appear, for once, desolate and unwelcoming. The threat proves mere bluster however: a narrow, drifted path avoids all difficulties, reaching the sun-burst summit just as cloud peels from the corrie wall to reveal eye-blue lochs and grey-green glens in every direction.

It is a sight startling in breadth and clarity even on a hill renowned for outstanding views. The Arrochar bens beyond the deep-set trench of northern Loch Lomond. The Braes o' Balquhidder leading the eye round to smaller, nearer Trossachs. The long, low line of the Campsies drawing a half-curtain across much of the southern panorama. All these come and go, come and go, as torn shreds of cloud scud below and around. Westward, where the Kintyre and Cowal peninsulas droop, willow-like, from the trunk of Argyll, the Clyde lochs stretch in silver streaks to Arran - looking too near to be an island - while further south higher cloud allows Tinto to be picked out behind the glint of a Lanarkshire glasshouse, together with the dark, squat shape of Dumbarton Rock. Also, barely discernibly marking the great city itself, are the high-rise blocks of Glasgow's Summerston.

Almost everything and everyone filling my thoughts, giving meaning to the word *Home,* lies within a four-mile radius of this last landmark - a thought I'm surprised to find almost too emotionally trying to accommodate, forcing a look away, across the broad sweep of land already traversed - now tantalisingly haze-free at the last possible moment before the Highlands envelop all view of it. It strikes me that having been denied sight of the city and its environs in passing has been a good, even crucial thing. The strain of being physically close to home yet psychologically so distant might otherwise have broken the spell of progress, and with it my spirit.

As it is, having evaded that particular snare, I now rest on trampled snow beside the trig point, musing that if the Ben had seemed huge, Himalayan almost, through the swirl of spindrift below, then the three bare iron legs of the long-lost view indicator will suffice for the Chinese summit tripod on Everest. I'm beginning to discover the best method of subduing unsettling fears about home, weather, or simply the sheer magnitude of the walk is to focus on trivia and meaningless distractions. Think small, not big.

Before heading down, a precautionary bearing (292° off true north) is taken back to the ridge climbed today and to be descended the morrow. The summit might not be so clear-headed then, with the upper 50m skiddy enough to demand precision and care. Then along the undulating south ridge, down the firm snows of the well-trodden highway. Here, in laughable contrast to the solitude and other-worldliness above, I meet a strung-out procession of eighty-six people and four dogs plodding and padding uphill!

The afternoon is dozed away behind the toilet block in the lee of a wind rising from occasional gusts to a gale carrying in showers with gusto: few of the masses will emulate my half-hour on top. Later, I return to the hostel in hope of early opening, but the wind obviously fails to register as "inclement weather" on the SYHA's own, impossible-to-gauge, Beaufort Scale. A large crowd gathers to cower against the wall: mainly Lomondeers, they include another school party, thirty-two this time, one of whose ghettoblaster (whether any ghettoes exist in the Highlands is open to question), brings news of Rangers winning the league at Pittodrie. As one, the kids are disconsolate, pre-empting enquiry as to the type of school they attend.

Inside, I watch the wind whipping white horses on the loch, write a few letters, turn thoughts to the imminent moving-on. For the first time since the Border I feel again the strange amalgam of excitement and fear which comes from blindly walking into the future. But whereas the land itself was then an unknown factor, here I'm among familiar hills - hills I would in no sense claim to know, yet which have seen me before. Almost everything from here to the Great Glen, eleven or twelve days hence, has already been climbed two or three times. I look to these coming days as a renewal of old friendships - or, in some cases, old adversities - hoping only the reunion won't be too stormy.

First, though, comes the "official" Ben Lomond day and a real, rather than metaphorical, reunion. Being with friends again will be just the boost needed to send me northward, and I go to bed full of the sleepless anticipation of a small child on Christmas Eve: tomorrow will be a day of excitement and half-expected surprises. The forecast is mainly dry, wind moderating through the afternoon. I'm not unhappy about that either.

Seven o'clock. I dash clumsily about - appropriately at the same time and in the same manner as on the previous big day three weeks past - packing last minute items, dumping unwanted food in the spare pigeonhole, making peace with the warden by proffering Jack's cardboard box, separating clean clothes from dirty ones. The latter I take down to the car park in two carrier bags, like the old girl in *Streets of London*.

With the gale blowing off the loch even more venomously than yesterday, it is a relief to dive inside the first of the cars to come horn-honking round the corner. Another car follows, then a full-to-the-roofrack minibus. In all, nineteen people to hug and shake hands with, and for a while I don't know which way to turn. Distractedly, I cram the rucksack with assorted edible

goodies - yet, despite the heaviest load since Moffat, I'm travelling light. Ray and Calum, fancying the role of sherpas, offer to alternately heave the burden uphill in a gesture both genuine and generous - although I can't help but think that just as a full moon supposedly provokes strange behaviour, lunacy even, the same seems true of a full rucksack. A Sherpa van would be more appropriate.

The climb through the trees is sweaty, but once clear of shelter the wind has its say: buffeting, pummelling, discouraging halts. Finding it strange to be ambling along, hands in pockets, after weeks of going it alone, I restlessly move up, drop back between groups like the wheatear chack-chacking from boulder to boulder high on the ridge. I'm aware of an absurdity in the situation, of the danger of mistaking this brief demonstration of support and solidarity as a sign of home. That, for all the present laughter, news and gossip, is still an inconceivable eight weeks and many hundreds of miles into the future: I must not let myself be deluded into thinking of today as anything other than a station on a very long line. Even while revelling in the company, I'm wanting away, to be moving on alone again. Only then will the end come and the company be there for keeps.

I'm last to the summit, fittingly with Frank, the Arch Bohemian - who once observed that *By yon bonny banks* includes the line "Albion, Scotland afore ye!", a statement on the relative quality of hillwalking if ever there was.

Many photos are taken, but lunch is a short, huddled affair, cringing against the slope from the searing wind. Proposed kite flying abandoned, we content ourselves watching a Sunblest bag, caught by a gust, soar high into the air before plunging, hawk-steep, to the hillside below. There is no fresh snow here, but Ben Lawers is sharp and white to its roots while northward the Blackmount has become the very antithesis of its name: a snowbound jumble of ridges and corries, daunting and serious. Should I have sent for an ice-axe? Too late now.

Too late and too cold. Friends are as eager to head down as am I, and the first few metres of descent snap off the view of them. All that remains is a mental freeze-frame of red- and blue-cagouled figures waving and turning away. I'm not alone quite yet however: the sherpas opt to reverse my route of Saturday, thus staying close until their ridge jack-knifes back southward where mine extends north. Then they too are gone, with a "See you at Achnashellach!". I repossess the rucksack, step up the pace a gear or two, try to forget all about them.

Even with the big hill out of the way, plenty still needs done before I can pitch somewhere near the Inversnaid road: another 600m of lumps and bumps starting with Cruinn a'Bheinn's neat cone. From here, a wire fence leads past a lochan to the twin tops of Cruachan high above Loch Lomond's Craig Roystan shore, where I sit looking down the aptly named Gleann Gaoithe, windy glen, and back to the snow-streaked summit of the Ben itself.

Swinging east to start the circumvention of Loch Arklet - indenting the watershed like the first line of a paragraph - I'm glad to feel the wind in my back at last. Rests come often as knobbly, pathless ground takes its toll. During one such pause, a herd of twenty deer trot blithely over a rise, then slam to a halt on seeing me well within stalking-range. As with the Moss Paul fox, I freeze (not difficult considering the conditions), and am again rewarded - this time by a couple of minutes of unsure, inquisitive attention ending only when, after several indecisive driftings-away and returnings, a large hind barks the command to retreat. With the number of deer usually inversely proportional to that of itinerant walkers, all this lends support to belief in these being greatly under-frequented hills in an otherwise very popular area. This, if true, is both surprising - with Glasgow little more than an hour's drive away - and sad, as the burn flowing down over lush green mosses beneath a schisty crag on Beinn Uamha is as lovely a spot as to be found on any well-worn path in the vicinity.

I consider camping here, but a cloudbase, albeit high, is forming: it seems prudent to avoid lengthening Monday's walk. From the cairn on Uamha the view is all water: Katrine, Chon, Arklet and nearby Lochan Mhaim nan Carn - where I pitch a safe distance from overhead powerlines. Weariness takes hold, such that after a perfunctory meal, worrying an unread letter from my sister has been left at Rowardennan, a long and varied day is ended by falling into deep sleep.

Somewhere in the shadowy depths of childhood, I learnt a maxim stating the best way of remembering the whereabouts of any lost object isn't praying to St Anthony, but concentrating on it immediately prior to sleeping. This process - somnolent seepage if you like - gains credence today, as despite being out for a twelve-hour count, I know in the very instant of waking that my sister's letter hasn't been accidentally sent back to Glasgow, but lies, crumpled and creased, inside my wallet, waiting to be ripped open and read in the dim morning light.

It contains two items of interest. Firstly, the walk has been given brief coverage in *The Great Outdoors* magazine, to which I wrote before leaving. Secondly, my sister Kath and her boyfriend Geoff plan to meet me at Ben Alder Cottage on 16th May. Why make mention of this? Because while both pieces of information delight me immensely, I scarcely suspect it will be the former, albeit tangentially, which will ultimately have the greater impact on the walk - and in such a manner that before a week passes I will think that to have genuinely lost the letter might have been no bad thing.

But that is all still to come. For now, I'm simply happy at receiving good news to brighten a dull grey morning. The anticipated warm front has brought light rain sounding like a sewing-machine at work on the tent fabric. Although a glance outside offers hope, I withdraw to bed. There is no rush: the three days, Rowardennan to Crianlarich, comprise a sandwich, today's hills thinly spread between two thick slices of walking. I'm content to stay put until ten-thirty, when the drizzle goes off in favour of a feeble watery sun showing no sign of permanence. The wind slackens to a more orthodox westerly, signalling the demise of the bracing, but predominantly fine, conditions.

I descend alongside pylons - towering like deserted cable-car gantries - to the isthmus separating lochs Arklet and Katrine. This is the kind of place often called *Tarbert* or *Tarbet* in the Gaelic, but here both waterlevels were artificially raised long after the allocation of such topographically precise names. Numerous painted wooden signs warn, in plain dull English, of dire consequences awaiting anyone caught so much as breathing in Glasgow's water supply.

Dense, damp bracken covers much of the steep pull onto Garradh, from where I look back down Katrine to the familiar Trossachs skyline of Bens Ledi, A'an and Venue. The *Sir Walter Scott* plies an early season boatload of tourists to Stronachlachar, its tannoy sending up an occasional clear word wrapped in sentences of distortion, like mica glistening in grey schist.

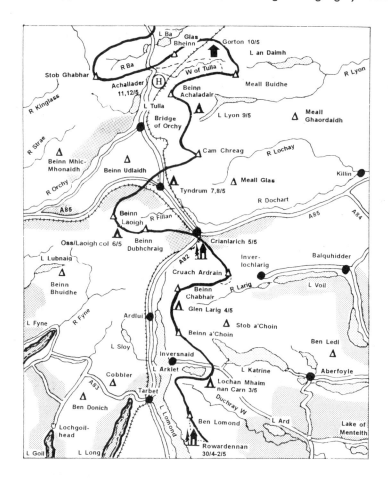

Rowardennan - Blackmount

I pause here a while, recalling an Easter outing in these parts when, with a friend, we cycled from Loch Ard to Inversnaid for a bar lunch, only to find the hotel in a state of total chaos. Circuits were fusing, pipes bursting, builders arriving unannounced and food orders being confused. We were soon ready to add voice to the chorus of chuntering customers, only to instead be reduced to mirth when the under-manager - at his wit's end - swooped in to clear our table saying, in his best catering college voice but with a Basil Fawlty smile of desperation, "Please let me take away all this crap".

Back in the here and now, I move on, past the stark white trig point and curious Half Dome-shaped pinnacle on Maol Mor, into a breezy squall sweeping Beinn a'Choin - at 770m the day's highest top. This soon degenerates to horizontal rain requiring full waterproofs - although fears of a repeat of the Beinn Bhreac meanderings vanish on finding a fence passing within yards of the summit cairns and on along the ridge. Green Glen Gyle, below and to the right, soon returns to view, while beyond rises Stob a'Choin: dark, steep, surprisingly clear. I mentally underline it in my list of unclimbed hills needing visited.

Cloud now finds its own level, settling precisely on the next few tops like a table resting on trellises. Maol an Fhithich is a rocky lump bristling with knolls and fenceposts, giving a fine uninterrupted view down across Loch Lomond to the busy A82 at Ardlui. The wind, having regained some of Sunday's strength, carries the rattle of a train across the water - its source invisible, lost deep in a tree-lined cutting, creeping beneath the massively dark Ben Vorlich like a centipede in a basement. I shelter behind a crag at Lochan Dubh for the mid-afternoon snack of chocolate and water, pleased to be high on tops seldom visited despite being clearly visible from the main road. An interesting kind of day.

A scrape of path leads onto Stob nan Eighrach, where litter crammed into the cairn hints at Waywalkers tired of bush-whacking through the rainforest below. Then it is over Ben Ducteach and down to meet the pylons again: they have taken the easy route along Glen Gyle, the wind singing eerily through wires and porcelain plates.

I'm startled by ghostly figures materialising from mist on the final 250m pull over Parlan Hill. I hadn't anticipated anyone until the Crianlarich Munros on Tuesday, especially not as unlikely-looking a pair as this smart, cheerful Englishwoman and Billy Bunter schoolboy. Contrary to first impressions, however, they know what they are doing - returning down Katrine after a visit to Lochan Beinn Chabhair.

The wind has long since put paid to hopes of camping by their lochan, a lovely place looking across the Falloch toward Vorlich. Instead, I cut down from the next col into upper Glen Larig and the long, almost straight river flowing eventually into Loch Voil. Even here, finding a sheltered site takes time: I finally pitch a mile or so downstream beside a large boulder. Gusts tousle the grass, but cooking is just about tolerable.

No sooner is food ready than the sun reappears, allowing the meal to become a picnic with views down the erratic-strewn glen to the ever impressive Stob a'Choin. As usual after making good progress in none-too-good conditions, I feel happy and relaxed, not overly concerned for the coming day - another long Tuesday and first of a new pattern of walks: high tops, big drops. Weather shows no sign of further deterioration, so hopefully, at worst, only the summits will be hidden - and known paths ease the way over these. There is also relief at being back in rough, wild country, where hills rise against the sky in subtly changing horizons, where the crashing of wind and water emphasise the silence of the land.

I'm moving by nine-fifteen next morning, chivvied by an uncomfortable campsite and a somewhat less calm and collected view of the day's task than noted above. Suddenly the daunting prospect of four disjointed Munros with a still-heavy sack seems to warrant a worried, fretful approach - perhaps in subconscious reaction to a broken night's sleep and consequent lethargy on finally waking to find daylight come too soon.

This is shaken off by recalling white splinters of ice showering across the sun on a recent winter ascent of Beinn Chabhair: first of today's hills and possibly the pick of the bunch. The memory is vivid enough to take me eagerly up there again, climbing directly to a craggy terrace from where a scramble is needed to reach the summit. The chosen gully turns out too loose and wet for comfort, but at least quickly brings easier ground and vaporous cloud on the curving, twin-cairned plateau.

The cloudbase has spent a less fitful night, starting the day much as it finished the previous one: slung from the tops at around 900m. Now, much to my delight, hopes that warm morning air might lift it clear begin to be realised, revealing a soft-edged foreshortening of hills further east. The high, elegantly smooth ridge linking Stob Binnein with Ben More seems worthy of prolonged consideration, so I cram into a neuk to escape the remains of the breeze, unpack the stove, make up for only having eaten a Crunchy bar for breakfast.

From here on, weather on my side for sure, the day slows: pressure off with pressure rising. Short, steep-climbing bursts alternate with long, drowsy sprawls in the sun. The rubbishy slope down to the Chabhair-An Caisteal col is free of the weekend snow - and, although the descent seems tediously long, I'm in the bottom of the acute high-sided V in twenty minutes, puzzling as to why glens pinching-in on both sides each bear the name Coire a'Chuilinn.

The next two Munros, An Caisteal and Beinn a'Chroin, are linked by a much higher col, orthogonal to the current one and suggesting an obvious short-cut to dump the sack before scampering up the muddy path. Technically, the watershed comes back down from the south top of Caisteal, but I can't resist going to the main summit for the long view down Twistin Hill and through Strath Fillan. Verdant hill-farm fields form a fine contrast to the great upsweep of glens on either side.

Back at the col, a battery of crags bar the *direttissima* onto Beinn a'Chroin, but the obvious line slanting up left is the one with the path. This soon brings a scruffy summit ridge, host to the assortment of crown green hollows and facsimile cairns which make a'Chroin notoriously awkward in mist. Another bowels-of-the-earth descent then bottoms-out beneath Stob Glas, the stubby southwestern spur of Cruach Ardrain.

This low pass, together with that dividing Ardrain from Stob Binnein, subdivides into three, two and two Munros the chain of high ground extending some ten miles eastward into Perthshire and straddling a gradual northward turn in the watershed. With the hills rarely climbed in combinations bridging these subdivisions, the frequent first impression of the whole range as forming a network of easily interlinked summits is somewhat misleading.

Another great plaque of smooth dark crag forces me into the corrie cradling the Ishag Burn, from where a climb amid light grey screes and bright rivulets gains the dip for Beinn Tulaichean - a southern outlier of Ardrain standing high above Rob Roy's old home of Inverlochlarig. Having come this far off route, it seems only natural to continue to the end of the ridge - not so much to go Munrobagging (I had already "done" this one in the days when that dubious pastime held me briefly in thrall), but to bid farewell to the waters of Forth, my right-hand companion for the past fortnight. The top, being out on a limb, proves windy, and the sight of cloud gathering round the higher summits ensures a hasty adieu. I hurry back along the broad ridge to a rapidly disappearing Cruach Ardrain, where silhouetted figures move dark against the skyline. They leave as I arrive: three women each in a different coloured cagoule. After peering over the cornice of Y-gully and recrossing the dimpled summit, I follow them off.

Tiredness offsets the excitement of having nominally reached the Tay, with the Grey Height ridge, as ever, showing little inclination to go downhill during the first mile of its course. I had come here one autumn to find virtually everything normally giving purchase to feet - rocks, gravel, paths - all coated in a thin, green verglas-like moss repeatedly upending me even on the flat sections. At least today brings no mishaps on the trudge to the slopes above the forest - where knowing the One True Way through the trees proves useful. (Until the bulldozing of a forest road some years later, all other attempts invariably ended in tears - both pronunciations of the word!)

Soon in Crianlarich - boots so coated in mud as to resemble Yeti gaiters - I'm well content at having otherwise left behind a critical eight-hour day. I clomp into the spotless five star hostel like a pauper into a palace - then, my handful of Munros making me feel fit to don the mantle of Hamish Brown, I brew a huge pot of tea.

There are as few occupied bunks here as there had been empty ones at Rowardennan - such that after dining on scampi in the Rod and Reel, after phoning my mother to wish her Happy Birthday for the morrow (when I will again be incommunicado), and after watching a white cloud-cap settle on the head of Ben More once the evening stops its swithering and opts for a deep, rich, all-corners blue - it is fine just to sit quietly in a corner of the lounge and work through a pile of up-to-date climbing magazines. Never doubting, of course, the only one missing would be *The Great Outdoors*.

I have always felt one of the great joys of hillwalking lies in being, very occasionally, in exactly the right place at exactly the right time, feeling privileged to be part of a day etched so sharp that only the earth's curvature limits the horizon, when simply looking brings the desire to walk, while walking demands constant stops to gaze in wonder. Today is to be just such a day, implanting itself so firmly in the senses as to serve as sustenance on many bleaker days ahead - quite apart from the more immediate benefit of allowing a sneak preview of the entire route to the Great Glen.

The morning starts misty-grey with a windless chill in the air. After buying stamps and milk from the village shop, I chat with a fellow hosteller - who differs metabolically in having been out for a week while still maintaining a crewcut. Conversely, my own month's growth already extends beyond that of a whole boatload of marines. Another co-sojourner of note is a mysterious Irish guitar player, *en route* from Oban to busk in the cities, who had succeeded in creeping into the dormitory in the middle of the night. Quite how this was achieved remains a mystery - there being no chance to speak with him later - but in light of the Rowardennan experience I feel this would be a very useful secret to glean.

Crianlarich has signs proclaiming it *Gateway to the West Highlands* - and while the Highlands have enough gateways to make them leak like a sieve, the climb above Wade's old road to the thin cairn on Craw Knowe does indeed feel like the threshold of a new and different land. Already mist is dispersing into nothingness, revealing the long line of yesterday's hills basking tamely under a cloudless sky.

The high tops for today, Beinn Dubhchraig and Ben Oss, first come into view as I crest the rise of Fiarach and look north. I'm on rough, watery ground studded with tiny lochans and *roches moutonées* (literally, sheep-like rocks), making great foreground for pictures of the clustered Auch hills and the massive, near-perfect cone of Beinn Dorain beyond. The latter is not only a sight for sore eyes, but also, it transpires, sore shoulders - the pause being good enough excuse to strip down to shorts for the first time, a decision paid for in skin later that night!

I hurry on across Cruachan Cruinn - a hill with so many contenders for the title of summit as to be describable, like myself, as topless. This brings the badly-drained ground beneath Beinn Dubhchraig's southern flank, where lunch becomes siesta as I half-doze through early afternoon heat, mindlessly tuning-in to background noises of birds and insects while gazing across western Argyll. The hills shimmer between a heat-haze and a sky so vast and deep, so resoundingly blue, as to give an inkling of what the old writers must have meant in describing the heavens as a *vault*.

Unable to muse on metaphysics all day however, I heave myself back upright after two hours of total stasis, then turn to the 550m pull onto Dubhchraig. This skirts the broken crags which name the hill and look so well in winter from halfway up Loch Lomond - although the reversal is perhaps even better: a full-length view way, way down to The Dumpling above Gartocharn.

Not that this can compete with the great northern panorama suddenly unleashed at the summit. The moment is memorable. My future - in the shape of clean-limbed Bridge of Orchy hills, tangled ridges of the Blackmount and the snowy horizon of Ben Alder beyond brown Rannoch Moor - intermingled with my past: happy days spent in Glen Coe, on the Innses, the Glen Lyon hills and, above all, Nevis - very white still and now taking over from Lomond the mantle of the Ben. All this and more has me turning round and round, smiling, laughing aloud in an involuntary response of delight. There too are Laoigh and Cruachan - trying to outdo each other in sharpness - Ben Ledi distantly jutting between Tulaichean and An Caisteal (was it really only two days since Ledi seemed so close along Loch Katrine?), and Beinn Dorain mirroring Ben More in the eastern quarter.

A dip in Dubhchraig's summit lochan seems an apt way of celebrating such an exceptional view, but with the water unbearably cold I settle for toe-dangling from a boulder instead. Apart from the lochan, the only water on the ridge takes the form of dirty snowpatches - so, waterbottle empty, I cut down to one of the burns feeding Loch Oss before my throat permits the tackling of its namesake of a ben above. Views remain epic: Loch Awe glows golden in lowering sunlight, pointing the way to hazy outlines of islands, making the day's main decision an easy one. Despite the first breath of a wind, a high camp will be made on the wide col before Laoigh.

The ground proves hard and bumpy, but after several false casts a reasonable site is found. This more than repays any discomfort with outlooks across Laoigh's vast, cavernous corries and straight down the trench of Glen Fyne. An ideal grandstand seat for both sunset and sunrise.

Fuel runs out after cooking the rice, denying me my mug of tea to clutch while watching the sun being shredded by low cloud behind Mull. With Tyndrum next up this isn't a problem, but does nothing to hinder a loneliness closing in as the sky darkens. Maybe I feel unease at risking a night in such a high and exposed place. Maybe the sheer splendour of the day, combined with memories of other times and places, makes me wish there is someone to share the experience. Maybe it is just one of my periodic depressions. Whatever, confidence ought not to sink so low: in mileage terms at least, this very hill marks halfway on the watershed.

Watch the sunrise indeed! The wind chaps the tent door, like the steelworks knocker-up, at five in the morning, flapping and flicking the fabric in confirmation of the previous evening's sense of foreboding. I don't feel much like wakening, or walking, or in fact doing anything - but, with two tent-pegs already yanked out, the rest will follow if I don't act quickly.

A surprise, then, when a second glance at the watch shows two hours having passed: I have lapsed back into sleep, oblivious to steadily worsening conditions. Now there is no choice but to move: the foot of the tent bucks like a rodeo horse, scattering cutlery into smirry dampness. Using both rucksack and backside to weigh down the lighter pieces of equipment, I bundle everything away before turning uphill into the storm.

The one redeemable advantage of camping high lies in already being two-thirds up an 1130m peak. This, combined with the wearing of clothes yesterday carried, means an eight-forty-five arrival at the edge-of-a-big-drop cairn - a time when most sane folk will be leisurely tucking into breakfast. I make do with shortbread fumbled from rucksack by numb fingers, eaten stooped against ferocious gusts. A coming-and-going wind-blown view down past Cononish to the distant main road proves the only present virtue of a summit capable of giving the most northerly sight of Glasgow. I have no real complaints however, this being the first dud in three visits and merely unpleasant rather than potentially harmful. One previous trip, a day of far-reaching seaward views, I sat here beside a north-of-England couple who totally ignored the grandeur around them to fiercely argue for fully fifteen minutes about techniques of cabbage-growing.

Cloud clamps down again, such that the hunched struggle along to the north top is in near darkness, the faint white blur of cornice used as a guide much as the centre line of a night-time country lane. A small cairn marks the top of the northwest ridge, where a good path occasionally breaks into short scrambles down crampon-scratched rocks. The path then pulls westward, headed for Glenlochy Crossing, and I'm alone among the black, crumbling slabs of the Ciochan. Fortunately under the cloudbase by now, I'm able to wander to-and-fro, peering over edges, occasionally dropping a level by way of some minor break in defences, until the final breakthrough beside the waterslide of the corrie burn. In the pass by ten o'clock, a second breakfast of chocolate and fruit is cobbled together, watching the cloud gather its skirts to rise clear off Oss and Dubhchraig.

For the first time all morning I relax: the 750m descent has taken over an hour of intense concentration. Later, I realise the day hasn't actually started badly at all: unused to the perspective of a high camp, I have merely been caught inside an unremarkable early morning cloud-rise with perhaps slightly more breeze than normal. From a camp in the glen floor, conditions would have seemed perfectly reasonable.

The experience is, however, to have a significant long-term effect. Only rarely will I now stay high of an evening, preferring both to avoid similar turbulence and to finish each day with some semblance of "going home". This gives the walk solid form, a way of shaping an otherwise chaotic collection of summits. As a stand-in for friends and pubs and the telling of the day's adventure, the green comforts of river and glen are to do a grand job.

The climb onto Beinn Chuirn mimics, height-wise, that onto Laoigh earlier, but is taken more leisurely with the day heating up. The summit, stony and bright under a blue sky, brings an unexpected bonus with its sudden view along the deep-shaded crags of Coire na Saobhaidhe to the pale greenness of fields beyond. I have forgotten this being the hill which looks so fine from the foot of the Cononish glen, often mistaken for its celebrated neighbour.

The downhill ridge snakes off from a tiny cairn: a crucial marker had conditions remained cloudy, all natural signs of the join having been long since sandpapered smooth by glaciation. After adding a stone to this helpmate, I pick a way down bouldery ground to a strip of young forestry guarding the final small hills before Tyndrum.

Meall Odhar proves another crunchy-heather top, giving dramatic, as-if-in-spite views back to Laoigh - where both summit and surrounding atmosphere look freshly scrubbed in their new lease of light. A strange rocky wart precedes Sron nan Colan and an unpleasant descent down boulder-hiding heather, then skiddy grass, to old lead mine spoil-heaps. From here, winding through ground as loose as a Cuillin corrie and strewn with *Danger!* notices, a track descends to the shade of old pines beside the railway and so to the village.

This last half-mile is churned into a morass of motorbike tyremarks, the perpetrator of which noisily antagonises me further once the tent is pitched on a campsite as worn and grassless as an end-of-season cricket square. Racing and revving as if enacting a Doppler Effect experiment, the wheelie artist puts paid to hopes of an afternoon snooze. Instead, I sit outside, simultaneously working through a large bottle of coke and a pile of postcards, before wandering along to Brodie the grocer to restock with gas.

Tomorrow is to be a virtual rest day: only Beinn Bheag, *little hill,* needs chalked off. This fills the angle between the Oban and Glen Coe roads - which divide at Tyndrum - and can be climbed sackless, allowing a second night in the village before Marlyn's Saturday supply run. With the weather becoming humid, threatening rain, this respite from higher things looks well-timed. A whole batch of big days are queuing up, and not until after the great loop around Rannoch Moor will things ease again.

The rest day passes quietly once the slightly irritating chore of climbing Beinn Bheag is completed. I think about extending onto the adjacent Corbetts, Beinns Bhreac-liath and Udlaidh, but from the summit of Bheag their grey, disappearing look adds nothing in the way of appeal.

I'm back in Tyndrum within two hours, delayed only by the absence of a marked railway bridge over onto the West Highland Way at the top of the pass. Recollections of there having been more than just pillars standing on an earlier visit are perhaps mistaken, but still cause me to wander in some confusion - before the patting of a gatepost (to ensure tomorrow's link-up) precedes a hurried stroll along the draughty, car-swept A82.

With the grocer closed for lunch, I go instead into the shiny tourist bazaar to buy postcards and chuckle at the array of kiltie dolls, Nessie tea-towels and boxes of shortbread adorned with Scottie dogs perched on tartan scarves. A coachload of arriving tourists treats these with considerably more respect.

Tyndrum's main claim to fame perhaps lies in being the smallest place in Britain served by two railway stations. I wander along to one of these, Tyndrum Upper (on the Fort William line), while waiting for a brand new glass-and-plastic phonebox to come on-line, then have the distinction of making the very first call from it, to my parents - who don't hang up properly, thus making it impossible for the lorry driver waiting outside to make his own call. A Telecom engineer is fortunately still on hand, but irritably adjudges the hitch my fault. It's bad enough suffering all your own hang-ups, I think, without taking the blame for other people's!

Staying on schedule means moving tomorrow, so Marlyn's arrival time is of some import. As she is keen to climb the first of the hills, ten o'clock is agreed - not so much as a precaution against the daylight (darkness takes a long summer vacation at this latitude: there are to be no more starry Loch Skeen skies), as to allow scope for weather-dodging. The newspaper forecast of light rain, some sun will do little to keep out the gusting wind and darkly-banked clouds now gathering in the west. Although the coming days will bring the first bed-and-breakfast since Biggar, they are also to be the longest so far and show no sign of succumbing easily. In light of succeeding events, this deep breath of a rest day will seem well-timed. Soon I will be floundering almost out of my depth.

A 2000m day with not a Munro to show for it! Whilst true that Corbetts - the next category down, heightwise - are notoriously difficult to combine, I now arrive at the major exception to the rule: a strung-out contortion of five, all in the 800m-900m range and all, remarkably, straddling the Orchy-Lyon/Fillan watershed. Nowhere else can so many ticks be so comfortably put into the book. More importantly, the day is the outward reach of a section which will see me camp beside Loch Lyon - very much an eastern glen, draining as it does beneath Lawers and down to Aberfeldy - before recrossing the hills to Achallader and Loch Tulla, firmly back in the west.

Rain has fallen through the night - the first, discounting the blatter over Laoigh, for five days - and becomes heavier with the dawn. Even intermittent breaks hold a dampness hanging in the air: with cloud down almost to railway-level there is little to look forward to once Marlyn departs. I pack all bar basics before sheltering under the canopy of a derelict petrol station to flag her down, repack the rucksack while trying to keep sopping tent away from dry clothes, then jump into the car and at last read about myself in *TGO*.

Supplies include a fair bit of reading material. Magazine apart, Rachel and Craig have sent an old school copy of Grassic Gibbon's *Sunset Song* inscribed: *Give it hell!* There is also a larger than usual batch of letters, including *Perkin Warbeck's Diary,* a rambling word-processed account of life back home sent up - in both senses - by one of the chief organisers of the

Ben Lomond jamboree. This is to provoke chuckles throughout the day, being read, paragraph by paragraph, each time rain becomes too heavy to walk through.

These are all waterproofed with freezer bags in the café as we sit, reluctant to face the downpour outside. Eventually, several snacks later, the rain unexpectedly goes off. We snatch the moment and drive full-speed toward a stunning, sun-caught, cloud-gapped Beinn Dorain towering through bright beads of windscreen rain. Mind you, we would probably have left anyway, come sun, rain or tornado, to escape a squad of American tourists disgorging from a coach. These rush indoors paying no heed to the sudden beauty along the glen in their desperation to buy shortbread and see Scotland.

The joint hill is to be Beinn Odhar, first and highest of the five: a smooth-sided dome of grass and scree now glinting as a watery sun keeps its foot in the door. Anxious both to utilise the weather and be on top by lunchtime, I set a stiff pace to which Marlyn - by no means a regular hillclimber - responds well. Occasionally we stop to look back south and west, where dramatic cloudscapes consist of equal parts sunlit patches and ghostly grey showers. Only Laoigh is hopelessly hidden. Far below, a tiny figure runs along the WHW toward the circular sewage ponds above Tyndrum - perhaps by design, perhaps hurrying to escape the shower of sleet and snow which slaps a chill poultice on our backs as we sit waiting for it to pass.

The final steepening is dry if misty, breaking suddenly to show a vivid rainbow arched over Bridge of Orchy. I shout Marlyn to hurry before the view disappears, then position her for a photo beside a big cairn giving good lunch shelter. *One.*

With our respective descent routes running almost parallel at first, and concerned the breakdown of plans for Marlyn to bring a companion means her having to go downhill alone, I stay close until scree gives out into tongues of grass, then watch her out of sight before turning to follow the ankle-high electric fence which meanders miles over these hills. Although I couldn't then know it, after Comb Hill with Jack, Lomond with the masses and Beinn Odhar today, every watershed hill from here on will be climbed alone apart from occasional chance meetings with fellow walkers.

The day seems on the improve in the deep drop beneath Odhar. A poor sun jaundices near hillsides and shines off the crags of Beinn a'Chaisteil, *castle hill* - tantalisingly only a mile away, but actually three hours distant in real watershed terms. The summit of the first intervening hill, Beinn Chaorach, comes as a relief after broad, dull slopes, and is topped by one of the new-style cylindrical trig points. These look nice while failing to give good old-fashioned, square-sided protection against wind. I shelter the best I can and gaze east to the camel-humped ridge of Beinn Challum. *Two*.

Although this hill and the next have been visited previously, familiarity offers no favours today. The worst of the weather hits the connecting ridge in a succession of sleet-filled squalls bearing down with all the menace of juggernauts in a rear view mirror. I withdraw into my hood, navigating face down by following the electric tripwires past their power source: a white wind generator whirring and spinning on a boggy col. Fortunately the cairn for Cam Chreag stands at the near end of its long lateral ridge and provides enough cover for the first real look down to Loch Lyon. *Three*.

After parting company with the fence - it turns southeast toward Challum - I follow one of its ampless antecedents to gain the second back-to-the-height-I-started pass of the day. A hen ptarmigan, first of the walk, limp-wings in circles like some demented clockwork toy while her chicks randomly scatter into the heather. Leaving them in peace, I descend back into grouse territory for a long rest at a lonely gate, eating most of Marlyn's left-over sandwiches and pulling on leggings as yet another heavy shower cruises in. (The hassle of unearthing and donning these has the effect of ensuring no more rain that day - a ploy I should have thought of earlier!)

The haul up a'Chaisteil's south ridge is lightened by repeatedly startling a pair of young deer into moving higher each time. They are finally seen silhouetted against the skyline on the last of many false summits, as though savouring the view from a hill as pleasingly shaped as its higher, more prominent neighbour, famed in poem and song, across the Auch Gleann.

Eyes need shielded for the steeply-downward sight of the horseshoe railway viaduct - pride and joy of the Victorian engineers and now throwing dark shadows onto sunlit grass. Reluctant to leave, I finally pull myself away, kick the cairn, start downhill again. *Four*.

Bogs before Beinn nam Fuaran give out onto the shortest, steepest pull all day - just what is needed at this stage - weaving through screes flattening to a summit with an uninterrupted, full-length view of blue Loch Lyon. I slump beside the cairn, suddenly tired enough to sleep. *Five. Thank goodness for that.*

The west end of Loch Lyon vies head-to-head with nearby Loch Giorra for the title of most remote spot in the Southern Highlands. Partly because of this, partly because it marks the beginning of a favourite glen (and, at thirty miles, the longest of them all), I have long nurtured plans to camp here. A surprise then - and initially a slight disappointment - to see, far

below, red and blue blotches which can only be tents. These belong to a
scout group on a two-day trek through the glens as a sampler for the hills,
and their presence rapidly replaces any selfish desire for solitude - *you've
had enough of that of late, good grief!* - with the pleasure of being amongst
laughter and wide-eyed vigour. I pitch beside them on the soft grey hydro
tidemark, thinking this is how the lonely places should be: alive and friendly
- as, indeed, many were until quite recently. Seton Gordon mentions
walking past the village school here as late as the 1930s.

The sleeping-bag is a touch damp from the morning, but that aside, the
evening is one of the most enjoyable so far. I sit out on the sand to construct
a stone windbreak for the stove, then look up and around to see hills on
every side, content in knowing the nearest road to lie a long, rough five
miles distant. The day has been arduous, leaving me drained - weakened
for the weekend - but the night's sleep will soon heal that. Ironically, for all
its three Munros and spectacular views, tomorrow will only involve two-
thirds of today's ascent!

ロロロロロ

The wind returns to a northwesterly slant overnight, bringing cool air to whiten the high Mamlorn tops with a coconut sprinkling of snow. Plumes of dragon-breath steam from lips and a pink flush tightens across cheeks in the cold-fingered struggle to tie off guys, then escape to the already-sunlit upper slopes and sharply-cut horizons for which the drop in temperature is a small price to pay.

Evening weariness replaced by energetic enthusiasm, I steadily climb the broad southern flank of Beinn Mhanach, tents shrinking to confetti beneath my feet. The cairn comes in exactly one hour. Mhanach is the junior member of a family of five Munros, horseshoed inside the curve of the Dorain-a'Chreachain ridge like a shooter crouched in a grouse butt. Brightness in the west allows two figures to be picked out on Mhanach's sidekick summit, Beinn a'Chuirn. I meet with them at the gate on the col.

We chat for several minutes, first about the clarity of the day, then, more unexpectedly, about the watershed. Mention of having been out for a month brings faint signs of cognition: I realise the others must have read the magazine article. This sudden renown chuffs me so much that after having been wished goodbye and good luck, I slip into a dwam interrupted only by a bout of waving as we again arrived on opposite summits simultaneously.

Who'd have thought it! I feel less isolated now folk know what I'm doing... how many more of those conversations will there be?... fifteen minutes of fame spread over two months!... must write to TGO again soon... progress report... I wonder if they'll take an article or two?... could even try writing a book... imagine that... being recognised!...

And so on, and so on, mind turned inward, on autopilot, oblivious to surroundings except in vaguely recalling *(NO!)* the direct route down to the next col, while not unduly steep, has the consistency of papier-mâché and is best left well alone. Somehow, though, this information is overridden *(NO!)* as I drop off the gentle plateau and begin contouring round *(NO NO DON'T!!)* to reach easier ground near the fence and an early lunch when *ohnonourrrrghhhhhelpppwhaumphnonowhawhashitphharrghfofuuuucksake-pleeassstoppfeetdigginshifouuphstopstopoowoomph!*

The daydream has ended. I had stepped out on a secure-looking grassy ledge which gave way, sending me head-first plummeting rolling jolting, arms and legs flailing, some ten twenty thirty metres to a juddering halt among mud and rocks below. I lie there, winded, dazed, glasses gone, aware only of blurred outlines of hills and a warm drip-drip of blood down my shirt to tell of still being alive. Other than that, nothing is certain. A thought immediately fills my mind and grows into more than a thought, into a realisation: *The walk is over.*

Then a vicious self-anger takes hold and my head begins to throb - more with frustration at my own stupidity than with any great pain. I hear myself repeating and repeating, as though spoken by someone else, the words *Shit* and *God help me.* Skewed and sprawled and shaking on the hillside, the name of the game is no longer Watershed, but Survival.

Mayday mayday mayday.

4: Recovery
(Sunday 10th May - Wednesday 20th May)

Everything had changed. Twelve-forty had me breezing along, as fit, confident and content as I could ever recall, so integrated with the walk that the opposing concepts of work/leisure, vigour/relaxation had loosened the bonds constraining them and gradually merged. The watershed was more vocation than vacation, a mould from which day after day was being shaped, each uniquely different, yet each adding to the rich stockpile of northward progress.

Now, at twelve-forty-five, all that seemed ended - the mould shattered, the walk wrecked - by a few moments of mental waywardness. I cursed the distractions which had led to a slope I knew to be dangerous, cursed the chain of events causing loss of both concentration and footing. If only I hadn't known about the *TGO* article, the glimmer of recognition could have gone unnoticed and my thoughts and feet gone elsewhere. If only I really had left my sister's letter at Rowardennan. If only... Just as on the drive to the Border I was if-only-ing again - but this time trying to rewrite the past rather than cheat on the future. Even in my present disarray I recognised this as pointless - what had happened had happened, like it or not - and I stopped the process short of reaching right back to the Garden of Eden to lay some blame at Adam's door. Mind you, he too had fallen! From the heights of a situation where the walk had been going like a dream, I had been brought low by drifting off into an actual one. Pride, as they say, comes before a fall.

These thoughts rushed out, like luggage from a suddenly depressurised airliner, in a stream too chaotic to immediately assimilate. I let them whirl and spin, on and on, turning instead to more practical matters. Arms and legs, although already stiffening, still seemed in working order. Indeed, apart from a deep gash to a cheek, all visible wounds were of the skinned knees variety. Spare glasses were used to find the originals mercifully unbroken and nearby: even the minute's wearing of the old, underprescribed pair was enough to tighten a headache behind my eyes. To have continued thus would itself probably have put paid to the walk. A handkerchief was held to face as blotter for red inkspots of blood.

Shock, like a circling vulture, would surely not be long arriving to pick my wounds. I decided to move on immediately. Besides, the remaining 100m of descent to the col would be a good way of assessing future prospects. These seemed grim on standing to put weight on my left leg: a sharp, hot pain stabbed through the thigh as though caused by an incompetent acupuncturist. The leg almost buckled with the shock of it. To touch, the skin was cold, numb, bringing a shivering fear of internal injury. Just what damage had been done was a mystery, but I knew even then it would certainly take longer to heal than the various cuts and grazes. Worrying too was a dull, indigestion-type soreness in my abdomen making me stoop in limping from a place I had, all in a moment, come to hate. A rueful glance back uphill showed no obvious sign of the accident. Streaked with scummy moss and loose wet scree, the broken slope looked as if things fell down it all the time.

Minutes after setting off, three walkers came into view on a collision course. I swung wide to avoid them, not wanting company just yet. Having no idea of my allegiance to the walk, they might insist on abandonment

forthwith - a decision too momentous to have foisted upon me, however well meant. I also felt so embarrassed at my predicament - evinced by blood solidifying to a tacky crust in my beard - that the word *shamefaced* carried an all-too-literal meaning.

Hence they passed at distance with only a wave, heading for harmless slopes beside the fence. A few minutes later - during which I washed in a burn and downed chocolate to keep energy levels high - my two friends from Mhanach reappeared. They were also following the fence, having presumably spent a pleasant, uneventful hour. They would expect me long gone, over Beinn Achaladair by now, so I hid behind a rock - feeling very foolish but anxious not to attract attention before deciding what to do.

I realised my primitive evasiveness was, in essence, an answer to the dreaded question: mental and emotional considerations had vetoed the physical proposal to give up. As long as the walk had life and breath, any thoughts of letting the head drop and turning toward the Auch Gleann and the road - toward the *tabula rasa* of a watershedless world - were inconceivable. The Glasgow bus was a threat to all I was living for: a symbol of lost hope, a tumbril hurrying to ambition's guillotine. I heaved the rucksack back onto shoulders and turned uphill.

For the first time in weeks came the experience of being left behind, of watching others pull away onto the ridge while I hobbled and rested my way up. In due course I was caught by another walker and now had no option but to answer face-to-face for my foolishness. Not that I need have worried: there was concern, not condemnation in my new companion's expression. The low-key support he was to offer during the ensuing few hours was probably the most significant individual contribution to the entire walk. Not only was he to ease me over two potentially hellish hills, he also helped calm a racing mind and - remarkably - virtually nullified the after-effects of shock.

My friend's name was Andy Dempster, an MBA member from Perth and kindred spirit. With long-held hopes of a deep south to far north, Mull of Galloway to Dunnet Head trek, he showed a more mature interest in my own progress than the standard curiosity/incredulity. I was glad to be able to repay a little of his encouragement in kind.[1]

If our gentle conversations were the first rung on my ladder to recovery, the second was far more dramatic. We contoured into shallow Coire nan Clach, then climbed between snippets of cornice to Achaladair's summit ridge with its breathtaking balcony view across Rannoch Moor: vast gapsite

---

[1] Andy's own book, *Classic Mountain Scrambles in Scotland*, appeared in 1992, published by Mainstream.

in a city of peaks. The Blackmount: nearer and more open now. The mighty glens of Nevis and Coe, high-walled and handsome. The White, Black and Grey Corries: all in view, all aptly named. Blue Loch Ericht beneath the low-slung saddle linking Ben Alder with Beinn Bheoil. Altogether a marvellous sight. In a word: *Lochaber*.

We moved on, away from the spy-plane view of Achallader castle and farm, along the flat, high terraced ridge, down to the dip for Beinn a'Chreachain. This I gained by a less steep option than Andy: the dodgy left leg meant downhill progress was strangely slower than uphill. On a'Chreachain's split-level summits swirling cloud blew in to catch us with snow. The day's colours had been dulling from gloss to matt all afternoon, until the perfectly formed scoop of Coire an Lochain now filled with a settling greyness as the edge-of-the-world view vanished for good. A pity, as for all Beinn Dorain's calendar angles, this long chain of hills improves, link by link, in a clockwise direction - especially in winter, when the northeastern shoulder we now used to skirt Coire Dubh Mor narrows to a lovely curving arête of windblown snow.

My original plan had been to camp at the foot of this corrie, then tackle 910m Meall Buidhe along with a run of low, boggy hills leading back across the Moor to Achallader, where Felix Aitken was expecting me. Still worried about internal damage however, I compromised between this and the other extreme of heading straight for warm comforts. Gorton bothy beside the railway thus became the objective. Andy, whose car was at Auch, would pop in on Felix and explain the situation. Whether or not I could then pick off the stray Corbett depended on weather and fitness.

We shook hands and parted - he towards Crannach Wood, I down long, tiring slopes jarring new-found pains with every step. Eventually, after nearly two hours and with the rain becoming heavy, the odd lump of Dun Laoghan was rounded and the small stone shelter reached.

In a reprise of Over Phawhope I simply unrolled the karrimat and collapsed in exhaustion - the difference here being sleep was kept at bay by soreness. Various scrapes either too large or awkward to be plastered had to be lain on raw.

Eventually I levered upright to cook all my favourites among the food supply: a candlelit feast intended partly as a crude attempt to lift morale, partly - the thought scared but was unstoppable - because if I did head for home next morning it made sense to leave the less tasty alternatives the ones forever dehydrated.

Unsurprisingly, this eat, drink and be merry policy fell flat in the cold, lonely bothy. I tried building a fire from old sticks and square chunks of wood, but the resulting meagre glow was a heartless, heatless affair. I read for a while, but with words merely shunting backwards and forwards along their lines I blew out the candle and lay staring up into blackness.

The initial fear of dying in the night through some lurking injury was now replaced by the more realistic, if only slightly less disheartening, prospect of stiffening so rigid as to be barely mobile by morning. I felt sad, confused at the wastefulness of my own stupidity. *What had I done?* It was as though I could see myself lying there in the dark, the weeks of walking crumpled and torn, thrown away beside me like letters half-written then discarded. The floor seemed the right place to be.

All night the rain poured: great driving gusts against the window and corrugated iron roof, each signalling its arrival with a hiss like that of wave-water drawing back through shingle. Added to a mouse scuttling in the grate and an all-over soreness aching, aching through the dark hours, this made for an unsettled night spent stuttering in and out of sleep. By the time weak grey light marked a lessening of the ordeal, fears of rigidity were realised: I lay as straight and stiff in my sleeping-bag as a cricket bat in its case. Attempts at rising proved both protracted and painful: only waist muscles seemed willing to function normally, demanding a series of sit-ups more appropriate to a high-tech gym than a dingy bothy.

At least the day's agenda had similarly tightened, the rain washing away any last hope that Meall Buidhe might yet be drawn back into the fold. For there to be any chance of keeping to schedule, of hanging onto the thread of the walk, the whole of today's loop would have to be short-circuited and rewired along the safely insulated track to Achallader. The decision to entirely omit a hill - thus breaking with the intention of treading the watershed as closely as possible - didn't overly concern me at the time, nor has it since. Several smaller summits had already been skirted when considered insufficiently alluring to warrant postponement of more pressing needs such as food and shelter, and the present adjustment was simply a large-scale version of these. I was realistic enough to know that as the walk transferred from paper to hillside, from idea to action, its texture would be coarsened by elements and ailments, knocked out of shape by the struggle to squeeze it into a too-tight logistical framework. Besides, having invented this game, I was surely entitled to occasional manipulation of its rules!

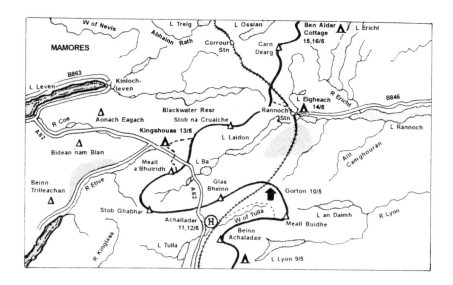

The resolve to reach Cape Wrath was as great as ever - perhaps even a little easier to grasp now the edges had been roughened - while my fallibility would perhaps allow scope for some future, equally-crazed walker to produce *Watershed Direct:* a straightened-out route realigned and renamed in the manner of a pioneering rock climb.

Mid-morning the downpour eased, but the four miles of track out to Achallader were nonetheless damp and drab. Cloud barely scraped clear of Crannach's old pines, while the Water of Tulla was swollen, peat-brown, well above its pre-night level. I was glad of the bridge at Barravourich. The white-walled farmhouse was in sight long before being reached at midday - an awkward time for Felix, who was dishing-up for her lodgers. The welcome never hinted at this, however: I was dispatched to the luxuriance of a hot bath before being fed the first of several meals of "scraps" - huge platefuls of gravy-covered meat-and-veg tenderly cooked in a shining white Raeburn.

Felix had taken a ten-year tenure on the place in the mid-eighties, thus firming-up the old, vague guidebook statement that "Accommodation may occasionally be found at Achallader Farm". Her main users were Waywalkers in summer, White Corries skiers in winter and spring. My own first visit had slotted neatly between these groups the previous autumn, and was memorable for an incident one afternoon. Chatting in the kitchen, I had seen a brown streak of movement flash diagonally down across the window, instantly followed by a dull thud as what transpired to be sparrowhawk crashed into the adjacent lounge window. From high on the Moor, having spied a pink fluffy toy perched on the sill, it had dived, literally at breakneck speed, for the "kill". Still warm and without a mark on its body, I had cradled it in the sunlit yard, supporting the unhinged head as one would a tiny baby's. The great bird was a thing of bold, intricate beauty: mottled light brown breast feathers, bright yellow legs, streamlined both in motion and colour. A friend had taken it next day, wrapped in newspaper, to a taxidermist in Cramond. It had returned in the interim and now stood, high on a shelf, surveying the lounge once more.

To be safe in a warm, friendly environment felt good: I relaxed a little with an afternoon of letter-writing and Scrabble. The pleasures were Damoclean however - the impending Blackmount day hung over me, held by only the thinnest of threads. On paper it stood out as one of the longest of all watershed days: well over 2000m of ascent, fifteen miles and no easy bisection. The only compensation came with the chance to travel light - hitching back for the gear and a second night of sheets and downies - together with an option to switch with Wednesday's rest day if the weather stayed bad.

Soon, though, this latter possibility vanished. A phonecall from Jerry and the Vicar told of their not being so flexible - only able to meet me with supplies late Wednesday morning. That left Tuesday, tomorrow, for the Blackmount, and as I went a post-prandial hobble down to Loch Tulla, looking across to invisible, cloud-wrapped ridges, I realised the logistical structure of two rest days per week to be nothing like as spacious as had earlier seemed. There was simply no time for recovery: I would have to mend on the move, with all the worrying possibilities that entailed. Although I hadn't dare say on the phone that room should be left in the car for an additional passenger back to Glasgow, I knew if I fell behind schedule there would be no catching up. Supply points were becoming too far apart, too specific to adjust. Tuesday would be a make-or-break day.

There was, however, one moment of relief that evening - a kind of retrospective optimism. While the TV spoke of little other than the newly-announced election date, June 11th, more immediately relevant to myself was the sudden realisation that today was *May 11th*. I had been out for a month.

When one door closes, another one shuts. Or so it seemed on stepping outside to be greeted by a drizzling layer of grey covering the hills down to 600m. The forecast had sounded quite encouraging, certainly better than this, and not for the first time I had allied hopes with millibars only to end up with both meteorological and psychological depressions.

Yet despite the size of the day ahead, the extent of mid-May daylight meant there was no real rush. I was able to sit down to a huge breakfast in the best Moss Paul/Biggar tradition. Felix's other residents planned walking the few miles of Caulfield's military road to the Kingshouse, and I envied them their short low-level day. I was heading for the same destination, but would have to sweat a lot more in order to gain a similar sense of achievement.

I was moving by ten, when cloud lifted enough to show a dazzling whiteness of fresh snow high up, and air began feeling dry and bright, hinting the day might hold promise after all. Three miles of road walking led to the hill - first beside Loch Tulla, then up the long raking zig-zag onto the Moor. Here black bitumen gave way to brown bog on the deep-heathered swelling of 492m Meall Mor, climbed only after a sweaty, dispiriting struggle. My leg was playing up already - a piercing ache beneath cold numbness of skin - yet this would be nothing compared to the four Munros ahead. Just as a hypothermia victim digs deep into reserves of fat in search of energy, so I turned in on myself mentally, searching for the sustenance to bring me through what I perceived, rightly or wrongly, as an extreme situation.

In so doing I all but ignored the marvellous view opening out to the east, behind me. As a child I had been taken to a stately home, Hardwick Hall, which boasted of being "more glass than wall". Rannoch Moor today was similarly "more water than ground": the jumble of major lochs - Buidhe, na h-Achlaise, na Stainge, Ba - all merging in one complex system with numerous nameless pools.

A boggy mile took me across the estate and old military roads onto the steepening for Beinn Toaig: the real start of the day's activity. Drier, red-soiled ground was a boost, allowing steady rhythm to be gained as I picked a way through scruffy, broken crags onto the broad northeast ridge. Here I almost stepped on a ptarmigan staying motionless, grey against grey stones, until the last possible moment - a case of camouflage working almost too well. The ridge - a gravelly, flat-stoned granite reminiscent of the high Cairngorms - brought the summit of Stob a'Choire Odhair easily, if somewhat protractedly, just before one o'clock.

Having been tight against steep slopes for much of the climb meant failing to notice the cloud's rising. Now it cleared from much of the range, lingering only in wisps around the stark white summit cone of Stob Ghabhar, my next objective. Spirits soared with the realisation this crucial day was suddenly so much easier: I could again see where I was going, both immediately on the hill and long-term in my mind.

A final spiteful snow shower blew across the ridges, forcing me in behind a crag. Then it was up a 300m boulderfield, through a convenient break in the cornice, onto the Aonach Eagach - nothing like as airy as its famed Glen Coe namesake, but still narrow enough to be fun. Ornate fenceposts led along a snow-skiddy path to the summit of Stob Ghabhar: a splendid high point from where the western arc showing Cruachan and Nevis confirmed the day's good intentions.

Bang on schedule, I paused to eat Felix's packed lunch before wandering down Aonach Mor: an extraordinarily gentle ridge considering its great height, taking three miles to gain the 900m from glen floor to summit. I was more relaxed now, aware that although difficulties were far from over, I had weathered the worst of this storm of my own making and could begin to settle into a routine once more. Even the leg pain eased as movement reasserted itself as the norm.

Above the Bealach Fuar-chathaidh - low point of and main pass through the massif - creamy-pink granite screes took me onto Clach Leathad. Here peace was shattered by two RAF jets scorching overhead: I plugged ears with fingers and ducked. There were fine views all round, especially to a sharp Bidean nam Bian and the slightly asymmetric cone of Schiehallion thirty miles eastward across the Moor.

Three lines of bootprints - like mischievous treading in new-laid cement - trailed through soft snow to the cairn marking the short, hanging ridge to Meall a'Bhuiridh: last and - at 1108m - highest of these hills. The first few metres of descent felt a little exposed to the snow bowl beneath, the rest merely exposed to a wind icily whipping up and over the narrow neck leading to the ski-slope summit beyond. Seventy minutes after reaching this I was downing a pint in the Kingshouse, having omitted tiny Beinn Chaorach and hurried down decaying pistes and wire-meshed log walkways with the bar as a full-view incentive all the way.

I hitched back on a road remarkably quiet given the splendour of the evening: horizontal sunlight gilt-edging shadow-black corries with cornices of gold, the Buachaille's great ziggurat of towers and ridges silhouetted against a reddening sky. The lift came from an executive in a shiny black limousine speeding from Lochailort to Edinburgh on a business trip. Not content with letting me travel in such style, he even offered a run right up the mile-long track to Achallader. As has been written elsewhere, a perfect end to a perfect day.

Worries quietened, I slept long and well, rising only when the rising aroma of burnt toast signalled the onset of breakfast time. Jerry and the Vicar (sporting a St Mirren scarf to mark their recent cup victory) arrived at eleven-thirty, having had a fright on the way up when a Lancaster bomber lumbered toward them, tree-height, across Loch Tulla as if on some delayed Dambusters raid.

After bidding fond farewell to Felix, we drove back to the Kingshouse. The bar was quieter than before, but walls hung with vertiginous photographs and old climbing ironmongery maintained interest. The others stayed until the tent was up, then left a squirrel-store of food, much of which needed eating before I could hope to move on. The barman told of several campers having sleeping-bags transformed into waterbeds after pitching on one of the enticing midstream islands the night before a storm, so I took good care to find a high, dry, landlocked site - only yards from the bar door, with the Buachaille in full view: satisfying all round.

For once, the Coe seemed to be getting the pick of the weather: the Blackmount hills were hidden away again. Not that I cared: they had been climbed, put behind me, and could be ground down to dust for all they mattered now. What constituted precious four-star fuel one day became as irrelevant as exhaust fumes the next.

I went inside the hotel to phone my sister Kath and discover boyfriend Geoff had become fiancé Geoff! Everything was as planned for the bothy rendezvous on Saturday: they would set off early for the eight mile walk-in from Bridge of Ericht. Things were definitely looking up.

After boulder-hopping on the Blackmount came the inevitable bog-trot over the Black Corries. Today I crossed the Moor again - the return half of the ticket bought at Gorton - determined to do so properly this time: via rough ground rather than Land Rover track escapism, on bogs topped-up by a torrential night of rain. So steady had been the drumming on the flysheet I was woken a couple of times by the sudden silence of brief stoppages!

High-pitched laughter backed by sounds of crockery-stacking and pan-clanging from the hotel kitchen finally roused me at eight. But despite the probing smells of bacon and sausages, my own breakfast was the usual mush of muesli and water, with a banana thrown in. Having started reading

Sunset Song the previous evening, I now settled to chapter two - only to doze off again as the rain turned up the volume, both aqueously and aurally.

I came to my senses just before eleven, when a hint of sun yellowing the tent walls suggested the day might at last be sorting itself. Sure enough, a dash to the bar for a pee showed blue acres opening overhead. I hurriedly packed, anxious not to dally any longer, and was walking before noon - just as a final two minute cloudburst signalled the end of the rain.

Two miles of dirt-track led back to the watershed. (I had willingly used the Kingshouse as an excuse to avoid the ground-in-name-only stretch between Lochans Gaineamhach and Mathair Eite.) The infant Etive churned through pools and small falls, already fast-flowing in preparation for its deep slot of a glen. Occasional backward glances showed the high tops clear and the Buachaille wearing a white hood of fresh snow.

By the time the Black Corries Lodge dog was within barking range, I had tired of easy going and was ready to strike off north - even though the long, gentle, heavy-heathered slope onto Meall nan Ruadhag was itself to prove tiring. The top brought a cool northerly breeze along with a full-length view of Blackwater Reservoir, but the cairn gave enough shelter to don full waterproofs as a heavy shower bustled through like a ewe chasing after the rest of her flock. Otherwise, it was to be a cagoule-but-no-sweater day: the steel-grey stragglers scurrying over Sunday's hills and skimming Loch Laidon avoided any further contact with the watershed.

The pay-off for dryness came in the form of another, less acceptable airborne visitation. Two pinpoint specks of blackness swelled like seeds in the south to scream in low-flying antics overhead: the RAF jet-set were back. Again and again as I moved slowly across the boggy col and onto Stob nan Losgann, the noise machines hugged the contours and left sonic shockwaves hanging in the air like gunsmoke. Again and again they were gone, smaller now than the black crows rising in panic from the heather, having covered a week of my walk within seconds. I suspected they had me in their sights and were showing off - especially when one completed a 20m-high, 180° turn around the mile-wide col between Ruadhag and Losgann, where I stood, heart-in-mouth, wondering what to do were there a crash. Perhaps, though, walkers go unnoticed at such speed: the Blackwater/ Laidon basins must seem an ideal aerial playground, far from roads, plenty of space for all kind of stunts. Whatever the reason, the hour-long performance was more torment than treat: an unwelcome politico-military intrusion into scenery singing of peace against ambitions of war.

By the time they were gone for good, I had almost reached the 739m summit of Stob na Cruaiche. A herd of thirty or more deer crossed just before the cylindrical trig point, restoring the quiet pace of normality. Across the Blackwater, the open southern corrie of Leum Uilleim matched the beauty of the name: *William's leap*. Further round, eastern Mamores huddled under the white wall of the Ben - while chisel-shaped Beinn Laoigh still rose to the south beyond the Bridge of Orchy hills. Only Schiehallion balanced the great western sweep - Schiehallion and the Moor itself, adding distance and foreground to almost every view. I was near the hub of the Central Highlands, with lochs reaching out in long silver spokes to link with the far-off rim of hills.

Some very wet and rough undulations, then a track winding down through forestry, brought the strange, outpost-like cluster of buildings at Rannoch Station - a convenient east-of-Scotland insertion into an assuredly west coast line. The place seemed deserted, reinforcing its frontier town feel, so I rang the tearoom bell. A woman - literally from the wrong side of the tracks - told me to camp down at a green bridge beside Loch Eigheach.

A labrador tagged along for the twenty minute road walk - worrying sheep, then watching intently as I ate a chicken carried from the Kingshouse. Palate whetted, the brute restarted its threatening tricks when I set off back to the station to make phonecalls. Shouting was of no avail: I had to resort to kicks, then stones when it trapped a lamb against a fence. Times like this I wondered why dogs bothered crawling from the primordial swamp - they were nothing but a nuisance right through the walk. While all this was happening the evening train arrived: an old tramp was met pushing his bike *downhill* from the station. He opined that the dog might prefer lamb to rabbit for supper.

A couple of calls confirmed Saturday's supply drop. This was turning into a complicated affair: seven friends all told and a backup system in case the main group had to cancel at the last minute.

Back at the tent - pitched facing south - the evening slowly darkened across the loch. I gazed out toward two Meall Buidhes: the higher, nearer one, a Munro, showing all the best angles, yet its lower, omitted neighbour inevitably occupying thoughts. Although its avoidance had been accepted as the right decision at the time, there now came a lingering sense of loss.

Solace came, as ever, from contemplation of northward progress. I had reached the end of a long, long stretch in which the watershed had been chiefly defined by major eastern rivers - Forth and Tay - rather than the more fragmented Clyde/Awe/Orchy systems. Now, for the first time since the early days of the Clyde, the west would have a proper say: taking a huge bite inland, forcing the route northeastward through Badenoch before the return due west across the Great Glen towards Knoydart. For the next two weeks I would be tracing the boundaries of Lochaber, Stob Ghabhar to Sgurr na Ciche, bridging the gap between south and north. With this change of direction already giving new impetus, hopefully the turmoil of the past few days would be out of mind just as it would soon be out of sight.

An early rise answered a call of nature in more than just the crude sense. I stepped out into the soft first light with the sun low and white over the loch, birds chirping and calling in the grass. Pre-walk resolutions of alpine-style starts had long since slipped away in the need to sleep ten hours or more, but the few occasions when I was part of the fragile beginnings of a fine new day were always deeply refreshing.

On emerging again, a council lorry honked a second dawn chorus, driver waving, as it headed for the station. After waiting for the edge of a shower to pass, I set off the opposite way into a bright, if chilly morning.

I had camped less than a mile from the Road to the Isles, possibly most famous of all Scottish through-routes. The section *By Tummel and by Rannoch* might be under tarmac nowadays, but *Lochaber I will go* retains the sterner character of hill track all the way to Glen Nevis. More than at any other time on the walk, the too-brief hour on the Road made me conscious of anonymous thousands having been this way before across the centuries, either for pleasure or as necessity. It was reluctantly I turned uphill near the rock of Clach an Fhuarain to climb easy slopes of dwarf heather and boulders onto the 730m end-top of Sron Leachd a'Chaorainn.

A fine view opened out, to improve bump-by-bump along two miles of upended, lochan-cradling strata. Schiehallion - now in its classic Mount Fuji form - and the eastern Mamores were again prominent. 941m Carn Dearg carried a huge tapering cairn, taller than myself. I battled down to the high pass of Mam Ban through a blatter of dry snow, but by Sgor Gaibhre - a less stony summit with a correspondingly less stony cairn - the all-clear had sounded. Variegated woodland shielding Loch Ossian's eastern shore now came into view, along with the sharp right-angled turn taking the loch's outflow into the near perfect flat-bottomed glacial trench of Strath Ossian.

I was entering the wildest area thus far: hills nothing like as reclusive as those of the far northwest, but shy and retiring all the same. Even though an ancient infrastructure of stalker's paths and tracks threaded these passes, this was no longer day trip country.

My home for the night - Ben Alder Cottage - could be seen far below from the twin Sgors of Gaibhre and Choinnich, paps well matched both in name and appearance, and conforming well to Scotland's glacial stereotype: gentle and grassy to the west, steep and broken to the east. Ben Alder itself loomed large and near now, massive brown slopes dribbling snow like a Christmas cake topped with icing. At 1148m, it stood as the highest obstacle on the entire watershed - but one which, thankfully, could be left until the day after next.

End-of-week tiredness combined with a brief return of leg pain made even today's last two tops - Meall a'Bhealaich and the tetrahedral Beinn a'Chumhainn - more hard work than pleasure. The bothy came in less than an hour by way of a jink through crags and a jump across a big burn, but proved dismally dingy inside. I preferred camping on the smooth meadow beside Loch Ericht: here I could spread myself in comfort. With five-sevenths of my visitation expected any time from late evening onward, I read by torchlight before eventually falling asleep straining to hear sounds of boots splashing through a river high enough to give a soaking in the darkness.

Loch Ericht is Loch Eireachd, *loch of meetings,* so it was appropriate the most populous day since Ben Lomond should occur here. Sarah, Michael, Bridget, Duncan and Big Steve had finally arrived at one-thirty a.m., via the shortest, wettest route across the Alder Burn. They were now laid out on the bothy floor like stretcher cases in a makeshift hospital, grunting slurred, sleepy greetings, calling for cups of tea. I didn't envy them their stone-cold, spidery-windowpaned black hole: for the first time all week my tent had felt really warm on wakening. I had stretched with sheer pleasure in prospect of the lazy day ahead. Early sunlight hung in the air, bringing scores of tiny thin-winged flies to bask motionless on the taut flysheet.

Much - probably too much - has been written of the ghost of Ben Alder Cottage, and while harbouring no interest in rummaging in the cobwebs to add or subtract from the myth, I was amused to be told that just as my friends settled to sleep, two further arrivals crashed open the door, bursting inside as noisily as a whole cellar-full of spooks. Doubtless one or two quietly simmering fears momentarily boiled over!

Once the others had gone off up the hill - by way of Cluny's Cage, fabled hide-out of Bonnie Prince Charlie and almost as difficult to pin down as the ghost - I wandered upstream in search of a crossing-place for Kath and Geoff, then sat among trees on the far bank, soaking in the sunlit pleasures of rock and water - the derivation of *Alder.* The bay was a lone neuk in the thirty-five-mile shoreline of a loch so splinter-like as to only here exceed a mile in width, and lying along the familiar southwest-northeast slant of a major fault. This one also contained Lochs Awe and Laidon, then ran on into Strathspey.

By three in the afternoon, after a couple of sorties for views along toward the dam and numerous syntax-wrecking upward glances from letter-writing, I was doubting there would be any more visitors. Had a sky turning sheet-metal grey and a breeze gently tugging and testing the branches suggested retreat? No fear! Kath and Geoff were hill-climbing, marathon-running, hang-gliding folk: they were suddenly on the skyline and the moment was a great one. I dropped pen and paper, pulled on boots half-laced and ran, shouting, to point out the crossing-place.

We sat on the grass to celebrate their engagement with two sackloads of goodies: mushroom soup, Marks & Sparks biscuits, and - remarkably - a bottle of champagne, albeit drunk from thermos mugs. I doubted whether the cottage had witnessed such opulence since the days of Victorian gentrification, when the means to cook slaughtered wildlife *in situ* was standard hillwalking equipment.

113

Sadly, with rain beginning to spit and spot, this *déjeuner sur l'herbe* couldn't last forever. The day-trippers headed for home while I went off with Big Steve - who had hared down Ben Alder ahead of the others - to collect firewood for the evening. For once, I didn't feel the sharp pang of homesickness usually marking the end of a meeting. The recovery from the fall seemed to have given a new stability and determination to cope with my continual living-for-the-moment existence.

Once the other Aldertonians returned - having been free of cloud all day - we brought huge loads of dead branches across the river, rucksacks sprouting wood like walkie-talkie aerials. The ensuing all-night blaze, along with the hiss of stoves, made the bothy warm and cosy not just in terms of heat, but atmosphere too. Any arriving ghosts would have been welcomed and given a mug of soup.

The rest day had been ideal: I felt prepared and confident for the four-day push to the Great Glen. This would start with a long and almost certainly damp crossing to another well-loved bothy, Culra.

One of the less obvious side effects of a big walk stirred to life today - although to label it such is almost to belittle its long-term importance. Before setting off in April, my subconscious assessment of just how "good" any particular walk had been depended primarily on external factors: company, weather, or simply the topography of the hills themselves. Now, five weeks in, with hill after hill after hill having been climbed, this cerebral quality control had changed its criteria to take more account of my own internal condition, less that of the world outside. The latter, like a silent movie car-chase sequence, tended to roll round endlessly until its salient features became wearingly familiar.

All this might sound strange given my being on a fundamentally linear, ever-changing route - from A to B with no going back - but while the hills differed marvellously in detail, in general outline they had a similarity causing slippage from focus to background when studied over-long. Hence while by any normal standards this was a terrible day - near-incessant rain, nil visibility, acres of soft, slushy snow - to me it proved the most invigorating, uplifting experience all week. Nothing specifically great, just a wonderful amalgam of enthusiasm, returned fitness and a shadowy good-to-be-alive feeling making surroundings and conditions all but irrelevant.

This, though, is largely retrospective analysis: only later did I come to fully appreciate the beginnings of a technique for bolstering and boosting morale by sifting the wheat of optimism from the chaff of day-to-day drudgery. Yet from here on this technique was quietly working away beneath the surface, making use of the weather rather than merely experiencing it, ensuring the summer-like weeks ahead were to reap a rich harvest of confidence which would in turn ration me through the psychological winter of the north.

More immediately, less complexly and for the third time that week, rain had poured down all night. Although reduced to drizzle by dawn, there was obviously no chance of a sudden Kingshouse-type improvement. I went in to waken the others - and be handed a cuppa by the bloke in the next room - before packing while Michael jumped about taking photos and making me feel something of a celebrity. Then the party split: Sarah and Michael accompanying me back up to the Bealach Chumhainn before returning to their car by a low-level route, the others opting for higher things by way of my Friday Munros.

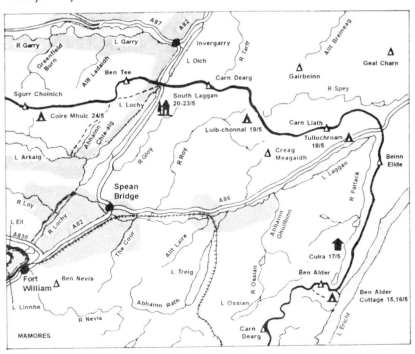

Loch Ericht - Loch Arkaig

There was no longer any need to plead injury as excuse for slow progress: the drag on my leg was over-ridden by energy gained from yesterday's all-day feast. I stormed ahead, delayed neither by a wetter-than-before path nor my huge restocked load. Michael took a rear-view picture of a sack-on-legs disappearing into the distance! In ninety minutes we stood at the pass - lowest, at 650m, of the three moating Ben Alder - where, after snack, a handshake and a kiss, we went separate ways. It had been good to restart in company, especially that of people I planned to meet again within the week.

Soon after leaving the cottage, a brief brightening had shown high crags, but cloud now settling again at 800m was obviously there for the day. 300m of well-defined ridge brought the disconcertingly gentle plateau. Here two sets of footprints trailed into the bright glare of the snowfield - made, presumably, by the owners of two rucksacks found propped against the bealach cairn. I took a bearing regardless - they may have walked straight over the cliff edge - then shuffled onward through snow the depth and consistency of that found in city parks with a thaw a day underway. A mile short of the cairn the other walkers appeared: a middle-aged couple retracing their own steps downhill. The woman lectured me as to the stupidity of carrying a camera in such conditions, but I couldn't be bothered explaining. They moved on, lost from sight within seconds.

With the stone summit shelter too wet and windy to elicit any pause, I swung southward, past the frozen Lochan a'Garbh Choire (vying with Lochan Buidhe on Cairn Gorm as Britain's highest standing water), then along the cliffs of the rough corrie itself. Cornices bulged into nothingness: the shape - and, no doubt, consistency - of shaving-foam. At least I could steer clear in safety, having found the remains of my friends' bootprints from yesterday.

Anxious to avoid seeing consecutive Saturdays burst into blood, I was glad of knowing to keep well right on the abrupt boulder-scree descent to the Bealach Breabag, thus avoiding treacherous slabs. A little knowledge isn't always a dangerous thing. Suddenly I was clear of both steep ground and cloud, able to see Alder Bay once more and to check the bearing for Beinn Bheoil. Lunch was eaten in the pass (which shared a name with a watershed hill in far-off Sutherland), where I mused on the apparent connivance of the walk's three geographical high points - Laoigh, Alder and Sgurr nan Ceathreamhnan - to form low points weather-wise. The first two having completed their part of the deal, wisps of cloud were doubtless already gathering in Glen Affric.

Beinn Bheoil (3333ft in old money), the traditional bonus after Alder, had a fine fore-top: Sron Coire na h-Iolaire. This looked both ways - like a child crossing a road - along Loch Ericht. The views weren't quite there today though: a thin wave of cloud lapped against the curves of the ridge to allow only occasional glimpses of screes plunging 600m to the water below.

With the sky still an overcast shade of grey, I was obviously in only a small pocket of dryness. This was sewn up as I slanted down to the stalker's path, the last hint of brightness vanishing like failed stadium floodlights as rain made up for lost time by pouring out of the west in a breached dam-wall of wetness. The heavens caved in all around - as though the Four Horsemen of the Apocalypse were out for an afternoon's dressage - and the moorland welled into wide weirs of water. I was fortunate to be walking with the storm and able to hurry on, splashing past two more walkers - the first overtaken for days - sploshing across the river, feet already too wet to care about going the second mile to the bridge.

Although soaked through on reaching the bothy door, all cares evaporated in the hot plaque of heat from a thriving fire: the place was crammed with school kids up from Leicester on an A9-West Highland Line trek. I was handed the day's second cup of tea even before unpeeling my wetsuit. The woodpile - logs dropped off by a considerate estate worker - seemed endless, the company - inquisitive kids and an instructor who knew all the local howffs - was good, and progress had been exceptional: less than six hours door-to-door. Hell might be raging in fury outside, but it was heaven in here.

I slept in front of the fire, just out of range of spitting embers, and slept well. The snores of the instructor were the talk of the youngsters when kicked from their karrimats at seven-thirty, but I was happy to quietly lie-in a while until the mayhem all around became too much to bear.

Having forgotten to include cereal on the weekend supply list, breakfast was measly rather than muesli: tea and biscuits, the overnight fast hardly broken. I stood at the door to watch the school party set off for the Bealach Beithe and Ben Alder Cottage, then swept the floor and read an out-of-date *Scotsman*. A walker from the next room (concrete floor, leaky roof) came in for a chat. He was heading for the Lancet Edge, one of three sharp, scrambly ridges leading onto high plateaux hereabouts which more than compensate the absence of the Cottage's lochside tranquillity. The circuit of Alder itself by way of both Short and Long Leachas has become something of a bothymonger's classic.

By mid-morning all the tops had come clear to give a hill-and-pass panorama in the looking-south-from-Aviemore class. I chose to ignore the gentle 500m swellings of Mealls Mor and Beag, heading instead along the parallel - and remarkably dry - path toward Loch Pattack. The air held the soft, washed-out, almost tangible lightness which often follows torrential rain, with high cloud gradually brightening into fragmentation. *A fine day ahead,* I thought - little anticipating just how fine, how long this "day" was to be.

A metal shed beside a track carried a sign telling walkers not to leave their cars as the horses would eat them! This was symptomatic of an estate showing above average awareness of the needs and mentality of recreational landusers. The delivery of logs the night before had been an even more striking example. Doubtless the teenagers - who, more than any number of adults, would perceive the inappropriateness of strict proprietorial rights applied to such wild country - drew more from this than from the "Keep out, this is mine" policy all too prevalent elsewhere.

I climbed beside trees, pausing every now and then for a look back across Loch Ericht to the Drumochter hills - trim and smart in white collars of snow. I was soon standing at a similar height on Meall Leac na Sguabaich: not a summit in its own right so much as an outlying top of The Fara, a strange, elongated maverick hill flanking four miles of Ericht's northern shore, nowadays neglected for the crime of just failing to achieve Munro status. For me, though, it was a special hill: here Tay gave way to Spey. Thirteen days had passed since I had picked up the threads of Scotland's longest river on Cruach Ardrain. Now I was to start edging round the second longest - although for a mere two-and-a-half days!

This change-over is probably the moment to make mention of what I came to call *compartmentalised walking* - ie my method of coping with the sheer scale of the watershed, of making the transition from weekend outing to twelve-week epic. The technique was simple: break the walk down into half-week blocks by using roads and villages as one would stepping-stones across a fast-flowing burn. I could then confine thoughts and hopes to the current block - each known to be manageable within itself. Thus Rowardennan-Crianlarich constituted a block, as did Crianlarich-Tyndrum and Tyndrum-Achallader. Events such as completing the Blackmount or reaching the Spey were subdivisions giving an extra sense of achievement and progress.

The blocks were held together only by thin strands of logistical planning and forward thinking, such that the upcoming weeks were deliberately left out of focus until actually visible. To have done otherwise would to have been overwhelmed by the task ahead - or, returning to the earlier metaphor, to have lost balance and been swept away by the current.

Curiously, this type of thinking also worked retrospectively, enabling me to stop fretting about my fall once the initial shock had worn off. There was also a paradox: in all but the physical sense I was nearer Cape Wrath at the Border than at any point thereafter. Even in times of crisis the eventual finish was blocked from thoughts lest despair set in. Hence my real destination today was the perfectly feasible one of Loch Laggan, now within sight to the north.

The easiest possible descent - carpet heather and green mosses - brought an equally easy climb over Beinn Eilde: a rockier hill than guessed from the map, with three or four knobbly tops. A track through the forest past the Falls of Pattack was reached down steeper ground concealing ankle-snagging boulders and a flock of small fidgeting birds I couldn't identify. The Pattack was still high after the rain, water rolling from a weir like newspapers off a print drum.

This was also one of the country's more confusing rivers, performing an abrupt U-turn toward the end of its course like a driver realising he or she is heading the wrong way at the last moment before joining a motorway. After my return home, several experienced walkers made the mistake of assuming I had skirted the west end of Loch Laggan - and hence that the Pattack flowed eastward to the Spey - whereas both Laggan and Treig were dammed in the 1930s to feed the aluminium works at Fort William.

Afternoon sunlight slanted through the trees of the well-kept farms above Kinloch Laggan. (This name should itself resolve any confusion, being Ceann Loch, head of the loch - although Kinloch Rannoch makes a mess of the rule in being sited at an outflow.) Another heavy-laden walker sat beside the village hall, evidently annoyed at an out-of-order phonebox: the nearest alternative was five miles away.

I thought of camping here, then plodded a mile or so west to Tullochroam, a small private house above a grassy promontory. The owner said Yes, of course, and even asked if I needed provisions. The family later went boating on the loch, their outboard put-putting toward Ardverikie Castle as I sat outside to cook a pot of curry.

Waterproofs - still soaking from Sunday - were hung from trees while I went back down to try my luck with the phone. I had to bang the casing to retrieve a jammed coin, but in doing so ended up with more than I had put in - as though Telecom produced a more traditional kind of slot-machine! The operator reversed charges to my father, who was delegated the task of ringing both John and Julia - to confirm my continued existence - and Little Dave, next on the supply list and London-based. He failed to reach the latter - as had I on every occasion since Achallader - so the last weekend of May still felt up in the air.

The return to the tent was in lovely low light with the hills looking great, splashed with snow as though buckets of whitewash had been thrown over them. A fitting end to an easy, amiable day - and the second of only six in the Highlands when I would climb neither Munro nor Corbett.

Tuesday being Tuesday, this was to be the longest day all week: a high, broad-backed ridge topped-and-tailed by lower, deceptively time-consuming peaklets - a sort of three-course-meal of walking. It was also a day which would bring the Great Glen within reach and mark the start of a walk within a walk - from my most easterly point in the Highlands to my westernmost, less than three miles from the great sea lochs of Knoydart. This fortnight-long trek - into rougher, more remote country than any yet seen, square into the face of any weather that blew - was on account of the monumental landslip which had, an aeon before, drawn the north of Scotland down to overlap the bulk of the land below it. Dauntingly, there were to be no more than five miles of northward progress during this fortnight - with all of these achieved in the next couple of days.

There was no rush, however. Logistically I had put myself on time-and-a-half from here, and the hills held no obvious terrors as yet. The Atlantic coast would come in due course, at a steady pace, and I would start by walking to Luib-chonnal, last of my central Highland bothies and conveniently near the Spey/Roy watershed. From there, the second self-enforced two-day break would be, as the song says, only a motion away.

First of all, though, came a stroll along to the Kinloch Laggan shop - left until well after eight to allow for Highland unpunctuality - and a chat with an assistant who was, like most folk in these parts, friendly and helpful. I had been looking forward to this brief visit to a favourite area, and wasn't disappointed.

Having spent an hour walking up and down the same stretch of road, it was a relief to branch off at Aberarder Lodge and climb into a breezy morning. I should, by rights, have gone another mile to Feagour, but steep woodland there and a well-constructed track here made the switch an obvious one. Four walkers were met heading the other way, having come over from Fort Augustus via a camp on the Corrieyairack, General Wade's celebrated showpiece of roadbuilding. They, like Wade's troops two centuries earlier, were on a long cross-country trek: the Ultimate Challenge.

This annual coast-to-coast event - about which I had completely forgotten (presumably yesterday's frustrated phonecaller had also been heading east), was conceived in the late seventies as a non-competitive walk on the wild side. Increasingly popular, by the mid-eighties it had become a peripatetic community of hillgoers in which everyone seemed to know everyone else. There was a choice of high- or low-level routes, with a minimum of twelve Munros or Corbetts being the tougher option. This group were going over the tops, bound for Dalwhinnie, the Gaick, Lochnagar and Stonehaven. As an afterthought, one enquired as to my own plans. Their faces were pictures of trying-not-to-look-upstaged when told!

As we wished each other luck, a worrying thought flashed across my mind: I would be struggling in Knoydart when they were celebrating through the Mearns. I hurried on, following a green path up rough, small-cragged ground onto 622m Creag Ruadh, where the summit was curiously undefined, holding a silver bead of a lochan like mercury trapped in a groove on a laboratory bench. There were good, open views down Laggan and through the Lochan na h-Earba faultline to the Tulloch hills. Little-known tops such as this often formed the staple diet of the walk: not only giving heavier going than higher, wind-cropped peaks, but sometimes stretching an otherwise ordinary day until it - and I - neared breaking-point. More enjoyably, they led into backwater areas, gave unfrequented routes onto popular hills, presented unexpectedly enlightening views of places already thought to be known well.

The day brightening after a scurry of showers, the stiff pull onto Meall Ghoirleig proved warm work. I then postponed lunch until a grassy ledge halfway up the 500m haul onto Carn Liath, lazing in the sun to let the nearby buzz of insects blend with the distant traffic hum, gazing across Loch Laggan to Ardverikie's fairytale turret.

The wind greeted my arrival on the high ridge with an icy blast from the north: being in the lee all morning had kept me ignorant of the gale that had blown up overnight. A sky scoured free of cloud gave another stupendous horizon, and I braced myself against the wind, legs apart, to look round. I had forgotten just how central these hills were: Braeriach, Lawers, Wyvis, the big western glens - all near enough to be identified at a glance. But due west made the real impact, shocking me into saying, out loud, *What the hell is that...?*

For there, at the limit of visibility, was a hill like a child's drawing of a hill: a dark, jaggy pyramid rising clear and unbelievably sharp. For a moment I thought I was seeing Skye: surely nothing was that sharp outside the Black Cuillin? Then the words Sgurr an Ciche, *breast hill,* came to me. The welcoming landmark for generations of seafarers and island dwellers was being seen from afar. One day soon I would be there, on its summit, and that day would mark my turning the corner towards the north. The moment of recognition was a sign of encouragement, beckoning me on.

But the view, the dryness underfoot, even the gentle rise and fall of the ridge were all offset by the gale. I swayed and staggered along as if drunk, hardly daring peer down into the slabby southern corries for fear of being blown over the cornice. The two cols after Carn Liath were narrow - notches between blunt saw-teeth - and here the wind tore through without hindrance, repeatedly knocking at the back of knees, felling me. Things eased a little on the higher, 1054m Stob Poite Coire Ardair, where to sit in the windshade of a rock was to watch a heat-haze rise from the snow - curious conditions! I was due to descend from the bump preceding this summit, but had continued along for a view of the mile-and-a-half of gully and buttress forming one of the major Scottish crags. Too vegetated to be much use in summer, Coire Ardair earned its reputation when the gullies - locally called *posts* - were choked with winter ice.

Angling down a grassy northern shoulder rather than continuing along to bag Creag Meagaidh seemed too sudden a departure, but it was a relief to be able to stand upright again. I saw three ptarmigan on Meall Ptarmigan, then deer on Creag a'Bharnain. Both hills abounded in rocky bluffs and scoops of scree. This was very much hinterland, the Back o'Creag Meagaidh in the manner of the Back o'Skiddaw, and immediately felt a world away from the bustle of Lagganside. Some of the quietest places in the country are not in wild, inaccessible areas - which act as lodestones to walkers and wilderness-seekers - but on the blindside of popular hills, where the proximity of roads discourages eccentric wanderings. What percentage of Ben Lomond ascents come via Comer, for instance?

I had seen the bothy - sunlit block amid green pasture - from on high, and arrived just after seven: a long-winded nine-hour day. The door wouldn't open, and peering in to see a rough stone floor led to a belief in the place being derelict. No bother: I simply cleared some stones and sheep droppings and pitched outside - only to jump with surprise on being hailed. The door had merely been stiff, while a ladder led to a loft renovated for sleeping: I went upstairs for supper. The three inmates were all Challengers - from Glasgow, North Yorkshire and Stoke: a mix making for lively conversation before they turned in for an early night. As at Ben Alder Cottage, I was glad of being outside. With the evening now windless and daylight lingering in the west, I left the tent door open and read until all hours.

I woke with no idea of the time, having lost my watch the previous evening - presumably while bending to drink from the burn below the White Falls, a mini-Niagara within sight and sound of my camp. Going indoors with a breakfast mug of soup failed to help - the others were equally vague - but from sunlight edging slowly bothywards, I guessed it to be moving-on time. A shepherd then arrived in a Land Rover filled with all shapes and sizes of dog, checking the Challengers were okay. It was almost ten he said: I had slept late.

After hopscotching the river, I headed straight uphill toward a prominent red scar of scree. The southward view was nicely balanced: yesterday's hills looming large beyond tiny Loch Spey, still beginnings of many a malt.

Glen Nevis giants made the nearer Munros seem mere foothills. The only disappointing aspect was the light and the angles being wrong for seeing the Glen Roy Parallel Roads - three green terraces running round the hills like visible contours, consequence of ice-age spillage through the wrong end of the glen. The glens here had Parallel Names, too: Roy, Gloy, Loy.

Creag a'Chail was cairnless, but Carn Leac wore an isolated stretch of dyke along its summit like a drystane tiara. Across Coire Uchdachan, the track and pylons of the Corrieyairack slanted down Glen Tarff to a just-visible Fort Augustus. Like the great pass, I had done with the Spey, and headed between two wire fences to the col for Poll-gormack Hill. Flatter, wetter ground then brought Leac nan Uan and lunch in the sun-trap of a large rock.

Temperatures had steadily risen all morning, until heat now shimmered above heather and a herd of deer waded into a lochan in search of respite. After a snooze, I found it hard to get going again - I would have been better crossing all two miles of bog before stopping - until an end-of-term exuberance suddenly took hold: I powered onto the steepening of 817m Carn Dearg.

More bogs led to Carn na Larach, but the final col was dry. I sat on Beinn Bhan looking westward to where Sgurr na Ciche again jutted left of Ben Tee, before turning to gaze south and east over land already covered - becoming quite maudlin at the thought of another section all but over, all its happenings trailing behind like a cast-off snakeskin. Yet this was only halfway: so much more lay ahead!

Enthusiastic once more, I climbed the forest fence before zig-zagging down through a large felled area giving telescopic blue-loch views up and down the Great Glen. A fenced slope of deciduous, loose-leaf trees stood lush-green, silver-barked against blanket pines.

Suddenly I was on the road - at 50m the lowest point since Rowardennan - and again trying to guess the time as I neared Loch Lochy youth hostel. Glory be, it was almost five-thirty: I was straight inside! Booking for four nights didn't seem quite right, but there were few better places to pause for breath. Quite apart from a lovely situation, Laggan hostel had been long and widely regarded as one of the friendliest on the circuit - a reputation maintained by the new warden: I immediately felt welcome.

Phoning home brought the message that Little Dave would arrive late the night after next along with his friend Richard. They were apparently eyeing-up Gleouraich and Spidean Mialach - two big western Munros - for Saturday's "rest" day. Michelle also spoke of coming north - to Cape Wrath to collect me! We talked and talked until the pips divided us. A shower was another forgotten pleasure, the first hot wash since Achallader - to be followed by endless cups of tea with John Brown, a Challenger out from Torridon on his seventh trip.

After lights-out, as the dormitory coughed itself to sleep, I lay awake suddenly scared at the pace things were going. The imminent remoteness of Knoydart formed itself into a dark, wordless worry, an internal manifestation of self-doubt, of unwillingness to face the crux of the walk. These fears - known for a week or more - made those of the fall seem past their sell-by date and gnawed at confidence so effectively that even now, years later, I'm tempted to retitle this chapter *Central Reservations*. Yet if I knew then what I know now, I needn't have worried. The journey westward into Knoydart was to prove the finest week's hillwalk of my life.

5: Crossing the Red Sea
(Thursday 21st May - Friday 29th May)

If a glance at the map suggests the Central Belt as a tightening around Scotland's waist, then by the same token the Great Glen is the country's neckline, plunging from Inverness to Fort William in a straight-creased, well-ironed collar of low-lying land, beaded silver with lochs as though strung with pearls. Beyond, set firm on central Highland shoulders, lie the headlands of the north: a rough, wild region defined as much by deep indentations of the sea - western fjords, eastern firths - as by hills themselves. A region with almost two million hectares of interior, over one thousand miles of coastline, yet only one hundred and twenty-five thousand inhabitants. Here, as though the Great Glen were a moat dug against invaders, the land adopts a more aggressively defensive stance - a trait traceable right down to the rocks themselves: southern Dalradian schists giving way to older, coarser Moines bulging through hillsides in outcrops and crags.

Water too takes on a different character. All the really weel-kent Scottish rivers, those meandering through popular ballads and flowing from the pages of encyclopaedias - Tweed, Clyde, Forth, Tay, Isla, Dee, Don, Deveron, Spey etc - are to be found in the wide-bodied lands south of the Great Glen. To the north, while almost every hilltop view gleams silver with water, the drainage systems - and, consequently, the river-names themselves - are much more fragmentary. Whereas before I was passing through areas named directly from rivers - Tweeddale, Strathclyde, Tayside - the map will now be strewn with names less obvious in origin: Morar, Kintail, Coulin, Assynt, Reay. Even the great series of West Highland through-routes: Shiel, Affric, Cannich, Strathfarrar, are celebrated more in their totality as glens rather than specifically as rivers.

During the coming few days I'm to be very aware of the significance of the Great Glen both as major dividing-line and natural stop-off point on long through journeys - an awareness no doubt heightened by the chance it gives this particular journeyman to catch his breath, to take stock of the six weeks completed. Much more than at Rowardennan I have come to terms with the walk as a temporary way of life. I'm thus able to treat it as such rather than as a frantic few weeks of activity or seemingly endless succession of summits. Halfway has been reached in more than just logistics and time.

There are certainly two, maybe three rest days ahead, starting with a trip into Fort Augustus in the guise of a tourist. I think about going the other way, to Fort William, but the Nevisport coffee shop loses by a short, shaved head to the Benedictine Abbey. Not having slept too well due to a dormitory window bang-banging in the breeze (but, annoyingly, asleep just enough to resist thoughts of shutting the damn thing), I finally rise - again with no idea of the time - to a dead-to-the-world hostel.

The kitchen clock showing six-fifty, I make an early breakfast before going out to start hitching. Barely has thumb emerged from fist than a fish lorry bound for Invergordon crunches to a halt on loose chippings. I'm thus deposited in sweet F.A. before the shops open, and somewhat unhappily - the prospect of a prolonged roadside wait having been such a part of my day's plan as to seem, perversely, more appealing than a prolonged mooch around town!

Had yesterday's warmth continued, I could simply sleep today away on some grassy lawn, but conditions are blowy and cold with occasional spitting rain. So I retreat into the Abbey, a beautifully light, open building holding an almost tangible sense of calm. This is something I'm finding strangely lacking in the hills themselves, due no doubt to a combination of periodically wild weather and my own jacked-up anxiety. I spend a long time inside - until the camera-clicking brigade arrives - wandering round the Stations of the Cross (half-time score: Christ three falls, me one), then drifting into the nebulous land linking thought, meditation and prayer. I'm later to realise just how badly I need this quiet break.

Lunch is fruit eaten in the lee of the cricket pavilion, watching monastic tutors scurry across the square toward the college, cassocks billowing. Abbey and college were both founded in 1876 on the site of the fort: formerly Kilcumin, renamed by Wade for William Augustus.

I can't be bothered going down to the lochshore, so opt instead to visit the five-lock staircase raising the Caledonian Canal from Loch Ness to Loch Oich. But boredom is the prevailing mood: soon tiring of watching replicate white-panelled boats, I start hitching back to Laggan. Another fish lorry obliges: I watch the same set of cabin-cruisers chug through into Loch Lochy. A dead slow-worm lies across the road, mashed by an anything-but dead slow car.

There are only three other hostellers: a motorised walker planning Ciche for the morrow and an elderly north-of-England cycling couple. The latter provide the evening's entertainment, especially the husband - who, with flowery shirt, trousers sawn-off at the knee, Chaplin moustache and broad Lancashire accent, could well be the role model for Michael Palin's Gumby character. He and his wife are also obsessed with trifling amounts of money. One overheard conversation revolves for several minutes around the relative merits of an 18p tin of carrots bought in the Laggan stores and another, cheaper version seen elsewhere that morning. Ideal companions for the Beinn Laoigh cabbage-growers!

We chat about mutually known parts of the Derbyshire Peak along with sharing plans for Friday. They are heading south, while I have devised a method of climbing the next batch of hills light-loaded and returning via the glens. This is the first of several such logistical schemings, to be a feature of the coming fortnight. If the weather improves even a little, it will make sense to use the time well.

I go to bed feeling glad of the rest, yet aware of the now familiar desire to keep momentum going. But tonight I chuckle rather than worry myself to sleep. My knotted-hankie friend clomps past the toilet as I'm secreted inside musing on life's profundities. Assuming the room to be empty, he looks in - I almost *hear* him looking in - then snaps off the light, leaving me to complete both meditations and evacuations in darkness!

More scatology. Despite having spent only six of the last eleven nights "under canvas", I wake in the small hours having drunk too much tea, convinced I'm lying in the tent, able just to walk a few yards and relieve myself on the grass. Fortunately a gritty piece of doubt niggles away in the corner of this misapprehension, keeping me horizontal long enough for the truth to creep in like the slow light of dawn. Thoughts of what might have been make me blush in the darkness as I fumble along the landing.

Enough of such things! The real dawn, when it comes, is indeed slow and ill-lit - but a brightening through the greyness revives memories of the Blackmount, prompting hurried making of egg sandwiches, packing of a daysack and a fast ascent beside the trees above the locks. I'm soon above Lochan Diota and into thin dry cloud on Ben Tee - most easily recognisable of Great Glen hills and clone of Schiehallion's cone. Short heather and boulders bring the summit much sooner than expected. Having forgotten to adjust my ETA for the lighter load means several minutes of circular wandering to check the hill does indeed slope off in every direction.

Although the sun is burning a hole through the cloud, I'm forced into taking a bearing for descent. While there is only one top to a hill, there are a million bottoms, and I can ill afford to go astray in the compression of contours below. The slope is ridiculously steep - such that the addition of another degree or two would surely send the boulderfield trundling downward like rubble from a dump truck - but I'm able to use a long, vegetated rake to give knees some relief. Halfway down this 400m treadmill the cloud rolls back to reveal the col - where soon I'm eating lunch beside a small waterfall and watching the summit come clear at last. The one-in-two slope continued right down to the pass without any run-out whatsoever.

The reascent onto the triangular eastern end of Meall a'Choire Ghlais is no less steep, but being uphill, where every step can be securely tested, feels more secure. Frogs are everywhere, a sure sign of spring: they flirt from beneath boots, belly-flop into pools of moisture, mate on the sunbeds of old snowpatches.

The green flattening of the ridge comes as release after the confines of the crags: the first col is spacious enough for a game of cricket - although recovering the ball would prove awkward. Indeed, the squareness of this whole massif neatly offsets the angularity of Ben Tee. The main top, Sron a'Choire Ghairbh, a Munro, can be seen well in advance, a mile around the rim. Although two silhouettes beside the cairn move on before I arrive, I know them to be marathon runners from Manchester due to this being one of perhaps only three Scottish hills to carry a visitor's book. (Mam Sodhail above Glen Affric and Suainaval on Harris are the others.) This lives in a coffee jar in a birdbox-type contraption, maintained by Richard Wood of Invergarry - who even before the start of my walk had climbed all these Loch Lochy hills more than five hundred times each! I write a brief greeting, then head down a long grassy rib toward the ruined cottage at Fedden.

A stalker's path curves round the base of these hills, linking Lochs Garry and Lochy, and here I turn back for Laggan. I take a mental snapshot of a conspicuous cairn a half-mile short of the ruin: my link-up point for the planned return via Gleann Cia-aig two days hence.

The afternoon rapidly heats up with the wind blocked off, so a snooze in the sun easily puts paid to thoughts of going back on high for the Meall na Teanga-Meall Coire Lochain horseshoe: a pleasant, sharp-ridged adjunct to the northern cluster of hills. I'm happy enough with my day's work, having made unplanned inroads into the week's schedule. Besides, tomorrow's rest day will be nothing of the sort, with Little Dave and Richard sure to be bursting with city-bound energy.

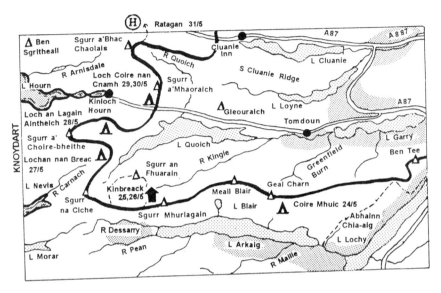

I wander back over the Cam Bhealach, reversing a trail of hoofprints, startling a small herd of deer. The dry, almost dusty path leads through a copse of birches before entering the long skirting-board of forestry above Loch Lochy. A white-sailed yacht glides gracefully onto open water as I reach the road after seven hours away.

Weekend looming, the hostel is much busier - a sight boding well as a basic weather forecast. I make spaghetti carbonara - relishing the brief opportunity to eat *real* food - then phone Sarah. She will be cycling from Spean Bridge along with Michael and her sister Lucy, having caught the first of Saturday's northbound trains.

Later, I find a quiet corner to finish reading *Sunset Song*. I have been deeply moved by the tragic love between Chris and Ewan, by the pathos of community breakdown at the whim of distant overlords, by the *feel* of the land and the all-pervading presence of the sea beyond the parks of the Mearns. And, above all, by the sheer, simple humanity of the story. How could I have lived six years in the northeast and never read this? It is well I'm alone in the lounge when the red Highlandman McIvor pipes "The

Flowers o' the Forest" at the end of the book: I'm near to tears for several minutes.

The Londoners arrive at ten-fifty, just as I'm despairing of them. Yet although this is after official lock-up time, the warden finds no problem in welcoming them in, even letting us sit up late for a pot of tea. There is no unnecessary pedantry here, merely natural kindness coupled with a desire to treat hostellers as adults and for the building itself to be seen as a temporary home. Rowardennan please note.

Weatherwise, Saturday turns out strikingly similar to Friday - marking the start of a trend of days neatly pairing-off like couplets in an eight-line poem. Also, for the first time, I realise I'm about to enter the last week in May: traditionally the best week of the year in the same way May starts with one of the worst. This potentially happy alignment of rough walking with smooth conditions isn't deliberate - I originally intended starting a week earlier - yet now seems more godsend than guesswork. A clear passage through this western section will be my humble equivalent of the Israelite's crossing of the Red Sea - an apt metaphor given the critical area, around the head of Loch Quoich, has the highest mean annual rainfall in the whole of Europe (as much as 500cm, or nearly a foot-and-a-half per month). If things go badly, Pharaoh's army and the drowning tide will merge into one and the same watery assailant. If things go well - and the weather hasn't really settled for close on a month - then to reach the ribbon of road running down to Kinloch Hourn will be to tread the verge of Jordan itself.

There are many tales to tell over breakfast, along with letters to read and slides to examine. Although slightly uncanny to see, the first two spools have turned out well. There is a new watch too - and, most important of all, two weeks' supply of food, fuel, clothes and maps. The coming weekend will be the first spent alone: with no road at which contact can be made until Kinloch Hourn, and by allowing myself an extra two rest days as a loophole in the weather, I have removed all possibility of arrangements being made for anyone driving up from Glasgow. Hopefully Shiel Bridge will be reached in good time for the eighth-week rendezvous, but before then different tactics are called for. Carrying a fortnight on my back doesn't appeal, so Richard and Little Dave have brought with them a spade, trowel, three biscuit tins, some gaffer tape and black binbags: a DIY food-burial kit!

We raise eyebrows and furrow highbrows among fellow residents, commandeering chairs and tables to noisily sort supplies into three different categories: their food, my food, hole-in-the-ground food. Eventually, both this chore and the official one of sweeping the dorm complete, thoughts turn to the day's hills. These, being near the cache-site, will give a sneak preview of the week ahead.

Although the drive down Loch Garry starts grey and cloudy, a strand of turquoise can be seen ahead, a portent telling of our heading in the right direction. Suddenly, near Tomdoun, clouds roll back like the soft top of a convertible to reveal limitless sky and squeaky-clean peaks between blueness of air and water. Sgurrs Mor, na Ciche and a'Mhaoraich unveil themselves as if to calm qualms and undermine fears: *See, there are no tricks, no hidden dangers. Don't worry about climbing us, you'll be okay.*

I'm so transfixed by this inrush of visual perfection that we park in the wrong layby and set off from the wrong cluster of trees. Gleouraich carries possibly the most celebrated of all stalker's paths, so to have expectations reduced to a flounder through ferns is very confusing - until I realise the mistake and point across the next burn, where the path is clear as day.

The day is clear as day too, speeding past as a romp along off-route ridges. Memories are a blur of picture-taking, story-telling, finger-pointing, of racing to be first to see Skye, of gazing northward in silence to the endless battery of summits, of lolling in T-shirt and shorts, sweltering on sweltering hillsides once the wind whipping up and over the corrie headwall has been ducked. A fantastic way to rest!

Near the peak of fitness, it is a joy to stroll over rough ground as though smooth and flat. I doubt whether all this takes any more out of me physically than did the dragging, shapeless day in Fort Augustus - yet even if so, the counterbalancing factors of good company and good food ensure a huge psychological profit.

Richard and I run the final slopes ahead of Little Dave - who goes the wrong way along the road and so loses his own car! Reassembled once more, we drive four miles westward to the watershed, then dig a deep rectangular pit in a slope above the middle of three scrubby trees. I stand guard for traffic while the others slave away. Every car that comes round the corner, we hastily down tools and pretend to admire the view - like Victorian grave-robbers caught in the light of a Bow Runner's lantern. Soil and stones are eventually out, tins and bags in, whereupon Richard makes a turf trap-door to finish the job. I memorise a few salient landmarks - the trees, the small concrete dam, the curve of the road - then we race away in the car, half-covered in glaur, laughing like schoolboys at the ridiculousness of it all.

Celebratory drams are drunk in the Tomdoun - from where Ben Tee and Sron a'Choire Ghairbh resemble an inflated version of Dumgoyne and the Campsies - followed by more imbibing in the "Swan and Cygnet" at Loch Oich Marina. This is with Sarah, Michael and Lucy, who have been down the same road and also seen Skye.

Sandwiched - or should it be three-course-mealed? - between these two bouts of drinking is a huge three-course-meal cooked by Little Dave. He obviously feels I should eat at one sitting enough food to see me to the cache. This has the consequence that after failing to finish a glass of orange in the nautical bar, there is little else to do but stagger to bed and let juices of the digestive variety do their work.

Seven o'clock. Predictably, the new section starts at the usual time and with the usual, frantic session of too-many-things-to-be-done. I manage some last minute letter-writing and the recording of yesterday's events - thus completing the second of four notebooks - before the others surface an hour later. By now, most of the taciturn young men sitting in pairs at breakfast tables like characters in a Pinter play have moved on, eager to be away into an already cloudless morning.

After laying the rucksack flat on the floor and pressing down with both hands - as though trying to resuscitate a heart attack victim - we too are ready for the off. The cyclists have long gone, Ratagan-bound, hoping to complete the haul over Cluanie before the heat really takes hold.

The Aonachs and the Ben, sharp against the deep, rich blue of the sky, draw us to the Commando Memorial for photographs. When a tourist coach arrives, everyone snaps away at the bronze soldiers, paying no heed to the marvellous vista in the other direction. The high coverings of snow are so dazzling as to make adjacent slopes jet-black in comparison.

We drive on past Gairlochy and through the Mile Dorcha, *dark mile*. This contradicts its name: thick yellow honey-light drips through overhanging tree branches. Just before Loch Arkaig, where the Eas Chia-aig crashes into a deep pool, we pull into a busy car park. Here I scribble a note to Jools and John, then wax boots while the others wax lyrical over swimming plans for later. Having intended switching back to heavy boots, I'm kept in the lighter pair by the prospect of prolonged good weather. As we set off, sweating already, a well-meaning tourist takes note of my huge load and

Richard's geological hammer (which he is to lose later in the day), and enquires if we are expecting ice!

Gleann Cia-aig cuts deep into the hills, a densely wooded defile. Richard, presumably inspired by the commandos, swings his hammer to force a path through. Sweat pours down backs as we struggle into a stride on rough ground beyond the forest fence. We cross the main burn by a rickety bridge a mile or so before Fedden, then flop down for a predominantly liquid lunch. The three miles feel like a full day in themselves.

Weight and heat drag down on me physically, while the imminent solitude has a similar effect on morale. Reluctantly, I leave the sack and follow the others across dried peat-hags to tie off the loose end of Friday's walk. Then the handshakes, then the depression: always hitting harder with farewells said on the hill as against ground zero. The fact of Richard and Little Dave also turning and walking away, rather than standing to wave, seems to double the anguish: a kind of relative depression along the lines of relative velocity.

Twice I hear shouts across the mile-wide void between my own steep ground of Meall na h-Eilde and their yellow-green slopes on the Sron. Then the tiny black specks disappear over onto the plateau and I'm suddenly glad of there no longer being any reason to sit and gaze wistfully back.

133

Deer watch from the ridge as I reach the 838m summit and turn to follow a rusty fence over stony ground to Meall Coire nan Saobhaidh. Saturday's look ahead notwithstanding, the views of Ardgour and Mull are new and exciting, while Ciche reverts to its sharp-end-of-a-pencil size. Whereas for two days the watershed marked the battleground between a western sea of high pressure and a cloudier, less settled area inland, today any dull conditions are vanquished to exile in the east. Horizons steadily thicken with haze, always a good sign.

More deer stand around a dried-out, crazy-paved lochan before the 150m pull to the trig point of an approximately trig point-shaped hill, Geal Charn. This takes less than fifteen minutes and reinforces the strange feeling that ascents are coming faster than descents. Maybe this is to do with the effect on balance of additional weight.

The long, tussocky mile over Carn Dubh seems dull: I nod off internally before wakening enough to decree the next obstacle, Sgurr Choinich, best left until morning: the map shows its gentle western slopes as a morass of bog and lochan.

The alternative nightstop - Coire Mhuic overlooking Loch Arkaig - isn't too great either. A steep-walled gorge forces me down, past waterfalls, until well below the treeline. Stony ground and a funnelling breeze then make for difficult pitching. But soon after six I'm inside, sipping soup, perusing the sports pages of a *Guardian* retrieved from a bin at Laggan. Annoyingly, having left behind the latest instalment of *Perkin Warbeck's Diary*, I'm denied the evening's most eagerly awaited reading. At least this extends the list of things to anticipate at Shiel Bridge.

Heat having left a legacy of a headache, I sleep early, zipping the tent door as high, pink, candyfloss cloud floats across the narrow skyward view. Hopefully this is harmless evening stuff. Hopefully tomorrow I will push on another ten miles to the security of the week's only bothy: Kinbreack in Glen Kingie.

The hottest day so far, by far. The clarity of early morning birdsong tells of the last few stirrings of breeze having slipped away into the night. The moment sun hits tent, I know it will be a roaster.

On a site comfier than expected, I lie-in awhile before cramming everything back into the sack and climbing diagonally uphill: already it is too hot to contemplate forcing the gorge. Sgurr Choinich's stony summit comes in an hour: here I rejoin the fenceposts for a long descent westward. Even gentler ground leads onto Meall Lochan nan Dubh Lochan - living up to its name in being strewn with tiny, dark tarns trapped in twists of the strata. The effect is that of pools left in a rocky shoreline by an ebbing tide.

A further rise brings Meall Blair. Here, once past a broken escarpment beneath the summit, I unroll the karrimat for an extended siesta-cum-sunbathe. Loch Blair - a sprawl of blue below - is backed by a long, uninspiring ridge leading to the day's highest hill, Sgurr Mhurlagain. I shut my eyes to this, pull a towel over my head, lie back. Sgurr Anything can wait. For now, in the heat of the day, I will simply rest.

One of the more frequently voiced misconceptions about the Highland climate is the year being a dreary, unending cycle of dampness. Nothing could be further from the truth: even this far west high pressures come and go just as they do further south. The basis of the erroneous theory is more likely the complex way Highland seasons are structured and interact, with the traditional three-months-each quartering of the year rarely seen. Instead, autumn - or, in this case, spring - often reduces to a mere buffer separating winter and summer. These abut onto one another like engine and guard's van lacking coaches between. Goodness knows to which season April's Central Belt heatwave belonged, but the icy northwestern winds and last-gasp snows on and around the Blackmount were surely the firmly attached tail-lights of winter. Perhaps spring came and went in the dousing on Ben Alder!

The three miles and 600m of ascent from Lochan Dubh to the summit of Sgurr Mhurlagain occupy nearly three hours. I slur feet uphill, zig-zagging from one shade-giving crag to another. Small knots of deer watch motionless nearby, too enervated to run. Only lizards retain former energies, each a blue-green whiplash of movement diving for cover beneath basking-stones. With no water on the ridge and no willingness to drop down and fetch any, I'm rationed to a sip per stop once a carton of juice is straw-sucked dry.

The neat cairn finally comes as afternoon cools to evening, giving a long view back down Loch Arkaig to the Great Glen. The loch, bright silver when first seen yesterday, is now a placid blue. In the distance - dissolving in haze - faint, soft-edged hills can only be Creag Meagaidh and her neighbours: already so far away! Nearer to hand, the Glen Finnan tops are pointed and good, while the ever more dominant west now offers a rival to Ciche: the two sharp tops of Sgurr na h-Aide soar out of Morar like twin cathedral spires.

I would linger until sunset if my throat didn't grate with thirst and give no choice but to run run run down grassy slopes until head can be buried in burn to drink myself dizzy. Refreshed, I sit to watch deer clatter nimbly down scree, then head off to join them in the purple-brown shadow cast by the high wall of Fraoch Bheinn. The only truly boggy ground all day congeals into a path leading to two stone cottages bearing the name Kinbreack.

Only the westernmost building is roofed, but contains another cosy, refloored loft. Surprisingly, I'm alone, the previous visitors having left that morning - a fact gleaned from a bothy book also telling of New Year carousing by the Lairig Club. Other reading material varies: Good News Bible, 197? bridge magazine, Telecom handout.

Even if the weather holds - which surely it will - I will spend two nights here. Tomorrow's walk takes in the south side of Glen Kingie before a return via a stalker's path conveniently crossing the head of the glen. I will then retrace this path on Wednesday, fully laden once more, to climb Sgurr na Ciche and so enter Knoydart.

In bygone days of Aberdeen Uni studenthood, I was often intrigued by a sign pointing to the Department for the Study of Sparsely Populated Areas. Never having managed to clap eyes on the course curriculum, I have no idea whether studies were confined to Scotland, or how precisely the word sparsely was defined. Yet the glen in which I now wake to a morning of grey, drifting mist forms part of an area so sparsely populated as to possibly fall outwith the course boundaries altogether. From the point where Glen Kingie docks with the road in Glen Garry, to the isolated coastal road serving the villages of Inverie and Airor, stretches a wild interior of some three hundred square miles with no permanent habitation and only a handful of remote bothies. The western half of this region, the Rough Bounds proper, is a peninsula renowned as the roughest, toughest, most remote of all Highland hill country - and rightly so, as I'm soon to see. But the broad, sluggish ten-mile windings of the River Kingie penetrate deep into another wild, remorseless area, one often overlooked by the more general guidebooks or merely given a sentence tacked on as afterthought to the paragraph on Knoydart.

Ever since first mapping the walk and being pleasantly surprised to see just how far west the watershed went, I have been conscious of the need to avoid falling into precisely this trap, of becoming so fixated by the real rough stuff around Sgurr na Ciche as to treat the Kingie hills too lightly. Thus I now look out of the bothy door and fear the worst: I have misjudged the weather again, just as at Moffat and on Beinn Laoigh. The late evening cloud has filled and settled, until now low enough to be seen as an endless smoke-plume billowing from the chimney stack. My first thoughts are to climb the loft ladder rather than Fraoch Bheinn, to go back to bed for the day.

But these two memories of fine evenings turning sour are replaced by two others: of the Blackmount and Ben Tee. Once again there is lightness, dryness in the air hinting of deception on a grand scale. Although to step outside the door is to step straight into cloud, not a bead of moisture settles on clothes or face. When something inside me says *Move, and quickly!* I dash back upstairs, wolf down breakfast, pack a frantic daysack.

By ten I'm hurrying back along the path which forms the main trade-route for walkers entering the glen. Already the grey monotone is away, the cloud piebald with patches of ethereal whiteness as the sun strains to break through. Then, a half-mile before the top of the pass, turning toward the base of a steep, slabby ridge fading upward into mist, I'm stopped in my tracks by the peaks south of Loch Arkaig jutting high and clear into an indescribably pale blue sky. I stand, staring in amazement and wonder, then grin and allow myself to breathe words waiting patiently at the back of my mind all morning, words too precious to be spilt over half-certainties: *Cloud inversion!*

I scramble straight uphill, taking in crumbling buttresses and overlapping slabs in haste to reach the fairytale land above. Cloud periodically swirls in as if trying to isolate my small cell of activity from the perfect stillness all around, but the view soon slips back into focus - now showing the triangular summit of Sgurr Mhurlagain along with the Glen Finnan hills - and I'm fully part of the morning once more.

I pop out into clear, clean blueness of warm sunlight only a few metres below the cairn of Fraoch Bheinn, *heathery hill*, then dash along to a slightly lower but more peripheral top for the view across the vast, pulsing whiteness to the north. Row upon row of ridges and summits rise clear from a featherbed of cloud, which has shaken itself down to settle on the 750m contour - broken to south and east, but clinging tight to the loch-filled basins of Quoich, Garry, Loyne, Cluanie. Writer after writer has described this wondrous phenomenon as a *cloud sea* - yet, at risk of being bound by cliché, I can find nothing better by way of comparison. So many and varied are the subtle movements among the gently furrowed waves of whiteness, the sight instantly, inevitably, suggests the lap and slap of a light swell against geos and seastacks.

The cloud eventually begins to dissolve, features of the land beneath slowly hardening into shape like a photograph in a developing tray. *Privileged* is too pompous a word to describe feelings at witnessing all this, just as *blessed* is too trite and twee. Perhaps *fortunate* is more accurate: fortunate not only that the walk's arrival in such spectacular hills has coincided with a spectacular day, but also in my having acquired a latent ability to sense the promise held by a dull morning. To have set off later and thus reached the summit in totally clear conditions would still have been memorable, only less uniquely so.

The rest of the day obviously stands no chance of maintaining this supreme standard, although the sight of Sgurr Cos na Breachd-laoidh - next on my list and looking as complex as its name - is enough to keep hopes high. First, though, I change into shorts to half-skip, half-run down the northwest ridge of Fraoch Bheinn until safely able to cut down grassy screes to the col. Having been so busy looking *from* Fraoch Bheinn, I only belatedly look *at* it and realise just how continuously steep and rocky a hill it is.

With water in the pass and perfect-angled slabs on the slope above, the 450m climb falls easily. I'm able to walk upright on rock most of the way - although things would be very different in the wet. Once up, this second Corbett is seen as two tops linked by a scruffy scuff of path, weaving through bands of exposed strata lying across the ridge like primitive sleeping policemen. The low point carries a huge, mansion-sized boulder where a pair of ravens perch, their caw-cawing as harsh and black as their plumage. A few yards further on comes the cowering bleat of a lamb, fatally separated from its mother: a scenario crude, basic and disturbing in its imminence. I hurry to the cairn for my own lunch.

Further west, short sections of sea loch - Nevis and Morar - peek from either side of Sgurr na h-Aide and draw the eye toward Rum, hovering on a cushion of haze. Closer, Sgurr na Ciche rises elegantly behind the ridge of the Garbh Chiochs, suddenly very close. Indeed, I could easily push on over its summit were this a mere midweek excursion. Instead, I have only a day-return to the next top, An Eag: a terminus soon reached after another abrupt descent.

I'm now right at the head of Glen Kingie: snaking away eastward, the colour of parched grass, utterly barren. Tomorrow's walk will bring me here again. But it is only mid-afternoon when I reach the stalker's path leading four miles back to Kinbreack - so, with weather and fitness both in perfect shape, only a modicum of thought is needed to respond *Why not?* to a plan milling in my mind ever since the inversion. I will stay high and return to the bothy along the north Kingie tops rather than the glen floor. The day is too good to waste.

An ever-improving path brings Sgurr Beag, then 1003m Sgurr Mor, both giving glistening views past Ciche, out along Loch Nevis to the distant square-on spine of Eigg. The *Big Hill* coincides with the hottest part of an already hot day, so I doze in token shade at the cairn before completing the ridge on Sgurr an Fhuarain. Here I see the eagle: silently turning, gliding, huge wings dark against bright early evening hillsides. Could there be any better end to such a day? If so, I would love to experience it.

Indoors by six-thirty, I'm further delighted to find three folk from Derbyshire having moved in - all from villages I know well. A couple then arrive from Lochan nam Breac, my hoped-for destination tomorrow. And there are two more reasons to gasp in astonishment. First, the male half of the newest arrivals, on reading in the bothy book of my having been out nearly seven weeks, says "Let me guess - you're walking the watershed". He apparently once thought of the idea himself, before rejecting it as "Too bloody hard" after an hour with the maps!

Second, we all wander out into the glen at sunset, each alone in his or her thoughts as lingering columns of yellow-gold light angle through darkened hills. The bothy bible is inscribed with verse one of Psalm 69: "Save me, O God! The water is up to my neck." For once, nothing could be less apt.

Woken by the hissing of summer stoves, I decide to join my co-bothyers in an early start. Cloud is right down again, but now constitutes a good sign: we all witnessed yesterday's inversion and hanker after more of the same. Two of the Derbyshire threesome dash off for Gairich, leaving their companion, a woman with a bad back, indoors to rest. I feel sorry for her, sad to see her miss another memorable day, so sit and chat awhile. She is heading south that evening, and happily takes a phone message to John and Julia - that I'm fine and planning to ignore rest days as long as the weather holds.

I'm over an hour later setting off than on Tuesday, and the morning feels chillier than of late. Otherwise, conditions are identical - even down to the first glimmer of brightness again picking out Fraoch Bheinn. The river, almost stagnant in its meandering, is easily forded. The path also meanders - through bogs maintained by the glen's huge drainage. I pass an old walker, his steady pace more suited to following the path than is my impetuosity. After going astray in a rough section under Druim a'Chuirn, I have to climb straight uphill toward him - embarrassed more at losing face than losing direction.

High in cloud now, I turn and turn up zig-zags to the bealach - astounded as ever at the quality of engineering needed to put paths in places such as this: paths built with generations of know-how but a minimum of more tangible resources. So efficient is progress that I'm back on An Eag within two hours, cloud thinning step-by-step. There is an electric-blue, almost ultraviolet tinge to the not-quite-visible sky above. With the top of the inversion evidently higher than yesterday, I find myself saying *Come on, come on,* as though words could coax the cloud down a few metres. For once, I wouldn't grudge the hill a little extra height.

Rather than wait, I decide simply to push for Sgurr nan Coireachan, 80m higher. This works sooner, more spectacularly than anticipated: within a minute of taking a bearing and descending the screes, ultraviolet becomes ultramarine as I step out into a wide-open westward view. The sensation: walking from a darkened hallway into a sunlit room. The actuality: the north-south divide of the Kingie range acts as a gigantic headwall damming back a great reservoir of cloud. Beyond, nothing, not a wisp. The change is so awe-inspiring as to send me berserk with the camera, then make me run, rucksack jolting, up the craggy path to Coireachan's summit ridge.

This version of the inversion improves yesterday's original design. With a much higher base - over 900m - cloud fuming from the summit of Sgurr Mor gives a volcanic appearance. The whole impression is of smoke rather than sea: the white froth boiling over the lip of the ridges around An Eag could be a bubbling concoction in a laboratory test tube. Only south is the surface calm, the Ben rising clear - to revert to the aquatic metaphor - like a whale coming up for air.

Two days in a row! Scarcely able to believe my luck, I sit beside the metal-spiked cairn an hour or more, gazing first one way then the next. Hearing voices off, I opt for an early lunch to be sociable, but no-one surfaces from any of the four ridges. Doubtless they have found a quiet neuk and are likewise admiring the view - which now, cloud dispersing, draws me to face westward. Today's hills dominate of course, but beyond lies the complex tangle of Knoydart proper, itself backed by a rich blue Sound of Sleat merging with azurine sky. Only islands indicate the presence of an horizon: Eigg's long razorback, Rum's deceptively smooth curves, the sharp saw-teeth of Skye's Black Cuillin.

Quickly down to the col on a path dusty enough to be skiddy, then back on high for the rollercoaster ride along the Garbh Choichs. Tuesday's hills may have seemed rugged, but they have nothing on these. An hour of constant twisting and turning to weave through, over, round countless small crags and ribs of rock. Mind you, when cloud returns from its too-infrequent sabbaticals, there is more than just a path to guide walkers through this geological mayhem. A high, sturdy drystane dyke runs right along the crest: a folly built by the slave labour of nineteenth-century estate workers to satisfy some landowner's urge to mark out his domain like a dog urinating against a tree. Criss-crossing the wall along Garbh Choich Bheag brings two small rock towers. The second forms a major summit, Garbh Choich Mhor.

I meet people on top, a couple who have paddled from Rum, up Loch Nevis, in a canoe. After we look for, and see, Cruachan and the Great Gash of Alligin, they generously offer an apple while telling of once having given a Mars Bar to a Scandinavian walker so hungry he didn't bother removing the wrapper! Happily munching, I drop 150m to the col for Ciche and the relief of water trickling from a slab, then scramble the slopes above with relish - revelling not only in the superb upsweep of one of the great Scottish hills, but in knowledge that, having reached the end of my long westward sidestep, I can start striding north again. And in there having been no rain - apart from Fort Augustus drizzle - since Ben Alder, eleven days back!

The summit of Sgurr na Ciche proves nothing like as sharp as expected, the merciless corrie steeps finally acquiescing to a short, stunted section of easy-angled ridge. There is, however, the yearned-for blazing seascape: although 1040m below, the head of Loch Nevis is only two miles distant.

In spite of this, immediately on arrival, I'm hit by the full force of anti-climax. This hill is what I have aimed for, lived for, all week - and now, despite being better than I ever hoped, the fact of it being in the present means it might as well be in the past. I'm suddenly desperate to move on, to set a new target, and only manage to cling onto the precious moment by concentrating on balancing the camera on the remains of a lightning-shattered trig point for a self-timed photo. How I hate this Tantalean paradox - the fruits of my labour whipped away the very moment I'm in position to savour them! I knew it before the walk - often in the form of wanting away when at home, then longing for home once away - and I will doubtless know it again. But this doesn't make things any easier right now.

Picture-taking is eventually achieved by the simpler process of handing the camera to another walker - who, along with his friend, had been bumped into on Sgurr Mor the day before. Their freedom and lack of obsessional drive, their chance to spend two, maybe three hours here, is envied. I wait only long enough to watch a strange little whirlwind scud across the summit - sucking up gravel with a high-pitched whine - then head back along the ridge into the safe, insular concentration required to pick a way down the huge northern boulderfields.

This side of the hill is even rougher than the southern flank: endless crags and slabs needing dodged. Nothing difficult, just continually awkward. The drystane dyke descends with me, usually showing the quickest route through ground less navigable in broad daylight than are many hills in thick mist. Occasional threads of path are relics of the days before Loch Quoich was raised, when this would be a more popular route of ascent. A slow-moving hour sees me down as far as Meall a'Choire Dhuibh, a small top swollen with slabs at the point where this most contorted of ridges makes its final spasmic jerk towards Ben Aden to end in a crescendo of cragginess.

I finally drop into the narrow pass linking Loch Quoich and Lochan nam Breac with relief at not having turned an ankle, then turn a corner to see the loveliest of all the day's lovely sights: the slot of Lochan nam Breac, trapped between the tree-clad plunge of Ben Aden and Sgurr a'Choire-bheithe's reverse angle, with a tiny triangular hillock standing as counter-point to the symmetrical cone of Luinne Bheinn beyond.

A place crying out to be camped in: I pitch at the near end of the lochan on a smooth, crescent-shaped strip of sand. Outwardly, this is the most sublime evening of the walk, with scenery, weather, progress all perfectly in tune. There is, however, still discord in my mind, a residue of the dissatisfaction known on Ciche, reinforced by the stark loneliness always lurking in the most memorable of campsites. I plan sitting up late to watch stars grow out of the gloaming, but in the end simply withdraw to the tent, zip the door, slip into the familiar, safe confinement of sleep.

Come morning I'm much happier. There is high cloud and light so soft as to make the hills seem slightly out of focus, yet the murmurings of breeze are from the east, suggesting another dry day. I potter about making breakfast and trying, unsuccessfully, to seal a leaky gas bottle with Elastoplast. Sand in the valve makes me wish I had camped on one of the nearby grassy terraces rather than the full-blown hedonism of the beach. In the end, unable to carry the quietly hissing cylinder in my rucksack, I bury it under a pile of boulders, furious with myself for sullying what seems an almost sacred place. (Only halfway up the hill do I realise the stove's own regulator could simply have been attached in the "Off" position.) I burn a pile of rubbish, wave goodbye to neighbouring campers - who have given glowing references for my coming hill while warning of recent rockfalls - then set off for the Quoich dam.

There are in fact two small dams, linked incongruously by tarmac. Here the avid conservationist of ten minutes back abruptly dies in me: it is good to be on something resembling a road. As mentioned earlier, these dams resemble that of Stirlingshire's Carron Reservoir in being raised above the natural watershed. Hence I stroll along the top without feeling guilty! There has always been a Loch Quoich, only the pre-hydro version probed the surrounding glens much less searchingly. On enlargement, water-flow westward decreased slightly, shrinking Lochan nam Breac and forming the alluvial beach. *Ergo,* I should sue the Hydro Board for loss of a gas bottle!

Midday fast approaches as I embark on a tongue of grass licking steeply upward between the jaws of two rock-filled gullies. This hill and the next, Sgurr nan Eugallt, form a pair of long, transverse, high-hurdle ridges blocking the Kinloch Hourn food cache. I consider doubling-up to cross them both in the one day - but feel relieved the lateness of the hour effectively puts paid to such plans. Marvellous as these Kingie/Ciche days are, they are also very long - and, while rediscovering easy rhythms of walking known before the fall, I know there is no point deluding myself energies have no upper limit. Besides, it is four days since the last break - six including the Gleouraich jaunt - and I have allowed *extra* rest days as bolt-holes from the weather. I'm glad to take things easy, well aware hillwalking arithmetic differs from that taught in school: two half-days add to considerably more than one full one.

This said, the weather begins to show signs of change. Soft light dulls, the heat-haze dissolves into an overcast layer of grey high above the tops. Bolt-holes might yet be needed.

Optimism dissolves too, in doubts whether the cache can be reached dry-shod - until all worries are shoved onto the backburner as I crest the ridge and burst into the big seaward view. Having hit the eastern top, Sgurr Airigh na Beinne, virtually spot-on, I'm suddenly given views of a rough, pinnacled ridge winding two miles westward to the higher top of Sgurr a'Choire-bheithe, with Ladhar Bheinn a looming shape in the distance.

The ridge is a delight. I stroll through several pockets of deer, then take hands from my own pockets to scramble over two pinnacles - on the second of which, like an eagle in its eyrie, I break for lunch to celebrate arriving at longitude 5° 27' west, westernmost limit of the watershed.

Although due to turn downhill from here, I dump the sack and hurry the remaining quarter-mile to the true summit for views down to Barrisdale Bay and Loch Hourn. Winds veering from east through south to southwest suggest I ought to head straight for the corries, but I'm eager to reach a summit which, at 913m or 2998ft, is one of a rare, iconoclastic breed of hills: the not-quite-Munros. The OS occasionally add a metre or two and thus promote one of these backbenchers to the upper chamber - Beinn Teallach on Lagganside being the most recent example - but this usually spells ecological disaster for the hill concerned. Paths appear, solitude disappears, herds of deer are replaced by herds of Munrobaggers suddenly short of a tick.

For me, though, weather is the main concern. Instead of the agitated, fidgety gustiness marking the end of the Central Belt heatwave, there is now a steadily freshening breeze and a grey metallic sheen to the western sky. I run back to the sack before dropping into one of the shallow northern corries by way of a steep but predominantly grassy slope. There is nothing to compare with yesterday's geological chaos, only a few slabs low down. The Rough Bounds are loosening their grip.

Unpleasant-tasting water on the col before Slat Bheinn doesn't augur well for what strikes me as a particularly unpleasant-sounding hill: *Slat* - ugh, ugly word! The 300m pull comes tamely enough though, echelons of seamless slabs bringing another stunning viewpoint high above Barrisdale. Soon the tent is pitched at the southern end of tiny Loch an Lagain Aintheich, near a stalker's path leading back round to the Quoich dam. Revived urges to push for the road are easily subdued: four hours should suffice tomorrow, whatever the weather.

While cooking a curry, I have an idea which will ultimately transform the next week of the walk. Perfect conditions having put me so far ahead of schedule, I now face an extended break at Shiel Bridge - three day's walk away - to await Linda and Doug's supply run. This possibly means as many as six inactive days: too much. Instead, why not push straight on through, get two more days in the can, then cut back down one of the Kintail glens to the head of Loch Duich?

The idea comes whole, complete with a map in my mind, so simple I wonder how it escaped me until now. Perhaps it has been there all along, hidden like a present under the bed, one I have merely been prevented from opening until the appropriate time. The chalking-off of everything as far as Beinn Fhada, thus creating more space in the critical ninth week, is to prove a tremendous boon.

A noisy night. I'm woken several times by a low humming, like a distant plane or an electric generator - although droning on far too long to be the former, while the latter is unlikely with the tent miles from a road. Perhaps I'm starting to imagine things - or literally have a flea in my ear.

There is also a mysterious creature lurking in long grass to the rear of the tent, emitting a gasping, rasping sound through the darkness. Despite all this I sleep late, wedged between bumps, until finally woken by the sudden heat of sun reaching the lochan: skies have cleared again overnight.

Sweaty and dirty, a dip seems in order. To simply step out straight into chill water - shining, sparkling with fragments of light like a thousand tiny mirrors - is marvellously refreshing, invoking vigour and sprightliness which remain all day.

I'm dressed and moving by ten, conscious the disappearance of the sun is for real this time. Fifty minutes brings the next ridge, with deer again everywhere: sentinel on skylines like snipers on a roof, fleeing behind outcrops like urban street-corner teenagers when a police car appears. There rarely seem more than a dozen deer together in these western hills - as against three-figure herds further east. Climate? Time of year? Consequence of excessive stalking? I don't know.

As with yesterday's hill, today's main summit lies slightly off-route to the west. I hook the sack round a fencepost before following the broken ridge to the trig point, bowled along by a wind which has strengthened and backed to the southeast in the hour since my setting off. Sgurr nan Eugallt, *sharp peak of death streams,* seems a little overstated: it proves the tamest hill since Kinbreack.

The morning loses its early glister, clouds banking in various dark shades to cover the south end of Skye and transform the Glenelg scree-dome Beinn Sgritheall into a massive reminder of Lanarkshire pit bings. Nearer - and, to my hill-saturated eyes, considerably more enticing - are the buildings and woods of Kinloch Hourn, where the ribbon road winds white down the glen.

Hurrying now, I return to the sack wishing I could suppress this desire to reach the top of any hill I'm on even if it entails, as now, a half-hour diversion. Normally this doesn't bother me - summits act as focal points around which days are built, while off-route ones give brief breaks from the watershed and an edgy, skiving-school feel to quicken the pulse. But in deteriorating conditions such as these I would be wiser to reach lower ground without delay.

The two eastern tops come quickly however, with the second - Sgurr a'Chlaidheimh - the only one all day to carry a cairn. There are occasional ptarmigan, but I'm more interested in watching even-more-occasional traffic on the road. This is in full view during the descent of Coire Beithe - a corrie, I'm later to discover, famous for one of the best-documented accounts of one Charles Edward Stuart's own eighteenth-century attempt on the watershed, albeit cleverly disguised as fleeing the Hanoverians. The poor maps of those days caused him often to stray east and west, yet he still managed to visit Ben Alder, go through the Laggan and Lochy hills, then cross the Cluanie and Affric ranges before giving up in Glen Cannich on hearing of problems with his Poolewe supply-point. There are no records of plans for a second attempt, but this must be presumed doubtful: he soon moved to France and lost the edge off his fitness.

The road! In only six days! I scarcely believe I have returned so quickly. But here are the three trees and the concrete dam, and here, on a grassy ledge above, is a treasure trove of food. Or is there? I'm beset with sudden fears of an inquisitive tourist or bloody-minded factor having spied on our antics and disturbed the cache once we had gone. Or some burrowing, tin-opening animal having sniffed at, then scoffed the goodies. Of course I know these things couldn't *really* have happened, yet the thrill of possible disaster is fine to experience. Hence postponement of the moment of truth until after tent-pitching beside Loch Coire nan Cnamh. Genuine finger-tingling excitement is so hard to come by, it needs milking when opportunities arise.

Swaggering back along the road - a dux student going up for a prize - I haul myself up the steep bank only to discover Richard made his turf lid so well its edges are invisible! After a few tentative leverings at firmly attached sods, it is *Sod it!* as the calm, self-satisfied approach degenerates into several minutes of frenetic pulling and tugging. Eventually a loosening and a final gleeful heave reveal the stack of tins and bags. *Phew!*

I'm soon tucking into the finest tent meal all trip: chicken soup, goulash and pittas, apple flakes and apple juice with Tunnocks wafers to follow. I deliberately hadn't paid full attention when the others packed the food, hence some pleasant surprises - including three huge chocolate bars when I anticipated only one.

If this is an ideal end to a memorable week's walking - one in which I have been so entranced by surroundings as to never once let thoughts drift toward the twin danger zones of Cape Wrath and Glasgow - then the finish of the feast itself is fitting to the point of symbolism. Just as the water for the custard comes to the boil, the almost-forgotten sound of another kind of water has me dragging the stove inside and zipping the flap as rain becomes torrential inside a minute.

I lie back on my sleeping-bag to laugh and laugh. The Red Sea indeed! Almost miraculously, I have passed through the western wetlands dry-shod. Now, inevitably, the rains return to engulf hills in Knoydart no longer able to harm me. The idyll is over. Intuitively I know the best week of the walk is past. Things are never to be quite the same again.

6: Munropolis
(Saturday 30th May - Saturday 6th June)

The rain fell for two days and three nights, although it felt more like forty of each. Woken in the first of these nights by the sheer ferocity of a gust drenching the flysheet, I remember thinking this was to be no hurriedly passing shower, but a zealously stormy clear-out a fortnight's hoarding of rain, inevitable consequence of the cumulation of cumulus.

Not that I had any just cause for complaint after such a prolonged dry spell: I was well positioned geographically and well prepared mentally to cope with a protracted deluge. A mere two days of walking would bring the Cluanie/Shiel watershed and the A87. Here, much as I fancied pursuing my newly thought out time-saving plan, I could, if need be, retreat down to Ratagan or Shiel Bridge and sit out a whole arkload of rain.

First, though, was to be a rest day here at the Kinloch Hourn road. Even had the weather not broken I would still have taken time out. Tiredness wasn't the only factor: I also needed to hitch down to Tomdoun and phone base, then eat my way through the less transportable food cache items. But at twenty-three miles - the longest cul-de-sac in Britain - I was concerned the supply of potential lifts might, in contrast to the weather, run dry.

And for a while it did, before a Leeds couple starting their long journey south after a week's canoeing on Loch Hourn dropped me at the Tomdoun Hotel. Here I soon crammed into a warm corner with a pint and a bowl of kidney soup as the place gradually filled with fishermen: a coachload from Denny on their club's annual all-nighter. Full of west-of-Scotland patter, they were very friendly - more than could be said for the bar's other occupants, a stuffy southern-England couple. The male half condescendingly questioned the most garrulous angler as though conducting an experiment on a member of a lower species, one somewhere on a par with the fish nobody seemed to have caught. His attitude marred an otherwise enjoyable hour. The proprietors - a Welsh couple with the fine Scots name Fraser - were very welcoming, making no complaint about cast-aside galoshes and waders soaking their carpet. On leaving, I noticed a montage of wall maps which could almost have been put there with a watershed walker in mind. I was thus able to swot up the next three weeks, to the Fannaichs and beyond. So much more lay ahead...

The phonebox - a dash-through-the-downpour away - was made good use of. Money refused to go in the slot, but allowed instead a long long-distance chat for free. Torrential Tomdoun seemed a strange place to learn I was to be an usher at my sister's wedding.

A lift in an old, cluttered Clubman estate took me back to the tent: a fine place to laze on a wet afternoon. I whittled away the hours making a meal and reading a paper donated by the Frasers, listening to the drumming on the flysheet and the white-noise gush of an ever-rising burn.

The evening was a tedium of dozing and eating until darkness came as early as it had in April. All in all, a nondescript day, perhaps the least noteworthy of the walk - not that this prevented me from realising, as I wrote up the log and snuggled into my sleeping-bag, it had also been the fiftieth day.

That large quantities of rain had fallen through the night could be deduced from more than just the rapid-fire gunning of the heaviest blatters. An irregular shaped pool of dampness soaked the groundsheet by dawn: the loch was over its banks, pushing long feelers of water across the hundred metre strip of grass. The Daily Express was a poor substitute for sandbags, and I quickly knew whatever unpleasantness was involved in climbing the hill would be nothing in comparison with the misery of staying put for even a half-day more. A nearby intake burn also threatened, roaring down with fearsome noise. Despite having appeared on Wednesday evening too deep-cut in its rocky bed to be a potential threat, this now crept toward overflow like a fast-filling bath.

As a prelude to packing, the tins and bags had to be restocked with rubbish and reburied - a hostel-type chore started in a momentary dry spell, completed in the dripping greyness of another downpour. The hole was already half-filled with water.

Back at the road I met a couple walking to Fort William via Kinbreack and Strathan. They doubted whether the burns, particularly the infamous Abhainn Chosaidh, would allow access to the south side of Loch Quoich. I concurred. On days such as this - when the quickest, safest route was over rather than round - the watershed seemed a perversely good idea.

The one virtue of the weather was the wind having fallen away. This made striking camp easy: the wet fly stuck to the grass once down and could be ignored while food and clothes were wrapped and squeezed into place. Then I climbed steeply through greasy, schisty bluffs, under a line of pylons, my own energy supply fuelled by Opal Fruits and the encouragement of a more substantial brightening. Cloud, never low, now slid back to show

Gairich's shapely summit across Loch Quoich. My target, Sgurr a'Mhaoraich, was shapeless by contrast - a big, brutal broad-flanked lump of a hill barring the warmth and comforts of Glen Shiel.

I pressed on, thoughts drifting back to a similarly miserable day on a similarly stout hill - Beinn Heasgarnich above Loch Lyon - when merely finding the summit cairn took over an hour of plateau-wandering. Today's peak was much sharper, so the resemblance would always end there - although the slabby northern outliers, Am Bathaich and Sgurr Thionail, posed potential dangers.

The glimmer of meterological hope continued as I hurried past a white-fuming gorge at half-height, across an unnamed top, onto rockier ground overlooking the tide-drained Kinloch Hourn. Here, at a cairn marking the best viewpoint down the loch, I stood several minutes, camera ready, in hope that swirling mist would solidify into something photogenic. This didn't happen: it was a shutter of cloud which closed, not one made by Pentax, ensuring the 150m of scrag leading to a'Mhaoraich's 1027m high point were as wet as anything in the past two days. Only later did I discover this to be my thirty-first Munro in the thirty-one days of May.

The next hour was all concentration and compasswork: picking a way down the dog-leg ridge, stopping every few minutes to wipe smirr from specs with a saturated hanky, stepping out unsurefooted onto slip-sliding scree sloping, rooftop-angled, over unseen crags. Not wanting to stray down vast western slopes, staying as close as possible to the ridge-line, I was momentarily rewarded by a clearance showing the col for Am Bathaich: a green square just below. The black, water-pouring slabs of the 100m rise were then turned by an abrupt scree-wall, where fears of becoming cragfast calmed on popping out onto easier knobbly ground leading north to Sgurr Thionail.

Cloud repeatedly thickened and darkened like gently billowing smoke as rain poured down as if from super-efficient fire-sprinklers: a wave of asphyxiation and some wailing sirens wouldn't have been out of place. The situation held too great a sense of urgency to be in any way enjoyable. And to think only a few days earlier any thoughts of burning were the result of painfully non-metaphorical rays from the sun!

The day's only real clearance was well timed - just as I reached the butt-end of the ridge - and showed yellow sunlight patching the green parabola of Easter Glen Quoich. It also gave chance to select a route down another very messy slope - where scree avalanched beneath feet and secure-looking boulders could be trundled with only a touch.

By mid-afternoon, already four-and-a-half hours on from the road, I stopped beside Loch Bealach Coire Sgoireadan for lunch at the high point of an impressively dry stalker's path. Sgurr a'Mhaoraich now showed clear through the clouds, black slabs shining, every water-filled groove seemingly veined with quartz. The quantity of water being shed by the hill was frightening to see.

Clear thoughts accompanied the clear conditions. I began considering my situation objectively, seeing the original plan of climbing the next hill, 885m Sgurr a'Bhac Chaolais, then descending back into Glen Quoich for a camp, as nothing short of foolishness. Everything was soaked: glens, hills, tent, groundsheet, clothes, boots, maps. Even my sleeping-bag was uncomfortably damp. Why not descend north rather than south from the final bealach, then hitch down to the hostel at Ratagan? This would bring Glen Shiel a day sooner than anticipated and add the complication of being ten miles off-route, but seemed far and away the best plan.

I was slightly wary of jumping ahead of myself in this way, of overwriting plans carefully, lovingly formulated, yet was thinking logically enough to perceive any notion of "roughing it" as totally preposterous. All the week's good work - soaring morale, time-in-hand - could be washed away in a few disastrous hours. These latest hills might be nothing like as rough or remote as those just traversed, yet were consistently higher: demanding respect, as indeed would every metre, every step of the way here on.

These were thoughts accompanied by awareness the best part of the day was liable to prove the only good part. The brief minutes of sunshine rapidly disappeared under another bank of dark, dank, rain-heavy cloud. With no time to waste, I hurried from the lochan, up 300m of grassy bumps leading to steeper ground, then along a rocky ridge. Here light dimmed, rain hit and I was again glad of a drystane dyke as navigational helpmate - even if it did swing eastward five minutes before the Corbett summit.

I cringed under a boulder in vain hope of the storm passing, then plowtered down the path to the Bealach Duibh Leac, *pass of the black slab,* where the path from Kinloch Hourn crossed an hour earlier itself crossed the ridge. With the gravelly zig-zags a burn in all but name, I opted for open hillside and a more direct line of descent. This quickly brought a genuine, full-time burn ten times its normal width and strength, where I fantasised the headline writer's glee at my drowning: "Watershed man swept away in Highland torrent". But with feet already so wet, to wade the broadest, most easy-flowing point was to suffer no additional discomfort.

Romping down to the road, I wondered if my chief reason for wanting a night at Ratagan wasn't so much concern with safety or comfort, more a fundamental desire to be among people. Locals, tourists, walkers, workers - anyone would do, any number of extra miles would be covered to be with them. So began an aspect of the walk which grew and grew during the remaining weeks. I was tiring of being alone, of living in the wilds, mind saturated with solitude just as clothes were now saturated with rainwater. The sight of a grey band of tarmac busy with coaches and caravans held a more pertinent, more resonant beauty than the towering ridges to either side. No amount of fitness or fine weather could now have the slightest effect on this: their purpose was simply to hasten the north coast, the only real cure.

A second, deeper burn was splashed across before I deposited some of its water in the fourth car to pass. Belongings soon dripped alongside others in the hostel drying room. One change of clothes had fortunately been buried deep enough to escape the deluge, ensuring a contented evening, feet up by the fire, chatting with Nic Lancaster, the warden.

Postponing all thoughts of tomorrow until tomorrow, I turned in early to relish the comfort of a warm, dry bed. Thus May ended as had April before it: in dismal weather, in a far-famed youth hostel, water lapping just outside the dormitory window.

Ratagan! Kintail! June! The sea! I had been too tired the previous evening to fully appreciate these things, but now, on waking in the momentarily confusing surroundings of the dimly curtain-lit dorm, there was an all-at-once realisation of where I was: *somewhere different!* I couldn't recall when last I had woken so excited by the day ahead - and this despite the discouraging splash of car tyres in the rain outside. I struggled into clothes, dashed to the main cause of this enthusiasm: the blue-grey waves and wind-whipped salt air of Loch Duich. After the grim, disappointing end to May, June had started with a sea-change!

The sea had of course featured in hilltop views since the very beginning - the Solway on a crystal April morning - yet the fact of its being merely a view had confined pleasure to one of the senses, sight. Now the experience was total: full-blown winds and waves, slap against shingle of green-swelling water, flicked drops of spray landing cold on skin, the taste of the air, colours fading from green to grey along the Inverinate shore. I savoured the moment, drawing from it a kernel of sustenance for the week ahead. There was a newness, a life in this I no longer perceived in the familiar postcard view of the Five Sisters beyond the head of the loch. It wasn't I was losing touch with the land, more I was now so close to it that only when something strange or exciting appeared could a reference point be found from which to fully appreciate its beauty.

A heavy shower eventually drove me back indoors. The weather, improved only slightly, made me far from sure of the wisdom of immediately continuing along the South Cluanie Ridge. I liked it here, had time in hand, was aware the rain's break-up into showers gave a reasonably reliable hint of the depression being almost away. There should, by rights, be a fine day come Tuesday. But beyond that? The local meterological curiosity (show-piece being too complimentary a word) was the "Cluanie Curtain", a veil of rain and low cloud prone to remain stationary over the area days on end. At least present conditions were bright and breezy, if still predominantly wet. Besides, I would relax much better with all possible progress achieved and rest days taken *en bloc*. Over a bowl of muesli I weighed these pros and cons - then decided to move on.

At Shiel Bridge campsite, prices were checked for later comparison with those at Morvich in Strath Croe. Then, after sitting out another heavy squall, I set off, half-heartedly hitching, along the four miles of A87 leading back up Glen Shiel. Lorries and coaches careered past, spray fanning from wheels, while the Achnangart quarry was a noisy, fumy, ear- and eyesore. But it was good all the same to be among familiar sights and sounds in one of the major hillwalking areas - and to temporarily be just another anonymous walker embarking on a three-day round trip through Kintail.

A slap on a gatepost completed the link with Sunday's walk. A little wearily, yet climbing quickly, I reeled in the long grassy slopes of Sgurr a'Chuilinn. To have regained the ridge via the descent route would have immediately negated any good work done on boots by the drying room. A pause to let a shower scurry through gave chance to watch a herd of deer come close, grazing like horses at grass. A steep muddy path then completed the ascent of Creag nan Damh, westernmost point of a Munrobagger's dream: seven ticks in a ridge-walk scarcely longer than that of the two-Munroed Sisters across the glen.

Here began one of the walk's more bizarre episodes. On turning to study the summit view - cloud low and leaden to the west, more broken elsewhere - I noticed an orange-cagouled, rucksack-less figure scuttling away down-hill. I first knew something was in the air when, after ignoring a brief shower and so overtaking him as he crouched beneath a boulder alongside a black mongrel, I heard and occasionally saw him chasing hot-foot over Sgurr Beag and Sgurr an Lochain, evidently irritated at being left behind by someone carrying the mother of all rucksacks.

Eventually stopping to check the compass in thick mist, I allowed him to catch up. Conversation started well enough: confusion over our having been on different Sgurr nan Coireachans for Wednesday's cloud inversion - his the Glen Finnan namesake of my Kingie hill. Soon, though, he was announcing The Lord to have specially blessed him that day, the lead-in to a spiritual word in season on discovering I was raising money for Nicaragua.

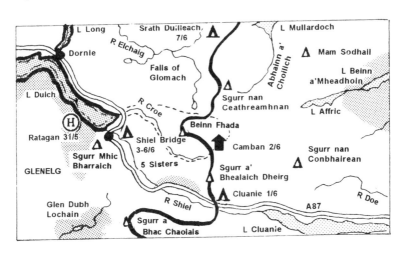

Cluanie - Loch Mullardoch

(This was my first discussion of the subject since leaving Glasgow, having deliberately kept distance between the twin motivations of walking and fund-raising to avoid the simplistic if-I-don't-climb-this-hill-some-poor-niño-in-Rivas-will-starve mentality. The only concession to this had been leaving the address of War on Want in each bothy book for possible contributions.) The fact of my being backed by a group called Scottish *Christians* for Nicaragua only fuelled the fire. Didn't I know the Sandinistas to be a communist government while the Contras were a righteous majority fighting a just civil war?

We walked as we talked, following a path-worn line of summits looping along like slack telegraph wires. I would occasionally tire of the tirade and let my mind drift to the surrounding hills - only to be hauled back into the thick of things by a proclamation that nuclear weapons, the privatisation of the NHS or the dismembering of the unions were all part of God's Plan for the World. It was as though my companion had John 3:16 emblazoned across his chest like the sinister believers nowadays appearing at every major televised sports event.

Maybe I was so out of touch as to be over-defensive, resentful at this intrusion. Maybe, with a general election only ten days away, I was the only person not embroiled in political debate and opportunist canvassing. Maybe I was simply displaying deep-felt wariness of evangelical fervour, be it religious or political. Whatever, on being told the four Nicaraguan cabinet ministers who were also priests "weren't godly men", I mouthed my own little prayer of thanksgiving at being able to branch off down the northern Druim Thollaidh spur. My companion continued eastward, dog and beliefs at heel, for the remaining Munros. I was alone again, cloud peeling from the high tops, afternoon sunlight flooding the glen below. Praise the Lord!

One good thing about all this was my desire to escape having dragged me along the ridge quickly. Having no more been in the mood for a day on the hill than for a Diet of Worms, I found myself treating the two-hour ridgewalk as a dull day at work. The only real interest came with pitching the tent and reading a newspaper acquired from Nic Lancaster that morning.

This had been easily achieved. For once, I knew exactly where to camp: a previously-used roadside pitch beside a patch of forestry. From the tent door, the parallel northern ridges of Maol Chinn-dearg stood out in sharply-defined sunlit lines, skies having cleared into cloudlessness.

A post-prandial stroll along to the Cluanie Inn was a late evening delight. Here, having a pint with other people met on the ridge, the evening was blethered away in non-spiritual, non-political hill talk. Later, annoyance now fully dissipated by alcohol, I was able to laugh rather than fume at the day's events. There was, however, one serious point to be drawn. I had reacted with unnatural tetchiness at the time, probably due as much to tiredness as criticism. Tomorrow would be the last walking day for a while. I badly needed a rest.

Every car speeding through the night spat stones down the embankment onto the tent, wakening me. This was, at least, preferable to the mysterious noise-spitting creature of Knoydart, and I slept well enough to oversleep - until eight-thirty, when a herringbone sky had me rushing to pack and move. Although a delayed action warning, I knew this as one of the worst of weather signs.

Tiredness dissolved into sharp morning air: I climbed the steep flank of Meall a'Charra without a break. This flattened at half-height, where an unexpected path appeared, leading through stonier ground to hit the main ridge just east of 1036m Sgurr a'Bhealaich Dheirg, *sharp hill of the red pass*. Deer, then humans, stood silhouetted against the skyline, one frightening away the other. I chatted with the bipeds at the obelisk-thin cairn - which, some way along a bouldery arête to the north, is apt to confuse bad weather visitors. No danger of that now, everything except the Cuillin standing clear under a whitish-blue sky.

The rush-hour for walkers arrived: I was glad to move on. The others were all headed east or west for more Munros, staying on the main line while I strayed down the northern branch. A disused scrape of a path showed that despite being the finest of three summit-supporting ridges, this had become a virtual backwater with baggers seizing the chance of six-in-a-day.

It would be interesting to speculate the number of walkers presently opting for the Five Sisters pure and simple, rather than the somewhat spurious, super-fitness-required "Brothers and Sisters" ridge. This figure could then be compared with a similar one from twenty years back, before the Munro craze really took off. Such statistics don't exist of course, but a fair guess would be that classic traverses such as the Sisters are having their individuality trampled in the rush to "do" everything asap.

On a lighter note, and in light of the narrative's current religious bent, a word of prophecy. Some day, somewhere, somebody will make a killing out of MUNROPOLY: a boardgame for 2-8 players. Climb the Scottish

Highlands in the comfort of your living-room! Features to include a "Get out of Knoydart free" card, a special risk factor for venturing out ill-equipped in winter, bonuses for completing the Cairngorms on ski or the Monadh Liath in a drought, a rope card for the In Pinn and sudden death/elimination squares applicable to the more scrambly summits of An Teallach and the Aonach Eagach. Whoever produces this, good luck to them. I, for one, would have no ice-axe to grind. But it won't be me! [1]

But enough of such flippancy! Fact was today I had the northeast ridge of the Sgurr to myself and it gave a marvellous descent - a sweeping high-wire of upended slabs never difficult enough to be a real scramble, yet still the narrowest section of the entire watershed. Views were impressive: back to the gullied headwall beneath the summit, down to an inkspot lochan.

Immediately the rock gave out I passed the *bhealaich dheirg* of the name: a red scoop of scree dropping steeply to the glen, the colour of a blaze football pitch. The ridge then crossed several grassy humps before boggily degenerating. Here I felt a sudden wave of fatigue for the last unending mile down the Fionngleann - presumably a consequence of having walked ten of the last eleven days, although I felt drained enough for it to be a symptom of illness. Beinn Fhada, intended as the day's second hill, no longer held any appeal. It became an ugly, threatening thing, well beyond capabilities. All that interested me was the green-roofed bothy at Camban. Here I wearily pushed open the door, climbed an awkwardly positioned ladder, ate cheese, drank juice, fell sound asleep for the duration.

Some hours later - I hesitate to use the inappropriate "at teatime" - I was woken by three returning bothymongers. Their provisions already hung in carrier bags from the rafters, suspended like flower baskets, betraying not only their owners' presence but that of a mouse. I went down for a communal brew, but the newcomers - on a through trip from Dornie to Drumnadrochit - were in dispute with one another and uncommunicative. They did, however, tell of the forecast for the coming days being very bad, thus reopening the question of my crossing Beinn Fhada.

Feeling much better for the sleep, I knew a whole day could be saved by a lightweight sprint over the hill that evening. I dithered only a few minutes, until the sight of greyness starting to gather over the morning's hill decided the issue. I stuffed myself with food, cut the sack back to basics, then

[1] Since this was written, such a game has in fact appeared! *MunroMania* is available from WildWare, 32 Cricket Road, Oxford, OX4 3DG.

virtually ran up the slope behind the bothy - sensing I was running as much from a rash decision as from the weather.

More than at any other point on the walk I obeyed my friends' *Sunset Song* inscription: *Give it hell!* Thirty minutes brought the ridge, sixty the first top, eighty-five the trig point. 800m of ascent, three miles distance: not, perhaps, fellrunning standard, but Naismith well trashed all the same!

I was just in time. While Trotternish in Skye and the whole northern arc remained clear - with Sgurr Mor Fannaich enticingly close - the herringbone sky to the south had grown fins and scales of cloud. The Cluanie ridges already gone, I lingered only to complete a film with a snap of the Plaid Mor plateau and western ridge system of this curiously hybrid hill, then hurried down the northeastern spur into Gleann Gniomhaidh.

Soon eastbound along a stalker's path, I no longer worried about cloud licking the corries above. Although happy with progress, the earlier tiredness returned as I swung away from the remotest of all SYHA hostels - Alltbeithe - to follow paths back round to the Fionngleann. All day I had been running on empty. Now I was fit for nothing other than a night's rest and a few easy miles down to Shiel Bridge come morning.

Drizzle was falling as I returned to the bothy after three hours away. Washing draped over a dyke told of further company. The earlier threesome had moved on to the hostel, to be replaced by Derek, a friendly gangrel from Embra. Swapping stories and food, I ended up with tales of a trek from Glen Coe through Knoydart and with bacon in my bolognese! We cooked by candlelight on bare floorboards, wind and rain rattling the skylight, a mouse scrabbling in the grate downstairs. Derek was on a genuine *stravaig,* going wherever the weather and his inclinations suggested. Also - best of all! - he didn't know what a Munro was!

The mouse stayed quiet through the night while the rain gathered noise and strength. A surprise, then, to step outside after a ten o'clock lie-in and find the weather mild-mannered, well-behaved. Although cloud was well down, the rain was no worse than an intermittent drizzle: the wind had been making all the fuss. Relieved - a food shortage would have made for a stomach-rumbling stormbound day - I went back inside to pack. This was a task made onerous by feeling obliged to cram in a whole bag-load of cans and foil packets left by various litter louts.

A middle-aged couple popped in for lunch just as I was leaving. They were on a Tour de Mont Blanc-type circuit of Beinn Fhada (walking right round the hill without actually climbing it), and would return to sea-level through the Bealach an Sgairne - my eventual route back up on Sunday. For now, I could use the shorter option of Gleann Lichd, the craggy upper section of which was entered after a boggy mile back over the watershed.

The path improved dramatically as scenery did likewise, dropping steeply past the Allt Grannda falls. The damp dreariness of the day and my own heavy-footed tiredness were, for a while, forgotten in the pure enjoyment of following a river from source to sea: the antithesis of the watershed and as invigorating an experience as had been the presence of the sea itself at Ratagan. There being no urgency, I dawdled downward, stopping occasionally to admire the U-shaped glen below. A family of four were met, also on the low-level circuit. Already, barely a quarter of their walk complete, they were struggling. An epic day lay ahead!

The path bottomed-out into the wide green glen at Glenlicht House, becoming a track dropping only 40m in the four miles to the public road. These were interminable miles as fatigue took over completely and an internal war was waged with the desire to rest at too-frequent intervals. In contrast to earlier, much of the desolate beauty of the lower glen was lost on me, leaving only a vague impression of hillsides vanishing upward into cloud with no hint of ever reaching a ridge from which to descend again.

Morvich campsite was, as anticipated, pricier than its couthy rival, and run by a gruff Yorkshireman whom I found slightly intimidating. Still, I almost stayed: Shiel Bridge was a further two miles round the shore. But by twice interrupting the tarmac trudge - once to watch a cormorant standing among sheep amid seaweed, once to buy an ice-lolly from a deserted restaurant - the ramshackle collection of buildings came easily enough.

I booked in for three nights rather than the possible four - keeping weekend options open - then spent almost all remaining cash on food. A rake in the bins salvaged a supply of *Daily Records*. One of these was read immediately, the rest put by for a rainy day - ie tomorrow.

Apart from various unanswered phonecalls, only one aspect of the evening remained up in the air - and that literally so. The unhappy juxtaposition of stillness, dampness and, above all, westcoast-in-summerness could mean only one thing: midges!

A quiet, lazy day. A day of dashing to the lavvy through a curtain of midges. Of fuel running out halfway through breakfast, of drinking tepid tea. Of getting annoyed at myself for having wasted a precious half-bottle of gas at Lochan nam Breac, of now being forced into choosing from a tawdry selection of cold food. Of opting for pork pie and worrying about salmonella. Of seeing a long, dull day stretched ahead. Of wishing there to be some way of following the Old Trafford test starting that morning, of wandering the campsite in hope of hearing a radio-whispered commentary, of wondering why even this made me feel tired and lethargic. Of questioning the wisdom of having stormed over Beinn Fhada, of worrying fitness may have been burned-out for good. Of looking at the chopped ham and cheese and recalling something said by Felix at Achallader: *Maybe the reason you fell was your concentration and strength were affected by lack of good food.*

A day of lifting mine eyes to the hills, to the three Sisters visible from here, of seeing Saighead drift clear while her siblings stayed locked up in cloud. Of lying in the tent to read papers cover-to-cover: small ads and horoscopes, gossip and van hire. Of realising how the hustings had passed me by, yet how little I had actually missed. Of studying the marginal listings like a political pundit. Of remembering how the South Cluanie evangelist picked his argument, his fight, by asking if I was going to vote, then using my vagueness as a weapon against me. Of realising how, despite longing to be with people in the abstract, I was increasingly finding them difficult to handle in practice: the Tomdoun snobs, the preacher, the unfriendly, untidy bothyers at Camban.

A day of turning to crosswords and struggling to finish them. Of wondering what it said about me that I could solve *Guardian* puzzles but not those in the *Record*. Of sitting to read Wednesday's four-page Derby Day pull-out, of studying form for the first time in my life and of losing myself in stalls springing open and good-to-firm going churned by hoof-pounding breath-gasping thoroughbreds racing in front of row upon row of open-top buses, champagne corks popping, blanket-spread picnics, top-hatted cheering and betting-slips crumpled then torn as the winning roar came. Of knowing all this to have happened away on the sunlit South Downs, *elsewhere,* of feeling an emptiness from having no way of knowing the winner. Of relapsing, deflated, back into quiet, damp, midge-ridden Loch Duich stillness.

A day of time dragging slowly. Of filling five minutes by counting down to the hour *beepbeep*. Of making watch noises. Of strolling along the Ratagan shore in an all too short blue-skied break-up of cloud. Of waiting till six - no! a few minutes longer, the watch might be fast - to ring through to Doug. Of hearing a poor, crackly voice saying: *Ah Figure! Warbeck here. How are you? Found any curry shops? You're awful faint, you'll have to speak up. We're splitting the journey and arriving on Saturday morning. Was up the South Peak of the Cobbler last Sunday. Mightiest of summits. See you soon. Brrrrrrrp.* Of that being the best thing all day.

A day of wandering back past an SDP notice: Public meeting tonight, Loch Duich School, 8pm. Of deciding to go, not to hear Charlie Kennedy speak so much as to maybe scrounge biscuits and tea. Of plodding two miles round the dead-calm loch, of wearing a woollen balaclava: stifling, but sooner that than a helmet of midges. Of the cries of seagulls skimming the water like stones. Of the water itself giving grey, warped, panel-beaten reflections. Of reaching the school to find nobody there, of waiting by walking the foreshore where midges rose from the water in a dense black spray. Of seeing a Range Rover/Volvo convoy roll up, windows luminous-bright with political stickers. Of Kennedy's father playing lovely, lilting Gaelic airs on his fiddle in the car park until the janitor says: *You'll be coming away inside now, Mister Kennedy sir, the midgies are something terrible the night.*

A day of the meeting being boring, of there being a mix of bearded forestry men asking questions on agricultural policy and wealthier, well-dressed women enquiring, concerned, about inner-city crime. Of embarrassment at being the only non-local there, of wearing big boots with odd laces, of being introduced to the MP by someone pretending to know me. Of mumbling something like *Here out of interest* when what I ought to have said was *Look, I'm on a long-distance walk and I'm tired and thirsty and skint. Any chance of a drink or something?* Of seeing the convoy speed off to Dingwall for the sleeper to London and TV AM. Of thinking *If they can't even produce tea at their meetings, let alone claret, how do they ever hope to gain power?* Of wandering back slowly beneath the knuckle-shaped ridge of Sgurr a'Choire Ghairbh, of passing the Portbhan restaurant where people were eating and drinking and lights shone bright in the gloaming.

A day of reaching the campsite and gulping down water. Of watching the weak-willed glow of a sunset, of diving for cover from the buzzing net curtain. Of drinking the last of the milk zipped up in the tent, of thinking I would climb a hill tomorrow, tiredness or no, rather than spend another shapeless day such as this. Of planning for The Saddle if sunny, Sgurr Mhic Bharraich if not.

A day of dissatisfaction, self-pity, of wondering how the hell I ended up here with next to no money. Of rummaging round on the floor to discover some coppers, making one pound in all. Of feeling so tired that I put off writing the log until morning.

But a day, above all, of much needed rest.

For the first time on the walk I experienced a genuinely poor night's sleep, rolling and fidgeting every few minutes. Or so it seemed: the reality was probably more like once an hour. Perhaps I was ailing for something, perhaps the restlessness was merely a result of having dozed off several times the previous day despite trying, like a mother gently chiding a child, to keep on the right side of consciousness for the sake of peace later on. Whatever the reason, I was poorly refreshed on finally emerging, mid-morning, to a campsite busy with noises of packing and moving. Tubular clanging of tentpoles, nylon swish of a flysheet being folded, recognisably different tone of revs of a car in reverse.

Cloud, higher than on Wednesday and Thursday, was still not high enough for my Saddle plan to be activated. Sgurr Mhic Bharraich was, however, ideally suited: only 781m of ascent as against The Saddle's 1010m, rising steeply from the site rather than five miles back. I knew, of course, another inactive day made more sense in light of my worrying weariness, but I had hated the abrupt aimlessness of Thursday's nothing-day, hated the way the lifeblood of the walk - onward progress - had felt to be seeping away as both atmosphere and aspiration lapsed into midgieness.

I sensed that while tiredness might well have its roots in Felix's nutritional theory, it might also be psychosomatic: a result of having had no genuine break from the watershed for nearly a fortnight and now suddenly finding myself with nowhere to go, nothing to do for three whole days. If this were the case, any form of distraction would help - and reserves of fitness and the coming, well-fed weekend would allow me to test it out. With no money to burn in the fleshpots of Dornie or Kyle, no enthusiasm for the tourist-thronged ramparts of Eilean Donan castle, I decided to simply slot back into the safety of my stereotype - and go for a walk.

As weeks had passed, I had come to recognise complex concerns such as these as integral to the nature of what I was trying to achieve: lines of weakness in the bedrock of the walk. They were difficulties to be endured, not problems to be solved, and could only be dealt with short-term. Over the longer period there would inevitably be deterioration in all aspects of my condition, be they physical, mental, emotional. The real problem was to maintain control - at least until I was near enough to lunge for the tape in the far north. The present short-term worry was keeping myself happy and occupied during the final twenty-four hours before Linda and Doug's arrival.

Hence I set off for what transpired to be a quiet, uneventful climb over Sgurr Mhic Bharraich. The deadening tiredness departed immediately on leaving the horizontal: with relief I felt the familiar blood-rush to legs as energy flooded back. I was soon on top looking across The Saddle's huge complexities and into Glenelg - Scotland's only palindromic placename. I counted at least seventy deer - the largest herd for some time - in a lovely grassy bowl beneath the summit, then strolled back down a path which popped into the campsite all-of-a-sudden, like a tube-train emerging into a busy station. The exercise had proved successful both in filling an awkward four-hour space and as a reference point for testing fitness.

The weather, too, was starting to liven up its act. A strong southerly, midge-removing wind sweeping the glen heralded a big storm. By the time I had finished a meal of bread and fruit and battled, buffeted, along to phone my sister Margaret, there was no longer need to search for an up-to-date paper for the forecast (although I was still keen to know the Derby winner!). The whipcrack of fabric on a neighbouring family tent and sudden keeling-over crash of a wheelie-bin showed far more clearly than any smudged newsprint diagram how isobars had tightened into a close-knit circle. I checked guys and pegs, pulled plate, mug, stove and all other lightweights inside the inner, retreated into my small, zipped-up world for the wildest night so far.

"...breakfast in Nevisport is fine and we're soon on our way. The loch that looks like Scotland doesn't when there's been so little rain. Driving down Glen Shiel we glimpse a mighty form through the mist, thighs thick as marble columns, beard like a hedge. It's the Figure, and he's a little bit peckish, so we buy him a sausage roll. This sets the pattern for the next two days: he eats at all opportunities..."

So began the eventual entry in *Warbeck's Diary* for a weekend continuing in the same vein throughout. For a while, though, I doubted whether my friends would make it at all. The storm had brought heavy rain and ferocious wind, tearing out of the southwest to hit every tent in the campsite square-on. Toward dawn the ridge-pole next door snapped like a twig in a wood, its occupants dragging their possessions and themselves into the car. My trusty Dalomite fared better, standing up well to the broadside despite a couple of nicks expanding to sizable holes. Predictably, the gale blew water under the flimsy groundsheet to make my sleeping-bag wet again, and I woke several times with the whole tent shaking as if under colossal G-force. I gripped the vertical poles tightly for fear that they, and I, might be carried off into darkness.

At eight-thirty, just when the storm was wildest, the wind stopped as suddenly as if someone had flicked a switch. I waited, waited for the next big gust, but it never came. There was only an eerie, pregnant silence and the occasional pit-pat of swollen raindrops on top of the flysheet. Eventually I crawled outside to retighten guys and edge nervously away to the toilet block, prepared all the while to dash back at the first hint of a whoosh through the trees. Soon, though, empty stillness filled with a gentle, less threatening breeze lacking the brute force and malice of its predecessor. The gale had blown itself out.

Thoughts turned to Linda and Doug. They too were camping, but in an older, more high-sided tent. Had it survived the night? Worries doubled on hearing someone mention Ballachulish Bridge being closed. Had their journey been broken in Glen Coe, as was likely, they could be hours late in arriving if Loch Leven had burst its banks also.

But no. Soon after eleven a battered old Metro appeared round the corner, all fears dissolved into laughter and hugs, and the aforementioned sausage roll was consumed. It transpired they had argued the relative merits of Glens Nevis and Coe the previous evening. Linda won, ensuring the bridge was crossed before the storm broke. Their tent - soon pitched beside mine - looked the healthier of the two. I patched my holes with sail-tape the best I could. Held together with bits of string and Elastoplast, this veteran of more than three hundred nights' usage was almost ready to be put out to grass. Although never *really* feeling liable to blow away this time, I doubted whether it could survive another storm of similar calibre. But this was summer: surely there wouldn't be another big blow in the next four weeks...

With rain and cloud choosing not to follow the wind's lead in heading for sunnier climes, plans to climb Auchtertyre Hill, a small, isolated peak above Loch Alsh, never got off the ground - or, more precisely, never got above sea-level. After watching a minibus-load of teenagers being kitted out for a miserable route-march up The Saddle, I, for one, was quite relieved when more heavy rain ensured we pushed on to Kyle for a pint instead. Not that I really minded what we actually *did* with the day: this was ultimately irrelevant. All that mattered was the two-week fast from friends having been broken: I could eat my fill of support and encouragement once more.

With the others still keen on some exercise, we drove north to Loch Carron, then up the winding, grinding, bottom-gear hairpins of the Bealach na Ba - at 626m the highest road in the west of Scotland. Conditions brightened here: cloud higher, stony tops occasionally sunlit. We pulled on boots to climb the remaining 84m of rubble-rough hillside to the summit of Meall Gorm. The Inner Sound sparkled silver in front of Raasay, while quartz-bright tops east of the road also came clear. But the hills I really wanted to see, the Torridons, first giants of the north, were lost in dense watery greyness to the north.

Then, as we drove back to Kintail, came a glimpse of sharp rock hills rising above Achnashellach. Again I felt the curious sensation first known eight weeks earlier on the drive south over Beattock - and, more recently, during the memorable Gleouraich rest day. The sensation was of looking a week ahead, of spying on my future - and somehow felt *wrong*, like flicking forward in a book to find out what happens. This time, though, there was a difference. My habitual lumping-together of days had been interrupted by a four-day block of non-progress. Now, with only one evening of respite remaining, I could think of little else but these hills. It was as if the past days had not only broken the linear mould of the walk, but also reawakened a desire for momentum, an urge to move on, that had flagged a little over the Cluanie ridges.

Thus even as we sat late into the night, eating oatcakes by torchlight, my heart and mind had already moved on from the busy A87 - which had, throughout the past week, never been more than three hours' walk away. Moved on too from the friendly campsite where I had spent only the second four-night stint of the walk. Already, in all but flesh and blood, I was far gone, away amid the complex cordon of hills leading into the north. A friend later summed up succinctly: I was beginning to feel the winds of the Cape in my hair.

7: Chrysanthemum and Cheesecake
(Sunday 7th June - Saturday 13th June)

Back off the road again! Munching nectarines, Linda and Doug in tow, I set off from Morvich into a dull, warm morning. We climb gently into Gleann Choinneachain along a path half good, soil-eroded setts, half bad, boot-swallowing bog. Soon the dramatic cleft of the Bealach an Sgairne takes shape ahead: so acute, so rockily defined as to feel almost a discard from the Black Cuillin. The pass - carving off Beinn Fhada to the north even more effectively than does the Allt Grannda to the south - is, geologically if not geographically - the most aptly-named of the "Gates of Affric": the fine, romantic title shared by all western approaches to a glen which, with its twenty-mile length and wooded lower reaches, the Victorian travellers came to regard as the finest, most romantic of them all.

Today, for me, the pass is more a gate back into a world of my own. Here I plan to leave the others and embark on a four-day, secretly remote stretch bringing the Glen Carron/Strath Bran divide and the opening of the north. Yet with more than a mile of the ascent still ahead, it becomes obvious the parting will come sooner than expected. Linda feels less than well, such that even at half-pace I'm pulling away, straining the distance between us like a dog on a leash. So after a stop for pâté and photos, the weekenders head back down the glen for the short walk and long drive home, while I zig-zag eastward over steepening, stonier ground. The parting hurts, as usual, but is offset by knowledge that the next contact lies only five days ahead - as against thirteen last time.

The final climb through immense, quarry-like rockfalls beneath the well-named *pass of rumbling* gives the most enjoyable walking for some time, capped by the sudden change from the narrow, dry, grey-black tightness of crag and scree to the soft, watery light of a long, open glen. But first appearances are deceptive. I know Glen Affric doesn't begin here, at its own gates, nor does the water draining the east side of this pass flow eastward. The true watershed is a nameless, almost imperceptible swelling a mile beyond and 150m lower. The intervening stretch of land seeps away northward to Loch a'Bhealaich and the sluggish meanders of Gleann Gaorsaic before crashing over the Glomach Falls into Glen Elchaig and the sea at Loch Long. The Highlands, home to many examples of geological illusion and glacial trickery, has few as subtly crafted as this.

After resting by the loch, I turn to the day's main task: the crossing of Sgurr nan Ceathreamhnan, third of the triumvirate of 1130m-plus hills which earlier gave batterings on Beinn Laoigh and Ben Alder. Ceathreamhnan is also one of the most celebrated of Gaelic tongue-twisters. Although easily phoneticised as *kerranan* by them that know, many opt for the safer (if more flowery) Graeco-Anglicisms of *chrysanthemum*.

Whatever the name - translating as *sharp quartered hill,* despite there being five, not four main ridges and corries - the massif itself is a sprawling, far-reaching exhibit to the power of glaciation. As on Laoigh before, the summit is twin-topped - but the watershed this time passes over only the western, slightly junior peak before winding down to the head of Loch Mullardoch.

Though long, this is one of the more eagerly awaited days of the walk. Such enjoyment is, however, largely contingent on the weather - and the high-cloud brightening of the hour after leaving the others lowers into rain as I follow fenceposts onto Sgurr Gaorsaic - an 839m foothill Corbett appearing anonymous and insignificant beside its high-sided neighbour, despite being only the second hill of the walk to be climbed from sea-level.

A compass-cut corner briefly brings a return to below-cloud clarity. Hillsides to the south, beyond the Affric, stand dramatically black against nearer, yellow-bright slopes of Gleann Gniomhaidh - a contrast as stark as a field of oilseed rape seen against newly-ploughed soil. But then comes the 400m slog of massive slopes beyond, where I soon have more than just my head in the clouds again. A glance at the watch. Two o'clock.

Four hours later I re-emerge, halfway down Sgurr na h-Eige - last knoll on the knobbly north ridge of Ceathreamhnan - looking over a mercury-sheened Loch Mullardoch with its coiling, magnesium-strip river. After so long in dark, dense cloud, even normally lustreless schists on grey, rock-strewn hillsides dazzle brightly. The feeling is of having regained sight after a period of blindness - a blindness which, the pre-Rowardennan episode aside, has given the most sustained compasswork of the walk: four hours in damp, swirling cloud, squinting at the map, wiping dew-like moisture from spectacles.

Having reached the west top of Ceathreamhnan without a break, I had sudden doubts whether the tiny, ankle-high cairn could actually be marking one of the high points of such an enormous hill. That it did was confirmed by taking a bearing along ten minutes' worth of path-scarred ridge to the true summit - a diversion intended not just as a navigational ploy, but to exploit a too-good-to-miss chance of reaching the highest summit in Scotland yet to have seen me.

Route regained, I then faced the long, compass-trusting sleepwalk over Stuc Bheag and Stuc Mor. After path and fenceposts gave out, the ridge broadened and the visual aid of the cornice dissolved as the eastern corries lost their definite edges. Again there was unwanted recall of Loch Ard Forest: conditions were very similar. This time, though, no sooner had the sound of running water told of my being too far left than a patch of drier ground with a dark shape looming beyond betrayed the whereabouts of Creag Ghlas - a craggy spine of a hill where I was able to confirm my position.

A few twists and turns later and I'm revelling in the shining greyness below, trotting down a waterlogged stalker's path into Srath Duilleach. Even the deer think it wiser to stay low on such a day: scattered everywhere, they include a young stag in velvet, bouncing away, startled, having failed to detect my approach. I'm in bouncy mood too, well pleased with my navigation and feeling again the poor-weather exhilaration accompanying Ben Alder. Having managed to remain on schedule through this, the rest of the week ought now to come easily. Conditions will surely improve, if only slightly.

I camp on a meadow at Carnach: a deserted cluster of estate buildings including a dilapidated, paint-peeling Anne of Green Gables summer-house, complete with verandah and shutters. I nose around a while, waiting for drizzle to relent and allow pitching and cooking in comfort. This it does - although the hanging dampness returns later in the evening.

Towards dusk, a 4x4 pickup drives slowly up the glen, but the driver - evidently more interested in sheep than in brewing and chatting with walkers - doesn't come over. This apart, the only sounds are background ones: calling birds, bright bubbling of the burn, occasional flickers of breeze. I sleep early and well, a healthy tiredness replacing the rest-break fatigue. The day has been long - much longer than fourteen map miles suggests - and has taken me a world away, both geographically and atmospherically, from the bus party bustle of Loch Duich. Now, with the big Affric ridges crossed, there is no ground of similar height before the north coast.

Next day begins on an amazingly steep Land Rover track winding up to the Loch an Droma pass. How on earth, I wonder, could a vehicle drive up it without tumbling, roof-over-axles, back down the heathery slopes? Steep hillsides follow before the levelling of Carn na Breabaig's lochan-cradling summit. The morning air, sharper than of late, seems to provoke vivid imagery: the tapering summit of Carnan Cruithneachd, split into slender buttresses by vertical gullies, resembles an upraised hand, while narrow, dark Loch na Leitreach, squeezed between hills and trailing its bright tail of river, is a mouse lurking in some confined space.

Yet the higher ground sweeping up from Mullardoch to wall-in Glen Affric is, for me, more evocative still. A light dusting of overnight snow combines with grey-green smoothness of slopes and a light, windless mist to remind of autumn days on bleak moorland to the east of the country: the Ladder Hills, say. This strange misplacement remains all day, even once extending to imagining I can smell woodsmoke - surely a trick of the senses, there being no habitation within eight miles.

There is no harm in reminiscence and reverie however: I'm content to be miles away for the featureless grassy plod over Meall Shuas and onto An Socach, *the snout*. (Even the name adds to the mental drifting, being shared with a favourite hill near Braemar.) The gentle 600m slope onto the day's only Munro proves tiring - I definitely prefer steeper ascents with the heavy, early-week rucksack - until short-cropped grass high up gives easier going. An airy, curving summit ridge comes unexpectedly after such a grind. My mind so far away, first sight of the long chain of hills stretching east causes momentary confusion. I'm half-expecting to see Bennachie or Tap o'Noth!

An Socach: most hard done by of all hills in an area where the OS seems content to give nothing but basics. The map shows a hill sans name, sans scree, sans crag, sans everything bar contours. Yet the upper part of Coire Mhaim proves broken, bouldery and rough. I drop a few metres below the lip to eat lunch (the trig point being too open to a stiff breeze causing constant wiping of my own snout), then return up top to study the view. This is short-range, despite high cloud occasionally breaking into shreds of blue: amorphous peaks to the northwest, Coulin Forest way, a coquettish curve to Beinn Fhionnlaidh across Mullardoch, but little else worthy of note. Greyness again predominates, as it will all week - always there in the background, showing through like a watercolour wash.

On eventually turning downhill I realise, with an odd sense of loss, Loch Mullardoch has disappeared from view for good. Such a major, long-awaited landmark (or watermark?), it has come and gone almost before I know it, like a picture shown too quickly at a slideshow. *Must come back,* I think, then walk on through the afternoon, down to and over An Cruachan - its ancient, sturdy cairn, its first sight of the next big loch, Monar - then down further into the broad, loch-filled basin itself.

I'm aimed for Maol-bhuidhe, one of the most testing of all bothies to reach, even by a direct route. Remote passes have always to be crossed, with the white-painted, red-roofed building virtually ringed by the headwaters of the Ling. Aware of this, I take the first easy fording I find, then squelch along two miles of path with one eye always looking back down to the river. It hasn't escaped my attention a more direct line back across would be needed come morning.

I swing open the bothy door feeling both weary and irritated - if only because the last hour has been spent trying to extract apple peel from between teeth - but spirits lift on finding a cosy, refloored room upstairs: a reassuring place to spend the pivotal night of an isolated week.

The bothy book proves the most interesting and amusing so far: an extended satire on the Ultimate Challenge, reference to a bothy frog rather than a mouse, a minimum of doggerel. The majority of entries come from people on big through trips, usually intent on using both Alltbeithe and Gerry Howkins' hostel at Craig at some stage. Most plans also include tomorrow's hill, Bidein a'Choire Sheasgaich - invariably referred to

173

colloquially, if not always affectionately, as *Cheesecake*. And in addition to all this, there are enough mis-spellings of *chrysanthemum* to beg the question of why people bother to complain about the Gaelic!

I'm loath to leave the bothy and its friendly, encouraging signs of humanity: candle stubs, whisky bottles (empty, needless to say), horseshoed door, boot-smoothed step. Without it, the glen would feel heart-rendingly empty. I'm loath, too, to face the problem of the Allt an Loin-fhiodha, the river running sluggish and deep near the bothy door. This stretch contains several tiny nodular lochans - not unlike the canal reservoirs seen in the Central Belt - together with the larger, more bulbous expanse of Loch Cruoshie. Beyond lies Beinn Dronaig, first of the day's hills.

I start by trying the outflow of the larger loch in hope of a shallow fording, until forced, with the river-bed lost under a metre or two of gently rippling murk, to head back east to a rockier section inspected the previous evening. Here I boulder-hop dry-shod to the far bank. Swings and roundabouts, even then: the diversion means now having to cross a mile of miserable, soaking moorland to regain the route, and the resultant wet feet mean I might as well have waded straight across in the first place. A further niggle comes when a path clearly discernible above proves frustratingly difficult to find on the ground.

Soon, though, these petty concerns are put into perspective by a more serious difficulty. I reach the 797m summit of Dronaig, with its westward views to Loch Carron and Applecross - both, inevitably, composed of differing shades of grey - then set about conceding all the hard-earned height to a slope which, according to the map, is crag-free. *Grass-free, more like!* Outcrops are everywhere, causing much weaving to-and-fro, up-and-down like a ball on a bagatelle board. *Bloody Ordnance Survey!*

Feet, on finally reaching the bottom, ache from a combination of wetness and steepness. I'm in a foul mood. Fortunate, then, not to know treacherous descents are to be the order for the day, to regularly recur like a discordant motif in a piece of music. Nor that the one just completed will rank only second on a scale of awkwardness.

While waiting for relaxed feelings to settle back into place, I have a proper look round for the first time since leaving the bothy. I can already see down to Bendronaig Lodge - and, once onto cairnless Sail Riabhach, an outlier of Cheesecake, am able to add the tiny sugar-cube of Bearnais, all but lost in the watery confusion of its eponymous glen. More captivating is first sight of vast Torridonian ridges: ghostly curtains of scree hanging like grey sweeps of rain amid genuine showers to the northwest. Yet even these are mere backdrop to the black pincer-corrie of Fuar Tholl above Achnashellach: one of the most startling of all Scottish hill-profiles, as weirdly craterous as a prop in a sci-fi movie.

With so much on display, I think about stopping early for lunch - before deciding the summit of Cheesecake itself will be more apt. This rises ahead, almost as other-worldly as Fuar Tholl, in a bald, bullet-shaped cone which, on closer acquaintance, transpires to be a gentle, loose slope of birdshot scree. The summit gives the finest view imaginable of Loch Monar: silver, remote, filling the upper eight miles of Glen Strathfarrar, and with no evidence of the tidemarks so scarring Lochs Lyon and Quoich earlier. The hydro-enlarged section looks particularly attractive in fact, flicking out, long and narrow - an anteater's tongue of water. Appropriately, an ant-sized plane flies low along its length, white-winged, tiny against dark, vast hills.

Tomorrow's agenda is also well seen: Sgurrs Choinnich and a'Chaorachain, the latter linking with the beautifully conical, beautifully named Bidean an Eoin Deirg, *little peak of the red bird* - grouse, presumably. More concerned with my own Bidein however, I reject an earlier notion to add the glowingly-reported ridge to Lurg Mhor, suddenly anxious plenty of time be allowed for the final third of the day's walk: already it is mid-afternoon.

And thank goodness I do! The first 100m of descent are no problem, but then comes the 300m plunge to the bealach. Here the entire northern end of the hill seems plated with near-vertical slabs overlapping into adjoining corries. The map is again pitifully underdrawn: I pace back and forth nearly an hour above the mile-long precipice, searching for a safe way down without recourse to backtracking over the summit. A promising grassy rake in the eastern corrie is barred by an horrendous scree-run I daren't touch. Only after having almost given up all hope of a reasonable route does a slightly more open gully tempt me down.

This proves watery and loose - scaffolding would have been handy - but eventually leads to grassy ground. Later, at Gerry's, I'm told I did well to find this, the only feasible unroped line, from above. For days after, I flinch at the thought of what it would have been like in cloud and rain.

Tired, drained by the descent, I think of camping on the Bealach an Sgoltaidh, before deciding to press on over Beinn Tharsuinn to the Bealach Bhearnais with a view to climbing Wednesday's hills light-loaded. This holds considerable appeal: sooner jam tomorrow than jam today.

175

Beinn Tharsuinn, *transverse hill,* is a hill-name usually given to an annoying lump standing between where you are and where you want to be. This one, although no exception, has the redeeming feature of fine views back to Cheesecake - showing no obvious line of ascent, let alone descent - and down Bearneas: innumerable rivulets gleaming like tangled rails in a marshalling yard.

The final drop to the twisted triple col of Bealach Bhearnais is, inevitably, craggy and confusing: different levels of ground linked by countless lesser flattenings, each formed from indentikit boulders-on-grass. Route-finding becomes unexpectedly problematic, the distorted perspective and concealed folds all the more exasperating given conditions being clear.

The watershed swings straight back uphill from the bealach, but having finished my quota for the day I'm in no mood for overtime. I cut down to the main glen at Pollan Buidhe, the muddy path squelching out information that tomorrow, like today, will start with wet feet. Ignoring the bridge, I splash straight across to pitch on an ideal greensward. Six-thirty. Eight hours for only ten miles.

Cloud turns an even greyer shade of grey as I cook, threatening rain which never arrives. Instead, in late evening, large areas of blue drift in from the west and a square of sunlight settles on Sgurr a'Chaorachain. This seems a fitting enough end to the most critical day since Ciche - and one virtually unwalkable in bad weather. It also gives hope for the first time in a long time that the sun might decide to shine.

Nae luck. The sun seems no more likely to appear for today's walk than it has during the brief hours of darkness serving as an apology for night in the Highland midsummer. Not that I'm complaining: dull though they may have been, the days since the Shiel Bridge storm have stayed mainly dry, while every phonecall home has, for weeks on end, been a litany of ruined holidays for neighbours, bedding plants washed out. A little more in the way of heat won't go amiss though: the drier-than-expected path back to the bealach arouses suspicions of earlier clear skies having caused a ground frost.

I leave the tent where it stands, quietly hoping that by chalking-off the morning's two Munros, then hurrying back for a feed and a snooze, a second pair of tops can be crossed in the afternoon. The climbing of these - Sgurr nan Ceannaichean and Moruisg - will allow me to hang onto the extra rest day gained by the similar double-shuffle in Kintail. Involving four hills rather than two, today's logistical finesse is liable to be much harder, but I feel fit and full of energy, fairly dashing up to the pass and onto the west ridge of Sgurr Choinnich.

Steadily-angled, this is regularly cut by narrow bands of rock, like a barrel ringed with hoops. Some give mild scrambling. The summit looks straight down to the tent - although views vanish in a flurry of snow before a'Chaorachain. I don't pause at the top, preferring to follow a bearing down white-swirling slopes, taking in mouthfuls of snowflakes, looking down to a mouthful of a lochan: Lochan Gaineamhach. But the descent is a doddle after Tuesday, and I tie off the loop by returning to the tent in just over three hours. A good morning's work.

Lunch is munched watching tracer-lines of flakes stream past the open tent door - neither this nor a post-nap drowsiness doing much to encourage thoughts of post-prandial walking. But an hour or so later cloud lifts, sky brightens, lying snow melts and thoughts of comfort and company at Gerry's have me hurrying to haul out pegs and bundle the wet flysheet.

I head back east before branching off at a small cairn marking the stalker's path onto Sgurr nan Ceannaichean, *merchant's hill*. Although the strict watershed lies a mile further on, this is too good an opportunity to pass up, too rare a pleasure to be left unsavoured: the finest path in weeks, leading directly to summit slopes 600m above. It comes in three sections: a series of short zig-zags between two burns, a steeper, straighter stretch, then some marvellous long oscillations across stony, open slopes beneath the summit. These could almost have been constructed by the self-taught engineers in celebration of simple harmonic motion. The ascent is effortless, relaxing even, with the gradient on the upper section so gentle as to barely seem off the level. I'm sad to reach the cairn - although the view westward refreshes too: road and railway showing as black lines through the trees. More easy going brings the high col and reascent for Moruisg.

Big water must be an annoying hill in mist, countless cairned points sprouting from a featureless plateau. Although half-clear today, its summit can be guessed, like that of Stob nan Eighrach on Lomondside weeks before, from a litter-crammed cairn. There is also a reprise of the sense of loss accompanying Mullardoch's departure from view: another whole section complete, and so quickly! I can scarcely believe the four-day crossing of these hills as the same length of time which dragged endlessly at Shiel Bridge.

The day's heaviest shower rolls in at the start of the long eastward descent to Luib. As on a'Chaorachain, the downhill walking is antithetical to that of Tuesday, being set at an angle almost *too* slight: dry dwarf vegetation up top quickly giving way to a gently sloping, seeping morass. Faced with such widespread water-loggery - heathery skerries floating on oceans of boot-sucking mosses - I cut leftward toward the railway in hope of finding a path. But there is none: it is a bog-weary walker who finally emerges onto the A890.

Although the hostel lies six miles to the west, the long walk is saved when the first passing car offers a lift. I'm soon sitting on the doorstep hauling off mud-covered gaiters while holding a shouted conversation with Gerry, up above mending the roof. Two Grampian Club members, Liz Stenhouse and Elsie Luke, are the only other occupants, so I have a dorm to myself. Presumably the imminent election is keeping people at home.

Almost immediately *this* feels like home to me. Converted from railway cottages, Gerry opened up his independent, non-SYHA bunkhouse-cum-hostel in the early seventies, providing countless bednights for famous and obscure hillgoers ever since. The way the place is run takes me back to the old-timer at Dolphinton, who mourned the old-style hostels with their hard-but-fair welcome. Here is a place where you settle-up on departure, not arrival, where you are trusted to take food from the tuck shop and make a shopping list to be paid later, where cooking and lounge facilities are shared with the proprietor (although to call the Aladdin's cave of rugs, books, old wooden furniture, foot-stools, carved tree-stumps and an open fire a *lounge* is to hopelessly under-describe it), where the door remains open 24 hours a day, 365 days a year, and where there is even a barrel of Alice Ale in one of the dorms (Gerry offers everyone a pint later on).

One anecdote should suffice to demonstrate the feel of the place. I ring John, who rings Calum, who rings back. He and Ray are planning to arrive late Friday evening, but how late is okay with Gerry? I shout the question through to the fireside, from where the reply comes instantly: "Anytime before midnight, because after that they'll arrive on Saturday morning!"

Thursday's concern is an area of moorland hills entrapped by the two branches of the Achnasheen road: a group of rarely climbed tops literally - and metaphorically - overlooked in views toward their vast Torridonian neighbours. By leaving most of the gear at Gerry's and hitching back round from where Glen Docherty begins its scenic plunge to Loch Maree, I'll again push the watershed to the limit of possible progress - and again go into a two-day break ahead of schedule. All week I have hoped to put this small plan into operation, suspecting - wrongly as it transpires - it to be the last opportunity for a lightweight day.

So after a dawn brighter than any all week, no time is lost in cooking breakfast, then hurrying outside. The luxury of listening to a radio is the only temptation liable to cause any delay.

A lift soon comes from a van bound for Inverness, then - as is now normal when linking-up - I return to a remembered gatepost before trudging across flat moorland to the steep rise of Carn Beag. (Fear of the walk accidentally losing continuity is almost as potent as that of failing to reach Cape Wrath.)

A shower cruises in from the northwest, provoking a brief query of the wisdom of walking, but all doubts disappear at the 550m summit and a sudden, startling confrontation with a close, jaggy horizon of rock peaks. The Lair hills, Liathach, Beinn Eighe, Slioch: first, and foremost, hills of the north. Showers breeze through, rippling light changes every second, yet the real perfection comes not from a hill, but a loch. Between Beinn Eighe's vast eastern screes and the castellated summit of Slioch lies the light blue fantail of a full-length Loch Maree. "Lovely", the old song calls it, and lovely it is today.

A gentle mile westward brings the bouldery rise to Beinn na Feusaige. The name suits: *hill of the beard*. Here the lower, wetter ground means a wider than usual variety of insect- and bird-life. I lie back to watch a lark directly overhead - both it and its song hanging, bobbing in the air like a ball on a fairground rifle-range fountain - while all around grasshoppers rub raw, exotic-sounding legs and black flies buzz like door entryphones. The hillside is interestingly varied too, the gentle northeast ridge of Carn Breac composed mainly of long flat stones and waist-high, rock-flaking crags. The watershed swings downhill halfway along, but I continue to the walled-in trig point for the exquisite view down through trees to Lochs Coulin and Clair.

I revel in the northwesterly airflow's hallmark, newness of light: remember Rowardennan! There is, though, a strange feeling which has, like the flies, buzzed around my head all morning: a feeling of the day being somehow *different*. This comes not from the spurious fact of it being election day, but is, I'm sure, something to do with the hills themselves. The mystery isn't resolved there and then: I'm too absorbed by spruced-up, showered-down views to really concentrate in any way but visually. Later, however, I realise what it was. All twelve miles of today's walk - bar the off-route Carn Breac - fall below the 600m contour, and it is a long, long time since that has happened - on Rannoch Moor, in fact, a month earlier. Every single top since then has been at least as high as the Donalds which so daunted in the Borders!

Moving on through the afternoon, I swing back eastward onto Carn Loisgte, a low, lochan-covered hill giving ever finer prospects down Glen Torridon. The showers also move on. My log makes short work of a view long savoured: "Torridon and Fisherfield gloriously clear: cloud galleons, many pinnacles".

Hummocky ground dotted with deer leads to the final - and finest-named - top of the day: Bidein Clann Raonaild. The old feudal family could hardly have picked a better eponymous hill than this, a well-made cairn emphasising the grandeur all around. Sgurr Dubh across Loch Clair excepted, I doubt whether a better viewpoint exists for Liathach and Beinn Eighe: both, despite their great length, appear almost unclimbable from here. The Fannaichs, too, look good - although they have hung onto their showers and are hammered, on off on off, for much of the afternoon.

With so little height to lose, the road comes quickly. After a preliminary search for a Saturday night campsite, I sit on the rucksack to await a lift. The road is exceptionally quiet - *Damn the election!* - although the delay is hardly tiresome with the famous glen-framed view of Loch Maree on hand, telegraph poles and all.

Gerry having cycled off to vote, the place is deserted when I return. The hoover lies uncoiled across the floor, hinting at chores to be done. A French couple book in, then Gerry, Elsie and Liz all return. The latter pair have walked in an inch of fresh snow on Maoile Lunndaidh. Another convivial evening is spent around the fire, drinking nips from Liz's hip flask.

Eight months later, Liz was killed and several other Grampian Club members injured in a coach crash near Bridge of Orchy. They had parked to unload rucksacks when another coach skidded and ploughed into their backs. It would be pointless to elaborate on the starkly horrific facts, or to dwell on the tragedy of something which could so easily never have happened: a few minutes here, a few metres there...

For many, the sense of loss was greater, the vividness of the pain and the shock more cruel than it was for me, who had spent only two evenings with Liz, then written and received a couple of after-walk letters. Yet the news shook with the thought of how, in the chaos of moments, the eager anticipation of adding to innumerable days on the hill was tragically lost in the suddenness of a life cut short. My own remembrance was of laughing, joking, arguing in the warm fire-glow of Gerry's room, of sitting, feet up on foot-stools, drinking whisky from mugs, of a brief friendship coinciding with the happiest, sunniest, most spectacularly enjoyable day in the two grey weeks since Knoydart.

Gerry's radio, hanging from a living-room rafter, is tuned to the nine o'clock election bulletin, so when my internal alarm goes off at eight-fifty-nine, I dash through, switch on and hear tell of the Tory landslide. The French couple eating toast are greeted in silence that morning. There is compensation, however, in a morning already warm and sunny: surely the hoped-for sunbathing rest day, the first since Cumbernauld. I'm also still pleased with Thursday's progress. As in the Great Glen, a first bite has been taken from the coming week's apple, and it tastes good.

But before lazing, a little exercise. A waymarker just west of the hostel points up the old right-of-way to the Coulin Pass, a mile or so of pine-needled zig-zags giving an ideal morning stroll. The path emerges onto a standard, stand-offish Land Rover track soon reaching the top of the pass

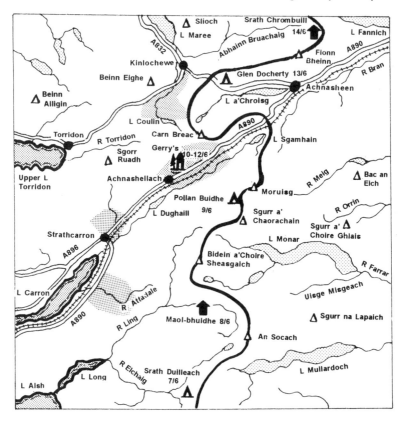

Loch Mullardoch - Loch Fannich

and a variant on Thursday's Loch Coulin/Beinn Eighe view. I sit out a light shower, then amble back down to Achnashellach station as a train clatters past through a tunnel of trees. (An American tourist once asked me: "When do we arrive at Acne Shellac?" - understandable, but sounding like a nasty disease nonetheless.)

There is certainly nothing nasty about the station, its white-painted railway cottage gardens a bright mass of rhododendra. Beyond and above, looking like a huge mound of cooling lava, towers Fuar Tholl's grey quarry-corrie. I doubt there is another station in Britain with such a spectacular open air waiting-room, and possibly not that many in the whole world. A warning sign reads: *Stop. Look. Listen.* I'm happy to do all three.

A car plastered in red rose Labour stickers gives the required lift to Lochcarron: an elongated waterfront town, Helensburgh minus the backstreets. Droves of mothers with young children are heading for school prizegiving in the community hall. I lie on the grass, just within PA range, and award myself prizes of the edible kind. A sharp sea-breeze draws a little of the day's heat, not that I'm complaining. Having waited a long time for a rest day such as this, I'm almost glad Calum and Ray aren't due until evening. It is great just to be among people, to have a wealth of options, yet simply to laze alone doing absolutely nothing.

Late afternoon, I hitch back to Craig in a Drake Fellowship minibus. This is being used as an ambulance, taking a youth with a dislocated wrist from Applecross to Raigmore Hospital. The driver chats about local bothies, the youth lies in the back and groans.

Calum and Ray, the Ben Lomond sherpas, arrive at the back of eleven, having driven the two-twenty-odd miles without a break. They look wrecked, the long drive having followed an even longer night of election-watching. Tomorrow will be different still: if the weather holds, the plan is to climb Beinn Alligin.

The morning is again bright first thing. I wake early to catch up on letter-writing - then, while Calum and Ray fry eggs and burn toast, set about the other time-honoured, time-consuming supply day ritual. But for once the selection of food and swapping of clothes from cardboard boxes proves too difficult: the added complication of a daysack for Alligin means I merely shuffle supplies from one box to another as though performing some complex party trick. Eventually the attempt rather than the equipment is packed in, and I go in search of Gerry to settle up.

Although having spent under twelve hours at the hostel, the others already feel sad at leaving. Doubly so myself, knowing that just as this is the final Glaswegian supply run, so Gerry's is the last intended port-of-call. Now, barring disasters, there remain only bothies and camps.

I'm even more loath to leave on seeing the weather turning: early promise dissolves in a sinking layer of grey as the corner is rounded into Glen Torridon. By the time the National Trust car park is reached, rain has increased from a timorous chapping at the door to heavy-duty forced entry. Although a brief clearance shows the *jewelled hill* already pearl-white with snow (the fourth such covering of the week: so much for flaming June!), it merely confirms what we already know: high tops are out of bounds for the day.

Instead, we sit in the car to watch band after band of rainwater slide down the windscreen like the sound bar on a badly-tuned video. A pair of tame finches flit from mirror to aerial to wipers, eager for window-thrown scraps.

Eventually, a brightening to the east tempts us back up the glen and into much brighter conditions. The climatic contrast with sea-level is astonishing: within ten minutes snow and high wind switch to warm sunshine and gentle summer breezes. The latter soon have me feeling very sleepy, content just to lie back and gaze across at the huge southern wall of Beinn Eighe, mottled screes draped over its ridges like a leopard-skin rug.

Midges eventually prompt an end to lounging and a drive to Kinlochewe, then to Achnasheen, in search of an open pub. It is pouring here again, the kind of two-hour cloudburst the BBC love to describe as a scattered shower. Driving back up Glen Docherty, *glen of the sacked football manager,* I worry the intended campsite will be awash. But all is well, the top of the road having missed most of the shower and the grassy layby being well-drained anyway.

We set up and sort out in a light drizzle - amazingly, the first occasion this potentially most awkward and unpleasant of all camping chores has been attempted in anything other than absolute dryness. One wetting in thirty-four attempts seems like pretty good value!

Also prompting retrospective thought is the fact of being beside an AA phonebox. The previous one I recall seeing was on leaving the Pentlands to enter the Central Belt - and there has been a lot of watershed under the bridge since then.

Not that I'm really interested in the past: the future intrigues far more. As the others wish good luck and drive away - one moment a navy blue Cortina gives life to the grey bends, the next there is only a cold, dead road - I know myself to be more alone than ever before, to be taking the first steps out on a very long limb. An estimate of the number of walking days needed to reach Cape Wrath gives only thirteen - four through the Fannaichs, four more for the Deargs and beyond, five in the far north - yet there are to be no more weekend lifelines thrown from Glasgow, no more definite schedules to be kept.

I will still have access to what rock climbers might term "points of aid": parcels waiting to be collected from hotels at the next two road-crossings, then a food-run by friends from Tain in a fortnight's time. These, though, are *all* I can rely on - and are disconcertingly few and far between. Everything which has gone before seems a mere preliminary to this final hundred-mile section. Now the hardest walking, the loneliest country, the fading levels of energy and short-term motivation are to be juxtaposed with the most weirdly wonderful hills and the ever-growing excitement of nearing the end.

What will this heady brew produce? I don't know, but the uncertainty worries me. To return to the climbing analogy, if things go well from here on I will be like an unroped pioneer, moving fast and free without constraints or delays. If, on the other hand, things go badly, I will be more akin to someone shooting off the loose end of an abseil rope.

8: Hitting the wall
(Sunday 14th June - Sunday 21st June)

The oldest, most northerly and perhaps most impressive of all Highland fault lines is the Moine Overthrust. Several hundred million years ago, during the period of upheaval known as the Caledonian Orogeny (from the Greek *oros* - mountain - and *genesis,* beginning), this great leviathan of primeval tectonics rose from the Sound of Sleat, lumbered across the northwestern corner of Scotland, then sank back to the sea bed at Loch Eriboll. To describe the resultant landform as complex and contorted merely scrapes at the topsoil of the subject. Layers of rock were thrust upward, folded and, in places, completely inverted by the subterranean show of strength, with the result that large expanses of one of the oldest rock formations - Archaean gneiss - now lie close alongside much younger exposures of Durness limestone, Torridonian and Old Red sandstones, granite, gritstone and marble, to name but a few.

Beyond this age-old divide lie the bulk of most people's top ten Scottish mainland hills, all with bare bones of rock literally thrust upward through the blanket bog of low-lying moorland: the Torridons, An Teallach, Slioch, Stac Pollaidh, Cul Mor, Cul Beag, Suilven, Quinag, Arkle, Foinaven. Collectively, these hills take on the characteristics of another, even rarer, form of rock: that of lodestone, magnetically drawing folk back, again and again, to this bleakest, most distant, yet most beautiful corner of Britain.

The watershed was largely unaffected by all this hurly-burly however, having been formed in a much later period. River-flow was primarily determined by glaciation, and glaciation was merely the icing on the geological cake. Yet it - or, rather, I - had surreptitiously drawn alongside the line of the Thrust. It was within three miles of the present camp - a polite distance to be maintained until the final crossing of the threshold near the Oykel headwaters in a week or so's time.

Until then, the change in landform would make its presence felt by its absence, so to speak. For the first time since entering the Highlands, the watershed wouldn't go out of its way to cross the most significant, well-known hills in the area. This was a trait which had, at times, seemed almost meticulously deliberate: take the geometric linking of the Tyndrum Corbetts or the precise picking-off of the Blackmount. But now high days on the Fannaichs and Deargs were to be interspersed with long, low holidays on smaller, less familiar hills between.

Not that thoughts of land structure were at the forefront of my mind at the time. They merely formed a backdrop to a more relevant fixation: the weather. Apart from the evening and morning brightness in Glen Cluanie, the showery sharpness of the Coulin Forest hills and the warm, relaxing rest day at Lochcarron, there had been no clear-skied sunshine whatsoever in the sixteen days since leaving Knoydart. For a week or so I had been anticipating a change for the better, but as time had gone on and false hopes piled up, I began to fear the exceptionally fine late spring had been a façade papering over a summer rotted through with dampness.

Again, this morning, as I hurriedly struck camp with the sky threatening another of the drenching, sleep-punctuating showers, I felt the worry of a wet fortnight ahead. A silent prayer was said for the second coming of summer: I was, after all, approaching the end times.

And lo! For once, dark clouds moved on without dropping in - one of the perks of being away from high peaks - and I was soon completing the short, stiff climb and long moorland plod to the 539m summit of Carn a'Ghlinne. Golden plover seemed everywhere, standing stone-still, thin-legged, on slight rocky eminences, piercing the still morning air with shrill one-note calls. As on Thursday, views down Loch Maree were a delight: ghostings of showers moving between big hills.

Anticipated heavy going to the next top, An Cabar, *the antler,* never materialised. Appropriately, deer scurried into the narrow, green glen of Feadan Duchairidh. More dry ground then led to Meall a'Chaorainn: short, wind-cropped heather, tiny stones, smooth tongues of grass. This, combined with sight of big Fionn Bheinn rising green and smooth beyond, made for the day's finest pleasure.

A lunchtime nap nipped in the bud. I set off again just before two with hopes of the Munro by three. This, though, reckoned without both the biggest peat-hag in weeks and the heaviest hailstorm of the walk. The former was seen only metres after leaving the summit of a'Chaorainn, allowing chance to cut across the doodling black lines of waist-high peat trenches at their narrowest point - a grassy Tarbert between two seas of treacly mud. Hardly surprising to note the slopes draining this featureless, useless stretch of land being named Coire Bog.

The second delay was more difficult to anticipate, catching me halfway up the 500m climb onto Fionn Bheinn. Sharp, pellet-sized drivings of ice stung me into inaction: I was forced to sit on my rucksack, turn my back to the wind (which formed a package deal with the hail, arriving and departing with it), and let the missiles rattle against the artificial skin of my cagoule rather than the real stuff on my face.

Eventually, after a stop-start ascent, the storm passed and the summit was gained - giving good views back across Strath Bran to Sgurr a'Mhuillin, the puzzling, pointed hill cropping up in many Morayshire coastal views. The northern side of my own hill proved much rougher than the trudgery-slopes above Achnasheen, and was split into two northern corries, Tolls Mor and Beag. The partitioning ridge was used as a descent route: a short-cut justified when another storm swept in just before the Land Rover track leading to the southern shore of Loch Fannich. Here I planned to camp.

First, though, came the day's most awkward obstacle - and one about which, like the electric fence way back on Stronend, I had completely forgotten. A huge red hydro-electric pipeline, seven feet in diameter, caterpillared its way across the watershed from the corries west of Fionn Bheinn: part of a scheme designed to supplement the east-flowing reservoir system.

Annoyingly - especially with rain now heavy enough to top up Loch Fannich of its own accord - my track was on the far side of the pipeline. I tried thrutching up the overhang onto an intake duct, but greasy-wet metal, lack of a chalk bag and weight of rucksack combined to pull me back down. Several attempts later I was resigned to a mile of bog-trotting to the loch-shore bridge - a miserable enough prospect in the torrential rain, but made even more onerous due to there being a tiny concrete hut only metres away across the cylindrical barricade. This would perhaps give shelter if only it could be reached. Then - *at last!* - came a place where gravel beneath the pipe's bulging belly had been washed away, allowing just enough room to burrow underneath, dragging gear behind. Soaked, covered in grit and dirt, head starting to throb, it was a relief to find the hut door secured only with string.

Although little bigger than a portaloo, windowless apart from a circular vent in the roof, cluttered with tins of industrial paint and sealant, the hut was itself sealed against wind and water - an ideal brew spot while hail lashed down. Needless to say, a couple of cups soon had me asleep - but on wakening I hadn't missed much: conditions outside were, if anything, even worse. Clouds raced through Srath Chrombuill at all kinds of levels and speeds, while a brief clearance only showed Sgurr nan Clach Geala, *white stone hill,* to be a snowy exaggeration of its name. I decided to stay put for the night. Even if thunderheads miraculously flattened to sheets of cirrus immediately, the ground outside would already be far too wet to allow a comfortable camp.

The storm-showers moved on overnight, leaving a morning sky of delicate cyan broken only by high, fluffy cumulus to the east. The snowfall had gone also, melted by the sun's first warming: the square summit of Slioch stood grey and imposing at the foot of Srath Chrombuill. With little packing needing done, I was soon wandering down the track toward the lochshore bog-flats, sad to leave my new-found bothy's straitjacket cosiness.

A grassy causeway led across a grid of drainage channels to drier ground on Beinn nan Ramh, *oar hill* - a name redolent of ancient fishing trips on Loch Fannich below. Here my predilection for steep ascents with the heavy sack was, for once, set aside. The two-mile ridge was so easy-angled, so smooth underfoot, as to be no more arduous than a stroll along a city street.

But what a street it would be! There were fantastic views westward to Slioch, its squareness now supplemented by a pinnacle-like eastern outlier: together they dominated a panorama also featuring the Torridons, the remote Lochan Fada hills and the high green loopings of the main Fannaichs to the north. Closer by, deer stood idly at my own summit before ambling off as I approached - only for a straggler to return and check, then panic and run on finding me still propped against the cairn! There were also two lizards within a minute: one alive, darting beneath a stone; one dead, brittle as a pottery cast of itself, glazed with turquoise.

Cars, windows glinted in the Kinlochewe sun away to the southwest, while less than two miles in the opposite direction stood the Nest of Fannich, a two-storey shooting lodge set among trees where I hoped to spend Tuesday night. It was hard to credit both this and my tiny painter's hut as coming under the heading of "bothy".

More easy going brought the headwaters of the Abhainn a'Chadh'Bhuidhe, main feeder for Loch Fannich. I couldn't face either of the two small tops at the point where the watershed swung northward towards Groban: the first, An Carnan, appeared to consist entirely of peat-hags; the second, Mointeach Leacaidh was shown on the map as home to sixteen lochans within a single square mile. Instead, I dropped into the ox-bowed glen, gulped a bottle's worth of water, then contoured the base of Meallan Chuaich - my next-hill-but-one - before plodding up 749m Groban, highest of these rounded tops.

The skyline was heartening. Even in the space of the morning Torridon had begun to drop back into insignificance, while far to the north, faintly, hazily visible beyond the Deargs, was a line of sharp peaks: Coigach. I felt a heart-leap of excitement. The west coast - and with it the watershed - was, at long last, nearing conclusion. Coigach was level with Conival - and Conival was where I hoped to gain first sight of the *north* coast.

Meallan Chuaich came easily after I cheated by dumping the sack beside a burn flowing from the Bealach na h-Imrich: *pass of leaving* - a sad, lingering name from the Clearances. A stray cloud drifted in at half-height to ensure the record of rain-at-some-point-for-the-past-seventeen-days had to be amended to eighteen. But even cagoule and gloves were soon discarded, weighted down with stones, once the shower passed and the afternoon regained warmth. Having allowed myself forty-five minutes for the round trip, I had to run downhill, gathering garments like a parkie chasing litter, to meet my self-imposed limit. Then the same length of time completed the descent along the Allt a'Ghleibh, past a wooded gorge to the head of Loch a'Bhraoin. Cows and walkers wandered golfcourse-green pastures at the water's edge - but with the one as uncommunicative as the other, I splashed straight across to Lochivraon.

This proved the dingiest hole since Ben Alder Cottage, the main room a dark, dirty, musty clutter of broken wood and decaying furniture. It looked and smelled as if cattle occasionally foraged inside - or perhaps the human/bovine analogy could be taken a stage further. I waited only for another shower to pass before going outside to find a flat stretch of grass.

Later, weather brightening, I chatted with two men heading to camp beneath the Fisherfield hills: visible from my tent door beyond acres of white-waving bog cotton. Not that I had quite finished my own walking for the day. Sunsets had thus far been conspicuously absent, with two tepid glows from the Campsies and Beinn Laoigh the only widescreen horizon efforts, while the Knoydart lightshows, fine though they were, suffered from

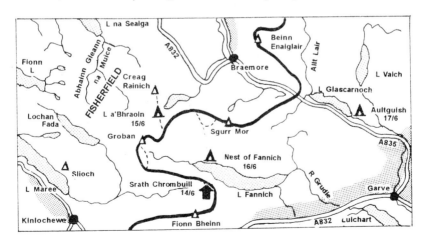

Fionn Bheinn - Beinn Enaiglair

191

being watched from the confines of the glens. Hence once cooking and letter-writing were completed, a pink flush growing across hills to the west had me hurrying, head down and determined, up the long slopes of 807m Creag Rainich immediately behind the bothy. It had been a short day's walk, after all.

Fifty-five minutes up, forty-five on top, thirty-five down. The middle section made it all worthwhile, sitting on a top just beyond the summit, feet dangling over a big drop, watching the golden glow spread across the northwest. An Teallach, with its huge bulk and cock's comb of pinnacles, dominated every other hill: silhouetted so black and featureless as to make invisible Shenavall and Strath na Selga at its foot. Beyond, islands and headlands stood clear against shining Minch waters, Gruinard Island and Greenstone Point easily identifiable. Further out came the long, low line of Lewis.

Both north and south were hidden in heavy cloud, blinkering the view and keeping attention fixed on the steadily sinking fireball in the northwest. This finally vanished into the sea with a momentary copper-green flash. Suddenly aware of starting to shiver as the temperature fell, remembering the need to regain the tent before light faded completely, I hurried down from my hard earned vantage point. The only pause was to watch a twin-engined jet high, high above, glinting silver in a second sunset, trailing white smoke-plumes across a sky as turquoise as the lizard on Beinn nan Ramh.

According to *Dwelly's Gaelic Dictionary*, the word *fannaich* means to grow weak, to become fatigued. This made it an odd name for a group of hills - "Won't be long dear, just off for a walk in the Knackereds" - but one which, after sixty-six days walking, now seemed remarkably apt. I was undoubtedly tiring, both physically and mentally, with any remaining eagerness chiefly taking the form of a general longing to finish, to put each new group of hills behind me, to get the job done. Short-term, there was only worrying dullness in my mind each morning on waking - an emptiness I knew wouldn't be filled by what I was to do that day.

This might sound strange with over four-fifths of the route complete. Surely by now I was in the home straight - or at least rounding the final bend? Yes, true enough, but a more relevant athletic analogy was that of the marathon runner's *wall*, the sudden physiological barrier which can almost floor someone in the latter stages of a race and transform the last few miles into a seemingly interminable treadmill. Now was the time I most feared the sudden appearance of its long-distance-walking counterpart.

There were, however, several factors still in my favour. The previous evening's sunset had reawakened perception of constant newness in the land - something with which I was in danger of losing touch. Despite having the whole wide world of the north as my home, I sensed an increasing lack of interest in things all around - surely a corollary to my drawing ever closer in on myself mentally. The sunset would certainly help delay this process. Also, the showery airflow governing the past few days seemed now to have moved on. The tent was oven-like on waking, marking the beginning of what was, at last, to prove a completely rainless summer's day.

Thirdly, the Fannaichs were the last group of hills of which any genuine knowledge could be claimed. Although hardly encyclopaedic, one previous visit ensured a degree of reassuring familiarity - like arriving at a job interview to discover you had once been for a drink with one of the panel. The Fannaichs were also the last genuine hill*walker's* hills. Everything beyond was a barren, stony wasteland where anyone arriving ill-prepared and ill-shod was in for a nasty shock. Comparisons were commonly made between the Fannaichs and Perthshire's Ben Lawers massif, and these were valid up to a point: each a high, back-to-back horseshoe ridge system, each six-Munros-in-a-day country. But the point came fairly early on. Here were no waymarked paths tripping down to walkways and car parks, no circle of roads covering for poor navigation, no well-drained corries easing the final miles of a long day. That said, in clear, dry conditions, the high, highly thought of Fannaichs constituted without doubt the most user-friendly hills of the north.

I planned splitting the group in two: a short hop over the western Munros of A'Chailleach and Sgurr Breac today followed by a longer haul across the main tops on Wednesday. In warm sunshine, wearing shorts for the first time since Knoydart, I had no ambitions beyond taking things easy.

Having cut a corner the previous evening, I now did so again by heading directly for the summit of A'Chailleach, *the old woman,* rather than back-tracking round to the gentler western flank. A hundred minutes accounted for the steeply concave slope, fine views all the while to the castellated buttress of Sron na Goibhre and back across Loch a'Bhraoin to An Teallach - now light and soft compared with its stark sunset blackness.

The summit view was even better, bringing the shock of the unexpected: far, far to the northeast, high above Sutherland moors, rose Ben Klibreck's distinctive cone. And away southward, beyond a still-prominent Cheesecake, a faint grey hump could only be Ben Nevis. Forty-five miles one way, sixty-five the other: not bad for a hazy, half-clear morning.

On along a broad ridge split by a groove-like channel, over an intermediate top to reach Sgurr Breac within the hour. Klibreck had now virtually disappeared, but was well compensated by the Cuillin's final bow, jutting over the left shoulder of Beinn Eighe.

The day's only other walkers - a young couple up from the road - were met on the path leading down to the 550m, massif-splitting pass. I thought of pushing on up the far side, over Sgurr nan Clach Geala to the A835 that evening, but to have done so would have tripled the length of the day - something even settled weather was incapable of encouraging. Besides, despite a stiff breeze on the tops, the west looking so hazily calm suggested another pleasant day tomorrow. I wandered down a path alternately boggy-dry-boggy to reach the Nest at two-thirty.

Having heard reports of this being the most commodious of all bothies, it was slightly disappointing to find half the rooms securely locked. Notices nailed to doors told visitors they were welcome one night only - which was perhaps partly why, on finishing a soup-and-cheese lunch, I opted to decant from the light, wood-panelled room with its views through to Slioch, and cart everything outside to camp on the meadow by the shore. Goodness knows what really provoked this, but the decision was certainly paid for in midge-bites later.

After-lunch drowsiness and a sore right big toe gave reason enough to shelve a silly notion to walk along the loch and climb Meall Gorm by its south ridge. I knew this to be counter-productive - the Creag Rainich sunset had more than used up the week's ration of off-route walking, and I might as well never have come down to the Nest if feeling so energetic - but the idea was only laid to rest completely once I had retreated to the sleeping-bag for a far more sensible plan: a siesta. This accounted for the afternoon, just as the cooking of chilli and the reading of an old *Observer* found indoors took up much of the evening. Then the breeze, westerly on pitching, swung to the east before, disastrously, dropping altogether. As it died, the midges came to life - and how!

It is difficult to convey the sheer anger and misery (or should it be midgery?) these minuscule black specks provoke. Suffice it to say I know people who would, as long as they live, only revisit the west coast in summer on pain of being coshed on the head and bundled there in chains. Wind, rain, snow, *donner und blitzen*: anything rather than have the blight of biters swarm around with their infuriating drill-whine, their ability to home-in on any millimetre of skin, however momentarily exposed.

194

A man who offered a lift the following evening told of there being 32,000 midges in every bush. Setting aside the fact of bushes hardly being the most common flora in the far north, there must have been half that number buzzing in my beard when I ventured out for a mid-evening pee - and the other half crawling around inside on my return. After a week in which wind had kept them at bay, they were now as bad as I could ever remember - a memory including August weeks in Glen Brittle and Arran.

I eventually retreated to the bothy, cursing not having been there all along, before dashing back outside to bring the gear indoors - whereupon the little monsters disappeared completely! Maybe it was the slight stirring of a breeze, maybe the temperature drop as another glorious sunset glowed yellow behind Slioch. Whatever the reason, they vanished as dramatically as had the big Shiel Bridge wind. Filled with a certain trepidation, I decided to risk losing another pound of flesh: I stayed out in the tent.[1]

The morning failed, thankfully, to bring more midges, but did bring wind and cloud racing in from the northwest. One glance was enough to send me packing. By nine I was across the bridge and hurrying back up the pass.

Despite the forbidding conditions, soft light settled in bright patches on the slopes - although to reach the pass was to be greeted by An Teallach smothered under a cushion of cloud. This almost provoked rejection of a plan to pop up off-route Sgurr nan Each before going over Sgurr nan Clach Geala, thus making Sgurr Mor the walk's fiftieth Munro. Contrived perhaps, but also fitting, it being the last hill of its height. The final decision was delayed by heading straight for the Clach Geala/Each col - before, with cloud still just clear of the tops, the sack was dumped and the extra hill climbed. Not that much more than minimum effort was required, Each's relationship to its higher neighbour being akin to that of Beinn Tulaichean to Cruach Ardrain: more outlying top than separate peak.

Clach Geala was easy too, although cloud now swirled down around the ridge. The earlier softness had hinted the day held no real malice however, and seconds after reaching the pointed summit overlooking a steep, stepped, snow-filled eastern corrie, whiteness drew back to reveal a now-clear An Teallach and a jauntily-angled Stac Pollaidh beyond.

---

[1] The beautiful Nest bothy was, sadly, destroyed by fire in December 1989.

Walking returned to the relaxed enjoyment of yesterday. Carn na Criche came and went - a nondescript top until the 250m crag plunging almost sheer into Loch a'Mhadaidh was seen - then I stood to hear deer clatter the screes beside the Allt a'Choire Mhor far below before turning to Sgurr Mor's final steep cone.

Fifteen minutes saw me kick the cairn of this great northern landmark, then sit down to lunch with a younger man wearing tracksuit and trainers. Remembering how chuffed I had been at having my own intentions correctly guessed at Kinbreack, I voiced a sudden hunch by enquiring if he was attempting the fastest-ever round of Munros. I was right, too! He had set off from Ben Hope on Sunday, with hopes of reaching Ben More on Mull within seventy days. Fifteen of the 277 hills had already been chalked-off, a further six to come that afternoon. His two companions soon joined us: climbing only occasionally, they mainly provided supplies and support. A happy hour was spent swapping stories and plans.

We parted with handshakes and mutual Good Lucks, then I distractedly wandered down and over Beinn Liath Mhor Fannaich. Here, once away from the twin-cairned summit, the going became much rougher. The grey, stony ground from which both this hill and neighbouring Beinn Liath Bheag were named was more a of type with the hills north of the A835 - reached at the head of Loch Droma in late afternoon sunlight.

I needed to visit the Aultguish Inn, five miles eastward, where a parcel containing food, clothes and maps awaited, having been deposited by Bridget and Duncan - part of the Loch Ericht entourage - at Easter. If it had

felt strange then, as I spent the weekend in Moffat, to think of people helping out so far ahead in both distance and time, it felt even stranger now to think of all that had happened since. Strange, that was, only until the receptionist handed over the carrier-bag, when I was suddenly interested in nothing other than gleefully rushing off to rediscover its contents!

With a night in the hotel beyond my means, I camped at the east end of Loch Glascarnoch. This differed from most east ends in being attractive and well kept, the elegantly curved grassed-over wall of the huge hydro dam towering above.

I later returned to the hotel - beyond which Ben Wyvis stood as a huge, natural dam wall at the foot of the glen - and treated myself to a bar supper: soup, scampi, crème caramel. A couple also down from the Fannaichs came over as I sat watching TV in the lounge. They were from Parwich, near Ashbourne: the third Derbyshire couple met on the walk, and this after years of never having encountered anyone from my old haunts! They kindly sold stamps and took letters to post. After the rigours of the four-day stretch since Gerry's, it was fine to spend an evening in good company and a comfortable armchair, well clear of midges. I arranged to return for breakfast next morning.

With the benefit of hindsight, this was a day of landmarks and endings. The fiftieth Munro, the last previously visited hill, the last people encountered on a hill, the last time for a whole week when I would feel genuinely happy. But only half of these were known at the time, and even they were of little concern. I was simply glad at having reached the end of another section, slightly uncertain as to the wisdom of pushing straight on into the Deargs tomorrow: in so doing I would commit myself to eight days without a break. It was a decision I preferred to leave until morning. By then, a good night's sleep and another look at the weather might clarify the situation. For now, all I knew was I felt - well, pretty fannaiched!

To move or to stay? I still didn't know. While a layer of high, furrowed cloud and a grey, gentle filtering of sunlight said Go, a heaviness in arms and legs argued strongly for No. But what else was there to do? Although the whole day could be dozed away at the dam, resources wouldn't run to both breakfast and supper at the hotel - and, with only five days' worth of food to see me through to Oykel Bridge, it would be a big risk to run supplies right down to the wire. What if I became stormbound for a couple of days? Almost by default the decision was made to press on. This next batch of hills needed crossing sometime, and it made sense to start in dry, light-winded conditions, tiredness or no.

After an extortionate hotel breakfast - £4 for a minimalist fry-up - I jammed in all the fresh supplies. These, packed before I knew my needs, included too few instant foods, too many clothes. I then hitched back up the road before climbing through small crags onto the day's first, unnamed, top. At 497m, this marked the end of an exceptionally long, gentle ridge snaking down from Beinn Enaiglair, which would occupy fully three hours before its high point gave the bombshell view down Loch Broom to hazily distant Summer Isles.

On a promontory far below stood the white houses and hotels of Ullapool, flecks of brightness against a grey background. There too were coaches swarming like bees around the tourist honey-pot of the Corrieshalloch Gorge, and the high Fannaichs, yesterday's hills, half-draped in cloud as though re-covered in dust-sheets now I had passed through and inspected them.

Today's quota was cloud-free, patches of soft sunlight falling through slots of blue sky: conditions on the improve. With much remaining to be done, lunch was pared back to raisins chewed on the steep, cautious descent to the head of the Allt Mhucarnaich and a stalker's path encircling the hill. A branch of this having earlier served me well on the crest of the long ridge, another offshoot - all the more appreciated for not being marked on the map - now did even better. Superbly drained, cleverly angled and kerbed with stones, it corkscrewed up Iorguill onto the main body of the Deargs. Not that there was any shortage of stones to build such paths: hillsides were more grey than green now, the upper slopes a slithering, clattering wilderness of large-scale scree.

Beyond Iorguill came the ridge of Diollaid a'Mhill Bhric: a mile-long scraggy face above the River Lael. Here was a drystane dyke longer, higher, more complete than either its Garbh Chioch or South Cluanie counter-parts, running along the watershed until clinging to the corrie cliff-top just before the summit of Beinn Dearg itself. A huge cairn crowned the most northerly land in Britain above 1000m.

Although cloudy overhead, views westward were excellent: light was already low and penetrating despite it being barely four o'clock. The horizon held a complexity I didn't bother trying to tease out, preferring instead the confusion of the unknown.

Having spent more than five hours over the day's first Munro, the next two took only an hour apiece. But I was tired now, tired and slow, trudging over Meall nan Ceapraichean and Eididh nan Clach Geala in a semi-somnolent state doing scant justice to a marvellous piece of land. Retained impressions were merely vague and general: black crags crumbling beneath the summit of Dearg; the wall beside me again, high and sturdy; seeing it loop and lope across the undulating plateau like a scaled-down replica of its great Chinese counterpart; setting foot in snow for the last time; the plateau a great grey sea of rock across which I floundered to rest on green islets of turf.

On the second top, *the web of white stones,* I felt as tired as I had ever known myself to be. The day had been no longer than many others - 2000m of ascent, ten miles distance - but the very fact of there having been *so many* others made this one particularly exhausting. I knew the last of the Dearg Munros - Seana Bhraigh, *the old grey slopes* - was beyond me. It lay three miles northward across more rough-rock ground. If I tried to go there, I too would become old and grey.

So down it had to be, although even that was tiring. The first flat ground was always going to suffice - and, as lochans were by definition flat, I headed straight for the string of watery beads in Coire an Lochain Sgeirich. Here, 700m up, I cleared a smattering of stones just as I normally kicked away sheep droppings and twigs, then pitched on a tiny, poor-soiled square of grass. A bumpy site, open to any weather blowing in from the west, but it would do. I collapsed inside, cooked the fastest meal of the trip, crashed into sleep through walls of sheer exhaustion.

Not that the day was yet over. Around eleven I was woken by the gruff, low-pitched growl of a wildcat somewhere to the rear of the tent. I dived outside, never having seen this most evasive of Highland beasts despite many times crossing four-toed tracks in snow. But the creature was too quick, the evening already too dark for my clumsy efforts: there was no sign of life in the stony recesses of the corrie. No life, that was, unless the sky counted a living thing, for the red glow of a sunset was building over slopes to the north.

Exhaustion temporarily forgotten, I pulled on clothes and scrambled fifteen minutes onto Meall Glac an Ruighe - the nearest available high point - to be marvellously rewarded. A wispy layer of cloud billowed like dry ice across the glen below as thick red sun-colours spread over the Coigach peaks to the northwest. The whole world came alive with intense, fiery crimsons, oranges, mauves and countless shades and subtleties between. Only the silver windings of the River Douchary far below remained unignited as the sun thickened to such a burning red it could almost be stared at without fear of eye-damage. On some ancient evening such as this, Beinn Dearg, *red hill,* would have gained its name.

A sense of unreality was accentuated not only by lingering drowsiness from the evening's sleep, but certainty in my being totally alone in the experience. It was as if the day, the walk, the tiredness, all were momentarily justified by one marvellous, mysterious sight. If Monday's sunset had been exquisitely precise in form, a quietly beautiful sonata, this was, by contrast, sweepingly symphonic, layered with power and emotion, impressive in complexity.

Fifteen, maybe twenty minutes passed before the sky burnt itself out and the sun slipped behind a low bank of cloud over the Minch. Suddenly the redness, the fire were gone: the land was grey, cold, unwelcoming once more. *How could it ever have been any different?* Tiredness returned as I hurried, deep in thought, back down bouldery slopes into the corrie. But I was hurrying too from the vastness of the world beyond: all I now wanted was my own small tent. In a distant echo of the Loch Skeen starscape, thought of benightment on the open hillside suddenly scared me more than I could ever recall.

So much for a red sky at night. I woke to the sound of light rain and the sight of slurry-grey cloud swirling outside the tent door. The late evening mist which made such a memorable sunset had, unfortunately, stayed put. Worse was to follow on realising both my sleeping-bag and the end of the tent inner were soaked. In the tired confusion of pitching, I had failed to notice the inner and fly being in contact: a beginner's error punished by my supposed shelter now being transformed into a dripping hovel. This depressed me immediately - literally putting a damper on the late evening elation - such that instead of being packed neatly in their usual places, everything was bundled haphazardly into the rucksack with not a care for the niceties of common sense. It was a disconsolate walker who turned his back on the flattened rectangle of grass: the weather wasn't alone in being miserable.

At least the seriousness of the situation concentrated the mind. I quickly realised a little pre-planning would potentially save hours of wayward wandering in rain and mist. I stopped again, sat on the rucksack, took out the map, memorised a series of bearings: to the crossing of a stalker's path, to a lochan, to the 804m Meall a'Choire Ghlais, to the lip of the Cadha Dearg corrie, to the twin summits of Seana Bhraigh.

This, against all expectations, worked well - and spirits began to lift even though cloud stayed clamped down. Once the corrie headwall was reached, I knew the worst to be past. A brief, short-sighted clearance showed a remembered rock formation, confirming my position - although it was still difficult to believe this dour, drab place had glowed golden as molten lava only hours before.

Scrapings of deer-track led to Seana Bhraigh itself - fifty-fifth and penultimate Munro and a hill which, more than most, I had hoped to have clear. The open, peak-dotted wilderness to the northwest and the nearby geometrically-straight edge of Creag an Duine placed this among the most

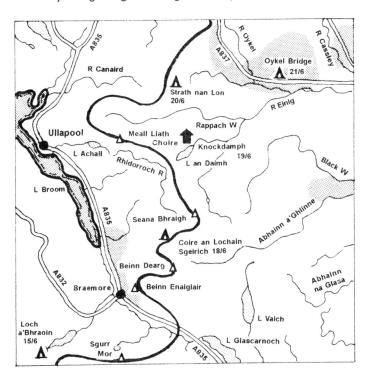

Sgurr Mor Fannaich - Strath Oykel

celebrated of all summit outlooks. But today there was only five-metre-ahead dampness and the frustrating sight of a shelter cairn facing the wrong way to be of any help against the elements.

At least the concentration required to find the summit had made the two-hour ascent pass quickly. The remaining two-thirds of the day, mainly downhill, ought to be considerably easier - plus they held the prize of another remote bothy at their end. There was solace, too, in unexpectedly popping out of cloud only 100m below the summit - albeit into a landscape dull with greys and greens. As on Beinn Laoigh, the weather had been playing dirty tricks on my high camp: conditions were merely mediocre rather than bad.

Bands of stones, a peaty col, upended strata led onto Meall nam Bradhan - a slabby-ridged hill where Seana Bhraigh at last granted views of its magnificent, below-summit corrie. Ahead lay very different country: the green woods of Glen Achall and the Rhidorroch River, which would dominate tomorrow's walk. All this was western water, due to enter Loch Broom at Ullapool itself - while that to the east wended via the Corriemulzie, Einig and Oykel rivers to the Kyle of Sutherland, thence the Dornoch Firth. Sometime yesterday afternoon, high on the plateau when I had been too tired to notice, the feeders of the previous firth, Cromarty, had finally been left behind.

A Land Rover track crossing to Strath Mulzie eased the descent past Lochan Badan Glasliath. Then a faint stalker's path - continually lost among plaitings of deer track - led round the shoulder of Mullach a'Bhrian Leitir above a long splinter of a lochan, too narrow to be depicted as anything other than a river on the map. I was tiring again, and boggy ground offered little assistance, but eventually the grey waters of Loch an Daimh came into view. Home for the night was less than two miles of well made track away.

At a boathouse at the head of the loch (virtually on the watershed), I chatted with a young couple - honeymooners? - strolling from a nearby shooting lodge. They had been over An Teallach the previous day, but evidently harboured no such plans now: there could hardly have been greater contrast between my unkempt scruffiness and their spotless white sweatshirts!

The lochside track was literally that, keeping right to the water's edge. Not that I complained: for the second consecutive day lochs were noted as conveniently flat when legs were tired. Knockdamph soon appeared, chimneys first. Unsurprisingly in this empty quarter, no-one else was around. With the downstairs floor too cobbled and rough for sleeping, I dragged everything into the cosy upper room before settling to read *I Samuel* in the bothy bible: a gory story for such a peaceful place. The only other reading matter was the bothy book - as opposed to the bothy Good Book - with its 1979 entry from Hamish Brown and his dog Storm, along with numerous tales of people tarzaning from trees to extricate firewood from the gorge behind the building. I was only the fourth visitor in nineteen June days.

Tired and slow-minded, I managed to melt the plastic coating on the kettle handle by turning the gas valve too high while making soup. Sleep seemed the best bet, so I chased away a sheep head-butting the front door, then brought in the now-dry sleeping-bag and turned in early. My own entry in the bothy book contained, along with the usual details, remarks on loneliness and readiness to go home. But the seven days of walking which would allow precisely that were beginning to feel insurmountable. As the old saying goes, night is always darkest in the hour before dawn.

Even sleep was losing its appeal. I was sweating and shaky on waking in the grey morning light, confused as to my surroundings, convinced as to the reality of a nightmare which had me strapped into a wheelchair. The fact of this being my first dream in weeks capable of being recalled made fears all the more vivid, and it was only on stepping outside I fully came to my senses. Not that the morning invoked much cheer either: heavy saggings of cloud seemed to vie with each other to deposit the largest, most malicious waterbombs on the bothy. There were three direct hits in the few minutes I stood and watched before retreating upstairs for breakfast in bed.

But by eleven, while the all-clear hadn't exactly sounded, there was a definite hint of blue in the northwest and tear-sized droplets had reduced to a vaporiser-fine smirr. I set off back toward Glen Achall, not on yesterday's track but along a higher, less stony-rough alternative contouring the pudding-hill of Cnoc Damh from which the bothy took its name. From here it was merely a traipse over grass to reach the 396m summit and viewpoint cairns of Creag Ruadh.

I was at last nearing the line of the Moine Thrust and entering the largest exposure of limestone in Scotland. This manifested itself in small, knobbly hills rising from a gentle plateau like dots on a page of braille. Nothing today would exceed 550m in height, and only the first two ascents were of any length - but with lower ground invariably giving heavier going, I knew these twelve miles would require as much effort as many a more impressive-sounding day.

Disciplining myself to stop only on summits and major cols did the trick (and helped with food rationing), such that with the afternoon brightening and plover calling from every slight hollow, the roll call of hills was slowly ticked off: Creag Ruadh, Creag Ghrianach, Meall Liath Choire, Meall an Eich Ghlais, Beinn Donuill, Cnoc a'Choilich, Na Dromannan. With so many subsidiary tops, and with the ground so uneven, I had occasionally to compass-check which lump I was actually on!

The third - and highest - hill, Meall Liath Choire, was undoubtedly the finest: bolstered by a small water-black crag, giving grand views of An Teallach: clear and jaggy, its corries streaked with snow. But while the views really kept me going today - Ben More Coigach's chocolate-brown wall of scree, Stac Pollaidh's impudent angles, the gradual approach of a totally surreal Suilven - even these failed to fire the burst of enthusiastic acceleration they would have done earlier. The same was true of the profusion of frogs underfoot and deer watching from low skylines. Once these would have been greeted with interest and curiosity; now they just seemed commonplace and dull.

Downheartedness was reinforced by the loneliness of the land. If forced to nominate the least visited of all watershed hills, the short leet would include three or four of today's quota. Lacking any great height, shape or remoteness, surrounded by many far more famous peaks, only the most ardently unorthodox of walkers would struggle not to be deterred by this quiet backwater. Even the likeliest ascendees - stalkers and their clients - would have little reason to seek out actual summit cairns. Years may have passed without visits, and the possibility of my having been the first person to string them together in this way was surely nearer likelihood than conjecture.

If, however, anyone had, they would surely have dropped down to broad Strath nan Lon feeling less tired than I did now. Although surprisingly dry underfoot, the final two miles between the Lochanan nan Sailean Beaga, over the long grassy slope to the river, took me across the grain of the hill and necessitated numerous annoying little climbs over furrows in the strata. At least the river gave no problems. Once across, I was soon camped beside an old ruined croft.

I was desperately tired once more. The stag standing bellowing outside the tent in a display of boldness usually reserved for the rut, and the view back to Seana Bhraigh and Creag an Duine - the latter balancing a circle of cloud on its sharp summit like a circus trickster spinning a plate on a stick - these were less akin to my mood than the hordes of midges I spent over an hour killing after a late trip outside.

Suddenly I felt I was struggling. Whereas a long spell without a recuperative break had been just within the bounds of my ability in the Central Belt and Knoydart, now the days weighed heavily, each hill more a millstone than the milestone it ought to have been. I was seriously doubting whether I could walk the final week to Cape Wrath.

But the downward spiral had to bottom out sometime, and it was ironic that June 21st, longest day of the year in terms of daylight, was to provide the darkest hours of the entire walk. Fears I would, eventually, reach the stage of being sick of the sight of hills, of losing touch with the very motivation for the walk in the first place, were today realised. I reached my lowest ebb.

Such things still lay ahead when I woke to a steel-grey sky and flatness of light warning of rain to come. Midges for once gave peace as I packed, and by mid-morning I was resting on Meall a'Bhuirich Rapaig - only 474m high, but the day's upper limit. Apart from the Kippen-Drymen trek and the flatlands of the Central Belt proper, this was the lowest high point of any walking day. The view west was clear and startling. For all the impressiveness of Cul Mor and Cul Beag, Suilven now stole the show: a sandstone spire towering over the smaller, nearer Cromalt Hills like a cathedral rising above slum-street rooftops. Gillean, Liathach, An Teallach might, I thought, be finer hills to climb - not least because their extra height offered more scope for variation - but in terms of appearance alone Suilven was surely the single most spectacular natural object in these islands.

I took a photo of Elphin village: a fertile island of lime-rich farmland which Frank Fraser Darling noted as a "geological emerald" - a lovely, if slightly tautological description. There too was the Ullapool/Kylesku road junction at Ledmore, yet I felt none of the usual elation at being reintroduced to humanity. Having been heavy-legged since the very start of the day's walk, the first indication of its end was greeted only with dull relief. *One top more, then you can go down.*

The one top more was Cnoc na Glas Choille, a slightly craggier moorland swelling criss-crossed with fenceposts. Here I ate my last non-dehydrated food before setting off down to the A837. New forestry diggings delayed arrival: it was wearily ! finally flopped onto a grassy roadside bank. The final section of the eight-day crossing from Glen Docherty had taken less than four hours, yet I felt completely, utterly done in.

The Oykel Bridge Hotel, location of a supply parcel, stood seven miles to the east - but, in strict accordance with Sod's Law, all traffic was heading the wrong way, including a Beetle-driving New Zealand couple who stopped to ask the name of Suilven. With both rain and an estate dog threatening, I plodded slowly down the road, calculating the current rate of progress combined with the need for rest breaks would entail anything up to a four-hour walk.

A lift finally came after half this - two men heading for Perth - and the thought flashed through my mind I half-wished to be going with them. Rain started as I was dropped at the hotel, standing beside the main road bridge crossing of the longest river in the northern Highlands. This was trout and salmon country par excellence (or should it be parr excellence?), the hotel a paradise for wealthy anglers and bon viveurs. £50 per night contrasted amusingly with my £70 for seventy-one nights' accommodation thus far - especially on remembering Duncan's story of how, on delivering the parcel, the manager had said "Ah yes, we know Mr Hewitt well: he stays here often"!

It was amusing, too, to stand in the thick-piled foyer in old clothes, with a bell-boy dispatched for the parcel. This reclaimed, I escaped to the recommended camping place beside the "Quarry Pool", a nearby loop in the river looking distressingly like the midge-equivalent of five-star luxury. But I was too tired to be bothered by anything - or so I thought - and wandered back along the road to phone Julia and John. This done - it was great to hear familiar voices again - I went into the public bar for a couple of drinks before retreating back to bed.

Then things seemed to go badly wrong. It was as though a number of small, insignificant-in-themselves factors combined to take me through a threshold of depression - or, more appropriately, across a beguilingly gentle watershed in my attitude towards the walk. For starters, there suddenly no longer seemed anything amusing in the stark juxtaposition of my material poverty with the lavish opulence of the hotel. Then there was the stifling stillness of an appallingly midge-ridden evening: I almost suffocated inside my cagoule hood trying to avoid being eaten alive while returning to the tent. Then there was the rain - suddenly, torrentially justifying the cagoule but cursed, not thanked, for so doing. And then there was realisation of this being the summer solstice - and that both it, and I, were gloomy as hell.

But later, looking back - and such was the depression it was a look back in anguish - I perceived the camel's back broken by the main part of my burden every bit as much as by these final straws. This burden had accumulated steadily, day-by-day, week-by-week, to become a top-heavy mass of bulging, burgeoning frustrations. Throughout the walk, problems had tended to be railroaded rather than rationalised: some, like the shoestring budget, simply laughed off; others - loneliness, the vagaries of the weather - over-zealously relished with something approaching religious fervour. Still others - the footsore first week, the persistent undernourishment - had been all but ignored, while both the Beinn a'Chuirn fall and the all-pervasive tiredness since Shiel Bridge had received the mental equivalent of a bodyswerve.

And now I found myself, for the first time, questioning my commitment. I had had enough of this shambition: I had become obsessed, addicted, fixated - and now wanted to be cured, to be free. For almost a year I had constructed, with painstaking single-mindedness, the towering edifice of the walk: first the groundwork, then the actual bricks-and-mortar, the walking itself. During all this time my gaze had hardly wandered, such that I had become blinkered, too entrapped in my own invention to notice how insular and isolated I now was.

I tried dwelling on the walk's more positive aspects: the support of friends, the friendship of strangers, what for want of a better phrase could be called my closeness to nature, the exceptional level - for me at least - of physical fitness. Yet the first three of these seemed only to point to the precedence of people over places - and consequently to the dehumanised barrenness of the hills and ultimate pointlessness of what I was doing. The Kinloch Hourn road wasn't Britain's longest cul-de-sac: the watershed was, and I had spent over seventy days ambling blithely up it, away from my real loves,

home and friends. And as for fitness, time was long gone when this brought *joie de vivre* to override all difficulties. The eight-day stretch just completed had left me hollow, the fitness just a brittle shell, a veneer covering an inside eaten away and eroded.

I suppose that night I suffered some kind of breakdown - although not in the commonly-perceived mental or physical sense, more in terms of momentum, in the drive which had kept me going so long. Just as a car cruising along the motorway breaks down - internal strains and stresses hidden under the bonnet until an abrupt manifestation of unexpected difficulties - so I was losing power, juddering toward a halt, frantically signalling to be allowed out of the fast lane onto the hard shoulder of static safety.

Lying there in the tent, mind restless when it should have been resting, I recalled a real vehicle: the proffered lift to Perth. From then on I could see only one way to relieve the pressure. It was so easy: come morning I would pack my ambitions along with my tent, shoulder pride along with the rucksack, head south to home and friends.

The final straw. Hitting the wall. Crisis of confidence. Call it what you will, I felt my wit's end had been reached before my walk's end. Only in the small hours, with midsummer daylight starting to filter through the tent walls, did my mind ease its racing and allow me to lapse into sleep.

9: Just and no more
(Monday 22nd June - Tuesday 30th June)

*H*ome. I have talked to myself a lot recently, and now wake with this most potent of words again on my lips. Home. I want to go home. Little seems changed from the previous evening: conditions outside remain dismally half-lit, clingingly damp, swarming with midges. Conditions inside are also much the same: I'm still chaotically - and, I fear, chronically - depressed. Having mentally rather than physically hit the wall, all I now want is to turn my face toward it.

There is none of the disciplined morning routine marking the start of virtually every watershed day thus far: no pulling-on of boots to step out for a stretch and a wash, no search for matches to light the stove for a brew. I lie inert, enervated, half-awake and only half wanting awake, mind still turning and turning in ever-tightening circles: a small boat caught in a whirlpool, sucked ever more dangerously down.

But things *are* different. They have to be: time has passed. The tide-race of thoughts has slackened - as all tide-races eventually must - and while a heavy swell still churns my brain, I sense things are becoming easier. For all my demoralisation, I know now is the time to get a grip, regain control, steer for the dimly-perceived harbour of safe emotional stability.

I lie quietly and listen: a car drives past, a bird sings, the rain eases. I smell the fresh morning smell of wet grass. Signs of life. Signs of a life beyond my own internalised, inhibited constriction of a life. For the first time in several days a degree of objectivity filters back into my thinking, and with it a degree of optimism. I see - complete and all in a moment, just as I had seen the Kintail walking plan while still in Knoydart - that although a time-span of twelve weeks is considerably nearer the dreary mainland of permanence than any romantic island of temporality, the crux of my problem lies not so much in the walk's magnitude as its sheer inescapability.

It is time to give myself a good talking to. *Look you idiot! Pull yourself together. You're acting as though you're depressed at the very fact of being depressed, as though you imagine you can get through without any low points. What do you think this is: a joyride? A jaywalk? It's twelve weeks of hard graft, damn you! OK, OK, so for the past week you've been lower than before and last night really put the cap on things. Well, that's over and done with: now you've a choice. You either lie back and wallow in your own unhappiness or bounce back just as you did with the fall. If this is your nadir, things can only get better. Almost all the hard work's done: there are only five walking days left, and you can go somewhere to recuperate before then. You're not tied to the watershed on rest days, remember! So don't just lie there, do something! Get out. Take a break. But for God's sake don't go home.*

Writing up the log also helps: soon a form of contentment starts seeping back like feeling into fingers on a cold morning. Degree by slow degree, depression thaws. There is distraction, too, in considering where to go for a break. The only real criterion is for it to be a town, and this gives two main options. Either I hitch some thirty miles back over the watershed to Ullapool, or twenty miles eastward to Lairg. The latter gets the vote not simply through being nearer: lying in the east coast lowland strip, it will provide a physical escape from high hill country. This proves my best, most clear-minded decision in a long while.

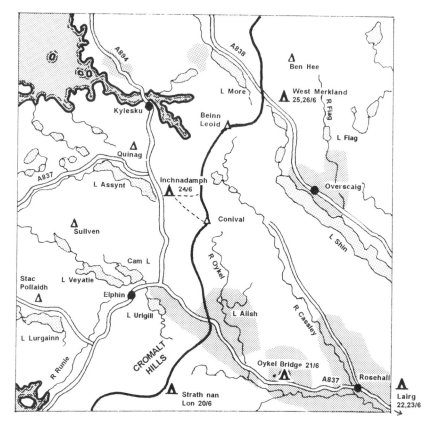

Strath Oykel - Loch Merkland

With the road desperately quiet - only two cars in the first half-hour - the modicum of cobbled-together morale starts dissolving back into frustration and self-doubt. Another proffered lift to Perth will still tempt me. Eventually, though, two lifts take me to Lairg, with the drivers, simply through the medium of normal conversation, making me feel more at ease with myself. In so doing they take on the role of Andy Dempster way back on Beinn Achallader. I'm much happier as I wander up Lairg main street to Kenny's Campsite and Freezer Centre - hoping the two won't prove synonymous.

Best of all, though, is Lairg itself. The small town, bleakly windswept, spindly with roads, is the largest place entered since Cumbernauld, fifty-eight days earlier. I arrive at eleven, the street busy with locals buying messages, visiting the post office or just standing around in twos and threes "having a news". It is great to be among ordinary people doing ordinary things. I feel again the extra dimension human warmth gives to my arrival in every village, hostel or pub - and which no number of hills, however spectacular, can ever hope to emulate.

The campsite is hard - and it feels odd pitching just as everyone else leaves - but I'm soon inside eating a cold lunch of sardines and chopped ham from Prestos. With damp, dreary conditions discouraging any afternoon activity, I sleep until evening, then sit in the Sutherland Arms to study the last of the maps: Sheet 9 - Cape Wrath. Magical number, magical name! Now, although I have long known only five more walking days will bring the great sea-cliff, to suddenly see it in the cartographical equivalent of black-and-white comes as something of a shock. I trace the days with my finger, just to be sure. Over Conival to Inchnadamph: *one*. Back over Beinn Leoid to Loch Merkland: *two*. Leave the gear to cross Meall Horn and hitch back round: *three*. Foinaven to Gualin House: *four*. Small hills and the Moor of Parph to the Cape: *five*. And a rest day with the Tain folk between three and four.

For the first time since the high Fannaichs I feel the old drive reassert itself - an eagerness boosted even further by phoning Michelle and being told she is planning to drive up, with a couple of friends, to Durness on Monday. They will collect me from the lighthouse next day.

Another sign of forces being mentally regrouped for the final assault comes in fresh weather worries. This aspect of the walk has largely passed me by during the last few days - partly because, sunsets excepted, conditions have been at their most grey and dull, partly through my having been too tired and logistically committed to really care. Only when there is scope for variation in what I'm doing - as with "floating" rest days - are the whims of the weather of particular interest. Other times it is merely a case of sufferance or enjoyment.

There is slight room for manoeuvre today, and on each of several occasions when I wake through the night it is to find myself in something of a quandary. If the weather suddenly improves, should I hitch back up and tackle Conival immediately, or stay here in Lairg a second night? The former is, I know, an option bordering on foolishness: I have time in hand, energy to recoup, a tentful of food needing eaten. But, as ever, restlessness gnaws, and it is with relief for my own peace of mind that the choice never becomes a live issue. On finally waking in the morning, I hear rain pouring into pools and puddles on the campsite, a state of affairs to continue for much of the day. The watershed, like Wimbledon and the Lord's test, is rained off - yet is surely the only one of the three great events where downpour isn't greeted with dismay.

Thus the only static Tuesday of the walk becomes a day devoted more to rest than action, the latter confined to a dash into town for a paper and a greasily poky poke of chips, then a lochshore stroll in a brief dry spell.

The afternoon is again slept away, waking only to listen to the busy noises of the town. I sense I'm starting to rediscover my enjoyment of the walk after a miserable week. My appetite for walking is certainly back: hollow emptiness on finishing the eight-day stretch now transformed into impatient hunger for the last great feast of hills. All that remains is for the weather to dry up during the night. Then, having spent the past couple of days making a mountain out of a molehill, I will return up Strath Oykel to set about changing things back into real rock-and-water mountains again.

I even sleep better than of late: no bad dreams, no tossing and turning, nothing. And, when I wake at seven-thirty, it is to the sound of birdsong in the trees: a good sign, as is the patch of blue sky directly overhead. Jam and pâté sandwiches are hurriedly spread, excess food presented to bemused caravaners next door, and by nine I'm standing at Black Bridge hitching both west- and south-bound roads: either are feasible routes back to the hill.

It is not long before I'm away - in a huge black Granada driven by a London couple who kindly offer to take me further than their destination at Rosehall. The car has a lovely lived-in feel - worn seats, scattered fag ends, maps and papers shoved into corners - and sparks memories of the succession of Ford Zephyrs in which my father ferried us around when we were wee. Now, as then, we dawdle along so slowly that the twenty-mile journey takes nearly an hour - but I'm glad of the company. They are genuinely interested in the walk, such that by the time we reach the top of the road, I'm almost as sad to leave the car as I had been Lairg earlier. The one feels like a mobile extension of the other.

With a long day ahead, I ignore the up-and-down climb of little Cnoc Chaornaidh and head northeast along a track to Loch Ailsh. A branch soon usefully slants into the upper reaches of an immature forest before giving out a mile or so short of the foot of Meall a'Bhraghaid.

A long, stiff slope stretches ahead, unusual in omitting all the standard intermediate stages of short grass and tussocks, switching instead from long-grassed bog to dwarf vegetation within 50m or so. This helps counteract a rigidity and lack of rhythm in legs which only fades completely once on the stony wilderness of the summit plateau - where the very nature of the terrain itself prevents establishment of free-flowing, easy-going movement. Anywhere else, the lessening of the gradient could be described as producing a gentler slope, but here, the more the angle throttles-back, the more like demolition-site rubble the ground becomes.

Four-fifths of the remaining days are to be on this type of rock, the country's highest exposure of gneiss. Pronounced *nice* - although the actual walking is far too rough for such a genteel-sounding word - gneiss is one of the oldest of all rock forms, and, like many old things, deeply reclusive. Apart from this northwestern corner and the outer Hebridean isles, most is buried far beneath the surface. Hence to see it out and about comes as something of a shock after the grey-green moorland days since Seana Bhraigh. The same is also true of tightening contours as the hills close in for one last crescendo of climbing. Even with cloud ominously curling round Suilven's sharp top, it feels good to be back in big country.

Soon the western hills are gone altogether, the well-named Dubh Loch Beag, *little dark loch,* blackening beneath its semi-circle of crag to a pool of spilt ink. Overhead darkens too, combining with the landscape's eerie ferocity to produce another brief reprise of self-doubt and shaky

confidence. Then the thought *In a week you'll be home* flashes through my mind like a subliminal TV image, and I take out the compass, take a bearing onto Breabag, march on across shards of loose stones tinkling underfoot like crockery in a poorly packed box.

Ground deteriorates along with weather as I cross Meall a'Bhraghaid, the southeastern top - marked by the white glare of a snowpatch - and navigate the two miles over Creag Liath. Occasional swirling clearances show grim darkness all around, until even these become fewer and fewer as rain comes on and cloud clamps down. Breabag Tarsuinn is all slabs, boulders, ribs of rock, making the climb much easier than the descent - but at least arrival on the twisted green col before Conival coincides with a clearance. I eat lunch as patches of watery sunlight yellow the vast scree-wall of Ben More Assynt, wondering if I have prematurely written off the day. Is there hope of salvage even yet?

No chance. Sunlight sinks without trace, as does all sign of Conival's broken southwest flank - up which I climb over runnels and ribbons of scree as rain starts to pour down. By the time the angle turns into the wind at the junction with the southeast ridge, conditions are every bit as bad as on Ben Alder in mid-May. Now, as then, the urge to climb drives me on just as surely as the rain itself drives down, with the struggle over a series of stark, black, looming towers almost perversely relished. There is scrambling - some bare-rock steepenings are exposed, although to what degree remains clouded in mystery - and gusts rasp the hill's sharp edge like a butcher's steel across a knife. Invisibly below, to the right, the Garbh Choire audibly epitomises its name: a rough, roaring crucible of crashing wind and water.

The ridge seems never-ending, a high-stepping stairway reaching on and on into the sky. I anticipate the summit, when it finally comes, to be rocky and pointed. A surprise, then, to emerge abruptly onto a dirty-green strand of grass broad enough to hold two waist-high shelter cairns. Somewhere in my mind a switch flicks from intense concentration to slight anti-climax: this is it, the summit of Conival, last of fifty-six Munros. Yet for all my unwillingness to savour the moment, for all my discontent at the 3000ft contour being a hillwalker's Plimsoll Line, I'm still unequivocally happy with the moment's significance. Mentally at least, it is downhill from here.

More immediately relevant is the actual route downhill, but navigational aid comes in the shape of a broad highway of yellowish gravel winding away into the gloom. I have forgotten my planned descent to Inchnadamph reverses the standard trade route up. The compass stays out nonetheless, to avoid inadvertent straying onto the ridge connecting with Ben More Assynt. Then, as slopes and path begin to fall away westward, the Silva is shoved into a pocket, to remain there for the duration.

Down a cairned scree-path through acres of boulders, down unusually steep peat to the head of Gleann Dubh, down below the cloudbase to find sky lightening, breaking, and water frothing white as burns begin to catch light. There is limestone in the glen, a lush greenness combining with the passing of the storm to dispel a headache troubling me for several hours. I cross, recross the River Traligill (*Giant's ravine:* named for a distant cousin of Bertram perhaps?), before opting for the north bank. Here a rocky gorge leads through trees to a bridge beside a Nature Conservancy Sign. A pleasant, sunlit mile - reminiscent in after-the-storm sparkle of the final mile to Moss Paul ten weeks earlier - takes me past the storybook cottage of Glenbain to a fine, half-hidden campsite at the confluence of two main burns. I'm tired - it has been another eight-hour day - but happy at having made such good progress.

215

After a huge meal, I stroll down to Inchnadamph for a chat with the bar's only other walker: Tony Wilson, a climbing instructor up from Devon on an extended wander. He plans staying out till August, so we swap stories and addresses.

Quinag, I think on waking, must be the most beautiful Scottish hill I have yet to climb. A long-limbed, many-topped, quartz-capped upsurge of gneiss rising steeply between a big freshwater loch and the seaboard complexities of Kylesku, it now shines and sparkles as though glistening with early morning dew. Having again come down to the road to admire this view - and complete a film in a futile attempt at capturing it - I stay twenty minutes or more, revelling in perfection of colour and shape: green field, deep blue loch, grey-white hill, pale blue sky. For the first time in weeks there is a twinge of the old, irrational urge to climb a hill on sight - something lying dormant in me during the tired weeks since Knoydart, and which requires a moment such as this, a moment of exceptional beauty, to be reawoken. But to spend a day on Quinag (pronunciation nearer *cognac* than *quinine*) would be to jeopardise the Saturday rendezvous with Catriona and Angus, quite apart from risking new-found momentum and "wasting" what is clearly to be a day of perfect weather - not that a fine day on Quinag could ever be considered wasted.

Examination of the map suggests another option however. I can rejoin the route by way of Glas Bheinn, a hill directly opposite and of equal height to Quinag, thus satisfying my sudden desire for views *from* the great hill by substituting the best possible views *of* it. This will require extra time and energy, so I hurry back to the tent and set about the twenty minute chore of restoring the weight of my world to my shoulders.

Climbing quickly on one of numerous local stalker's paths - the day starts and finishes on real crackers - I'm soon across the stepping stones at Loch Fleodach Coire, with its lovely hill-framed view back to Canisp. The path rakes leftward onto a wide scree col: here I dump all but camera, map and waterbottle before climbing a clattering stoneslope onto 776m Glas Bheinn.

The diversion is, as expected, well worth the extra effort. Quinag's three main tops are all lagged in light, vaporous cloud, while deeply indented sea lochs complement the hill's wildness with hazy-blue docility. Beyond, the last flick of a shower belt catches the Meall Horn-Foinaven massif: mysterious grey walls of scree hiding both the north coast and the end of my ambitions. South is of little interest: even a side-on Suilven fails to distract from new horizons.

The need to push on eventually sees me slithering back down scree in extended telemarks, then settling into a stride for the long, easy-angled ridge of Beinn Uidhe, *ford hill*. The summit comes without a break - due to the simplicity of walking along vast pavements of gneiss running longitudinally through a stone-crush of loose rock. With the whole area renowned for lack of high-top vegetation, it would be impossible to nominate the barest of all the bare northwestern hills - but this one is especially notable for numerous blocks of gneiss pitted like lumps of Tom-and-Jerry cartoon cheese. Clusters occur at regular intervals along the broad ridge, heaped into small, cairn-like mounds - at the last of which, a point named Mullach an Leathaid Riabhaich, I rejoin the watershed. My roundabout re-entry has occupied over three hours, yet I have enjoyed every minute.

Conditions are near perfect now, certainly the best since Sgurr na Ciche, possibly the best of the entire walk. A non-walker with hopes of sunbathing in the glens might demur at occasional stirrings of breeze, but here on high the absence of great heat makes the soft-edged light and fleecy, floating cumulus all the more delectable.

Hills to the south stretch in a long line, rising like an archipelago. Everything from Dearg to An Teallach, with Creag an Duine again distinct among them. Soon, though, they are gone: I drop into a section of lower, more greenly vegetated ground which occupies the rest of the afternoon: a maze of hummocks and lochans so rough as to evoke further reminders of Knoydart. There are just too many slabs to make descents easy, not quite enough to provide continuous rock-walks on ascent, yet all the while fabulous views revitalise every rest stop. Foinaven looks close - and *You don't have to climb it until Sunday* is a reassuring thought. Reassuring too are cloudcapped Ben Hope and spiky Ben Loyal: north coast hills!

Having spent a whole day inside the line of the Moine Thrust, I now cross back to gentler country for the grassy pull onto Meallan a'Chuail - although even this carries steep summit crags overlooking moorland blotched with lochans and cloud-shadows. I linger to gaze along the length of Loch Shin toward a fondly-remembered Lairg, then turn and hurry down the north ridge to a badly needed burn.

Water induces thoughts of food - I have hardly eaten in almost ten hours out - so I ignore the final 150m pull onto Meall an Fheur Loch, racing instead down elegant stalker's path curves to the birch woods and the road. Two miles of very quiet road-walking bring the isolated cottage of West Merkland, where an elderly, kind-faced woman lets me camp on a grassy promontory beside the loch. Fears of this proving desperately midgy ease with dark clouds, a steady northerly breeze and light rain. Not that I really mind either way: I'm zipped up and asleep straight after eating.

The rain unexpectedly stays on through the night and into the morning. Unexpectedly because, on noticing the clouds' approach from the last of Thursday's hills, I had been able to see, beyond, a blue cummerbund wrapped around the western horizon. Quite where this went is now about as clear as the hills themselves. At least the recent excellent progress gives enough logistical leeway for various possibilities.

Ideally, I will cross both the Meallan Liath and Meall Horn massifs today: this allows a drive back up to Loch Stack with the Tain folk, while keeping on schedule for a Monday finish. I can, on the other hand, simply stay put and rest, then add a half-day tomorrow once the others go, followed by doubling-up over Meall Horn and Foinaven come Sunday. But with all three groups of hills divided by long-distance stalker's paths linking Loch Stack with Gobernuisgach Lodge in Strath More, the prospect of escape routes makes planning a good deal more flexible. I decide to set off immediately, endure what must be endured on the morning hills, and leave thoughts of further progress until the lunch-stop at the first of these paths, the Bealach na Feithe.

Also helpful is leaving the tent where it stands, travelling light and fast. At last I'm in an area where roads run south-north rather than east-west, parallel with rather than orthogonal to the line of the watershed. But first things always come first, and breakfast is movable - tea and biscuits while pacing the road to escape midges - if hardly a feast. Then it is over flat-topped 372m Cnoc a'Choilich and down through bog-grass to the east end of Loch Eas na Maoile. Here drizzle stops as the high ridges ahead begin to come clear.

Meallan Liath Beag - second of three consecutive 300m climbs - proves dry and rocky, with the ever encouraging sight of mist rising from the slope ahead like steam off hot coals. Then comes a significant, long-awaited moment. I crest the steep, stony pull onto the Corbett-height Carn Dearg, and in so doing reach the point where north-flowing water comes into play

- ie where the watershed forks into east-north and west-north branches. I step across, back, across again, with the same childish glee which saw me do the same thing, years before, at a bridge on the Derbyshire/Nottinghamshire county boundary. Now I take things a stage further - and must confess to performing a little dance of delight on the ridge!

Significant moments are coming thick and fast. No sooner do I cross onto OS Sheet 9, last of the twenty-one maps, than the outlying top of Meall Garbh brings first sight of the north coast itself. How near the wide grey waters of Loch Eriboll look! It is with only half an eye to where I'm putting my feet that I trot down spongy slopes to the Bealach na Feithe and lunch. The other eye-and-a-half are fixed on the limitless ocean ahead.

With rain blowing in from the west, Meall Horn and its minions become a full-waterproof traipse through the lower fringe of a cloudbase. The shelving of plans to return down the stalker's path now seems a mixed blessing. Sabhal Beag is very wet both underfoot and overhead - such that despite slight improvement over Sabhal Mor and Meall Horn itself, I'm unsure whether to finish with a descent of the tricky crags of Creagan Meall Horn, or a short-cut direct to the path. Nothing ventured... and I'm soon wriggling between imposing buttresses in a less than happy re-run - or rescramble - of the Cheesecake descent. At least the path's silver snail-trail tells of easier walking to come, and I'm soon relishing its dry-shod passage beneath the southeastern flank of Arkle.

Rain off, waterproofs off, the lower reaches of the Allt Horn a sheer delight. Loch Stack reflects sun like a car bonnet, and with Ben Stack rearing beyond it is difficult to believe there to be a road squeezed along the far shore. Before reaching it, a pause in a pleasant half-mile of pinewood allows campsite possibilities to be checked out for Saturday. The best is good indeed: sheltered from any wind, with a superb tent door vista of Arkle's tilted crags and quartzite screes.

I regain tarmac at seven-thirty after nine hours away: another very long day. Later study of the entire walk reveals the biggest gaps between night-stops near the very beginning - when fresh and fit - and at the very end, when most tired. This paradox undoubtedly stems from attempts to substitute the comfort of being near a road each night for the community feeling which revived morale in Lairg. In literally going to great lengths to get down from the hills, I trade-in the short steps of normal daily sections for long, sweeping seven-league strides from west to east then back west again. Any detrimental effect this has in terms of tiredness is more than offset by its piecing together of fragmented confidence.

I need to phone Tain to confirm time and place for Saturday, so combine this with hitching down to dine at the Overscaig Hotel by Loch Shin. A huge Kinlochbervie haddock has almost to be excavated from beneath an equally enormous mound of chips.

For all the ease of the hitch to reach the hotel, there is now a hitch in the end-of-week plans. A phonecall back to base tells of Michelle's car being a doubtful starter for the long drive north. I might be forced to return alone on the minibus connecting the Cape with the Kyle of Durness ferry, then make my own way south. This isn't as disheartening as at first sounds: discovering the bus leaves at ten each morning and costs £3.50 return pleases in being so easy to ascertain. I realise just how close I now am.

I'm not at all close to the tent however, so set off into the still, half-clear evening with over seven miles of road ahead. Only three cars pass during these, not that I'm particularly bothered by the absence of lifts. The steady rhythm of striding through darkness brings an odd exhilaration. I become very aware of the simplicity, the purity of what I'm doing: pounding along with all but vital walking functions shut down for the night. It is as though walking, not resting, has become my state of equilibrium, where I'm most at peace with myself, most able to sort things in my mind. The steady beat beat beat of feet hitting tarmac provides a solid framework for thoughts - and seems, in the strangely sublime ninety minutes spent powering along beneath the snow silhouette of Ben More Assynt, all I need to survive and be happy.

The Tain folk arrive at half-eleven, although we are not to actually meet until nearer midday. This comes about through my blethering to the woman at the cottage while keeping an eye out for their distinctive orange Chevette. Hence when they drive past in a shiny black Cavalier I'm caught totally unprepared, nowhere to be seen!

Belatedly crammed into the car - now containing three adults, as many small boys (Andrew, Iain, Alasdair), a huge rucksack and a picnic - we leave the Shin basin, cross the watershed, re-enter the district of Reay. Here the weather, drizzly and midgy in the east, brightens. We park in a layby beside Loch Stack for a waterside lunch of pies and pieces. The screes and slabs of Arkle rise huge along the far shore: the Gray family backed by the greyest of hills.

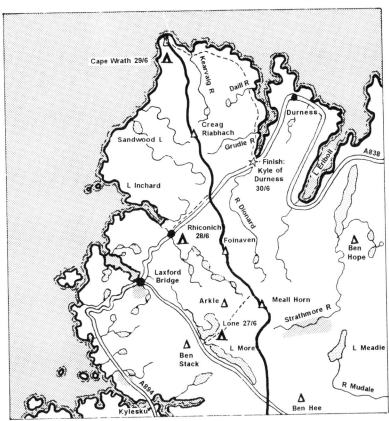

The boys throw stones into the loch. We adults chat about friends and hills. Two hours pass. Then I'm alone again, for the last time, as the others hurry back to Tain for an afternoon gala. It is disorientating to think of high summer in lowland towns. Returning home will require rehabilitation.

With unwanted clothes and maps sent back in the car, the rucksack feels lighter despite fresh stocks of food. It doesn't take long to return and pitch in yesterday's wood - entered through a narrow gap between two huge erratics. These stand sentinel, as if waiting to clash shut like the Wandering Rocks in the Argo myth.

Wind now rising, the shelter of trees is appreciated as I read through a wad of letters. One from my parents contains two fivers: handy if I do have to hitch home. There is also a block of Orkney fudge from Eildon and Ian, the Biggar suppliers: so more-ish that only by being hidden under the groundsheet is any sure to be saved for Foinaven.

Not that Foinaven is yet inked-in for tomorrow. Wind grows stronger, noisier all the while, such that on leaving the trees for a stroll to the croft-cum-barn at Lone, I'm surprised at its buffeting force. High, widening streaks of cloud scud in from the south - a direction of attack at least suggesting some hope of it staying dry. Whatever the conditions, I estimate a maximum of five hours for the crossing to Gualin - with options to repeat the travelling-light, hitch-back-round tactics of Friday.

Like a handful of pebbles thrown against a bedroom window, the wind-hurled smattering of rain wakes me with a start. This is around two a.m., and I lie awake a long time, fretting over logistical finesses. The louder the wind roars through the trees, the more I consider a lightweight charge northward.

But proximity to the end makes this dissatisfying: it seems wrong to finish in such a contrived, contorted manner. So it is with considerable relief I emerge after a further six hours' sleep to huge wind-torn gashes of blue above violently swaying conifers: apart from the early morning chuckies, the rain has stayed away. I try to recall ever before having been in such an aggressively dry gale - blissfully ignorant of this being only a loosener for the full-blown thing in two days' time.

The path, as before, is delightful: cleverly built to exploit nicks in the strata, providing a sense of enjoyment to complement food-induced fitness. I regain the pass in just over the hour. Sheltered until now from the wind's harshness, once onto the open slopes of Creag Dionard, Foinaven's southern outlier, the gale really takes hold. Again and again I stumble over boulders, unable to maintain a straight line across increasingly stony ground, the fiercest gusts forcing me down onto haunches. At least this gives ample opportunity for study of stunningly blue Loch Eriboll and clear, rock-terraced Ben Hope.

The 778m top eventually arrives, and with it the godsend of a circular shelter cairn - although this, having no non-clambering way in, takes over a minute to enter. Waiting for a pause between gusts is like waiting to ring someone's doorbell in a gap between blasted-out hi-fi songs! Once inside, wind pan-piping overhead, it is calm enough for the cagoule to be unpacked. To have done so earlier would have seen it ripped from my hands and carried halfway to Wick.

Cloud rises to reveal perhaps the most spectacular hill seen in seventy-nine days of walking. Three miles of ridge telescope into a series of pointed tops, eastern slopes carved into corries by spurs and offshoots, western flanks falling away in steep, uniform screes to lochan-filled gneiss moorland. I battle along the last broad-ridged summit, unnamed Point 806m, before things narrow and steepen dramatically as a path - itself narrow - zig-zags down to the Cadha na Beucaich, *steep-sided pass of roaring*. Although the wind appears to be slackening overall, here on the tightly-enclosed col it is at its worst. To step into the gap is to struggle across an exposed city street between two high, sheltering tenements. Crouching low, on all-fours, all I can do is avoid being forced over the lip of the corrie.

An abrupt rise taking me out of the jetstream also brings the range's finest feature: a bare, black rock tower apparently tacked onto the ridge, some 100m high. This goes by the name of Lord Reay's Seat - but may well be

the source of the more general Foinn a'Bheinn, *wart hill*. Having appeared insurmountable from a distance, an easy - albeit exceptionally steep - scree-path now leads up its western edge, showing it to be of a type with similar deceptive crags in the Lakes having the clever, punning name *Shamrock*.

Views ahead are easier to disentangle now, the coming hour's walk seen as a marvellously undulating tightrope of scree, Striding Edge to the power ten. But in terms of barrenness, of quantities of shattered rock, the obvious comparison lies in the Black Cuillin, not the Lakes. Yet even there the odd isolated patch of hardy, high-corrie vegetation survives - whereas Foinaven has scarcely anything above peat-covered moorland 500m below bar a strip of springy moss running along the very crest, thriving on erosion from walkers' boots.

The whole hill harbours an air of disintegration and decay - until at the far, northern end, on the two highest tops, Ganu Mor and Ceann Garbh, terrain changes character. Here, just beneath both cloud- and Munro-level, lifeless screes break into greenness and a long gully scythes through a cliff-face. Not that the view westward changes: still the same lochan-pocked moorland backed by line after thin line of Atlantic breakers white-foaming in to smash against a washed-up wreck of a coast.

I snap out of view-gazing for the steep northeastward descent off Ceann Garbh. This takes in an area of small crags - not for nothing is the hill named *rough head* - but everything is less fearsome than the map leads to believe.

A moorland hour brings a sandy beach at the east end of Loch Tarbhaidh - from where I stroll three road miles to Rhiconich and the first return to sea-level since Kinlochewe. A middle-aged couple bundle stacked peats into sacks in a scene unchanged since time immemorial. Rhiconich, likewise, has a timeless, almost quaint feel: hotel, police station, phone box all deserted as I pitch on kelp-covered wasteground beside Loch Inchard.

Quiet or no, the evening is one for celebration: surely nothing can stop me now. I phone John and Jools to be told of Michelle, Davy and Craig having hired a car and preparing to set off for Durness next morning.

The evening effortlessly matches my mood: wind dying away completely, a deep orange sunset lingering, thickening over the calm waters of the last west coast sea loch. The day has been one of superlatives, and the beauty of the whole walk, the seamlessness of all the past days, gives rise to a sublime peacefulness. Yet twenty-four hours will see it all over, the sense of achievement mingled with loss.

From across the road, in the bar, I hear sounds of drunken singing and accordion-playing. For all the bad times, all the moments of despair, how I have loved these past twelve weeks! Loved the walk's thin, anonymous path up through the country, loved the different places merging quietly into one another, loved how I have *lived* the walk, day and night, sun and rain, good times and bad. Loved, too, the way the walk is finishing with good weather, marvellous hills. Just as I will return again and again to my new-found-lands in the Borders, so I will long to be back in the wild country of the north, where the west's jumbled closeness meets the broad spacious-ness of the east. It is as though the watershed, having sewn together the two halves of the country, is now neatly tying-off the ends.

The great moment comes at 6.58 p.m. Scottish Watershed Time - which differs from BST in being calculated on a wildly inaccurate watch. In windless, clear-blue conditions, I stroll the last half-mile from the hillock of Dunan Mor, prop my rucksack against the whitewashed wall of the lighthouse, sit a long time on the cliff-edge simply gazing out to sea. There is no great emotion - that will come with people rather than places - just a deep sense of contentment and genuine heartfelt relief it is all over.

This lack of outward reaction is a little surprising, since it has been a day of steadily mounting excitement: the last nineteen miles counted down to single figures, then nothing. But perhaps the real crescendo came yester-day, on Foinaven's ridges, with today merely a quietly beautiful coda in a low key.

The last hills being far from spectacular is less surprising. In only a very few places does Scotland rise to great height directly from the seaboard, and this northwestern tip is no exception, containing a cluster of stony-topped moor-hills around 500m high. This, though, risks making the finale sound disappointing: it certainly wasn't. For all its lack of outstanding features, the day has been delectable, and I wouldn't have wished it any other way.

I had woken feeling in top form physically - which, together with the chance to wear T-shirt and shorts, ensured the miles came easily. A good hotel breakfast also helped: I had chatted with two women up delivering a boat from Exeter. They must have driven as far as I had walked!

But neither good food nor good conversation was ever going to delay me today. Forty-five long-striding minutes brought the top of the road, fifteen more the first of two Meall na Moines. From the last 500m hill, Farrmheall, I had looked back to the great screes of Foinaven and Cranstackie. As often during this last week, conditions were nothing like as sunny further south. I could, though, see a distant, pointed hill which I guessed to be Quinag.

Gravelly ground had led to a sharp drop and a crag needing skirted, before a dull plod onto the second Meall na Moine. Sight of the sea had long since caused loss of interest in the intricacies of the watershed, yet the last truly noteworthy river-system here reawoke some of the old curiosity. Below, to my left, the headwaters of Strath Shinary led in four miles to one of the most celebrated of all west coast lochs: Sandwood.

With a mile of east-facing crag beneath its summit, Creag Riabhach had proved the best of the day's hills as well as the logical lunch stop. An Grianan also looked good - steep and slender across Loch a'Phuill Bhuidhe - but not half so fine as the yellow-white sands and translucent waters of Faraid Head to the northeast. I had smiled to think this alone would make the journey worthwhile for my friends when they finally arrived. Certainly dunes and turquoise shallows made a finer sight than a long-bearded, weather-beaten hillwalker!

Last crag skirted, last bealach crossed, last Beinn Dearg climbed. The hills were shrinking away, smaller each time, until only the gentle rise of Cnoc a'Ghiubhais stretched ahead. Under 300m in height, this barely counted as a hill at all. I had hurried on, deep in heather, deep in thought, across the oddly named moor of Cnoc nan Tri-mile, down toward the road. This seemed a long time coming, and I had stopped awhile to watch a white minibus disappear slowly eastward. *Same time tomorrow I'll be inside looking out.* This whole area - the Moor of Parph - serves the MOD as a bombardment range, hence the absence of a vehicular ferry across the Durness Kyle. This makes the Cape suitably inaccessible - no gimcrack John o'Groats tourist shops here - but the manner of isolation is far from ideal.

There had been no more rests. The road, once reached, wound down to the dip of Clais Charnach, where shade and lack of drainage coalesced into a midges' playground - and I was wearing shorts! Arms and legs, pitted and pot-holed with bites, started resembling the poor-standard tarmac. But at least the road had led along the crest of the plateau, ensuring I finished with some of the easiest walking of all.

And so to the Cape. Any slight disappointment at being unable to descend to sea-level (known in advance) is offset by having first sight of the lighthouse hidden, like a well-concealed present, until the last possible moment. Now it is here to see and touch, lovingly, meticulously wrapped: manicured lawns, whitewashed out-buildings, tapering light-tower, HMV foghorn. Relaxation and relief outweigh any anti-climax.

After gazing out to sea - sky cloudless, the thin, hazy Long Island faintly defining the horizon - I return to the buildings and speak with the head keeper, Donald MacLeod. He says I may camp anywhere outside the

lighthouse area - which I take to its limit by pitching tight in against the only available shelter, the waist-high perimeter wall, just in case...

I fetch water to rehydrate the last of the food, then crawl inside to cook and doze. My last remaining lump of cheese has suffered in the heat of the sun - and so have I. All-day brightness having brought on a headache, I'm glad of a chance to lie down.

The nap does its work and the headache clears - unlike the western horizon, gradually thickening with cloud to produce a poorer than expected sunset. Again I sit on the cliff-edge, high above spiralling seabirds, high above the boom and crash of waves tide-surging into creeks and inlets. I lapse into a rare bout of stationary meditation (whatever deep thoughts ever come to me usually do so on the hoof), my mind drifting vaguely back over the walk: the green Borders hills, the hazy Central Belt dustbowl, the snowy corries of the first Highland bens, the hot heart of Knoydart, the grey weather of Affric, the grey screes of the north.

Oddly, memories of the early days are most vivid - as though recent sections are like a film sent away but not yet returned from the processor. There is a sense of wonder at having linked hills as diverse as Peel Fell and Foinaven, Ettrick Pen and Slat Bheinn, Ben Lomond and Beinn Leoid. I ponder, too, how the walk has changed me. Not so much in the physical sense - semi-detached toenails, bleached-brown hair and muscles bulging like bowstrings from legs are obvious, yet temporary, changes - but in the long-term psychological sense.

How will I readjust to city life? Will there still be the old desire, desperation even, to go out and climb hills? And to what extent will the walk accentuate the solitary, eccentric side of my character? These questions are, of course, unanswerable as yet. I'm content to let them lapse, to savour instead my mood of calm elation. I feel remarkably unchanged, unremarkably normal.

It is happy and relaxed I wander back to my small tent at the end of my world. What began on miserably damp moorland in early April has reached its conclusion, its fulfilment, on a distant sea-cliff at the very end of June. More than 850 miles of walking, 100,000m of ascent and an infinity of memories lie behind. I have done it. I have walked along the watershed in eighty days.

But, as the Americans say, the opera's not over till the fat lady sings. And sing she certainly does this eightieth night, singing out of the southwest in a high, soprano-pitch gale intense enough to shatter wine glasses - with force if not resonance - were such things to exist at the Cape. After the Foinaven crescendo and the Parph hills coda, today proves an unexpected, if marvellously appropriate, encore: an aria at the top end of the scale, weather returning frontstage to show off the extent of its range.

Just after eight a particularly ferocious blast rips the tent apart. There is a hideous tearing sound, poles sag sideways, a sky view opens overhead. For a moment I simply lie there and laugh. Again and again during the past twelve weeks the weather seems to have tailored itself to my needs precisely - if "tailored" is apposite in a situation of tearing fabric - but this is a ridiculously symbolic denouement. The trusty old tent, basis of my survival, succumbs to the very thing from which it has given protection at exactly the moment when no longer needed. Any sooner and the walk would have foundered. Any later and I would have been in trouble on some future expedition. Perfect timing.

There will be ample time for contemplating the mysteries of synchronicity later, though. For now, the need is to avoid being blown into the Atlantic. I think of letting the tent go that way - of watching it sail, wind-torn, to be shredded against the cliffs - until, unable to bear the thought of losing it, I bundle the remains into the rucksack.

Plans for the long-awaited reunion have also been ripped apart. I know, as I battle my way across to the old lookout station, there will be no ferry, no minibus today. Anything higher-sided than a Porsche would stand little chance of remaining upright on the road, and Porsche don't manufacture minibuses, nor could the Keodale ferryman afford one if they did. I hold onto vain hope all the same, deciding to stay until midday: by then the bus will be an hour overdue.

At least shelter can be found just now. The lookout is a ruin - hanging plaster, rubble-covered floors and glassless, broken-framed windows - but I find a corner free from the whirlwind eddying. Occasionally I brace myself to stand beside a window giving views of the approach road, but there is no real hope of seeing anything other than clouds hurtling toward me, speeded up, as in the time-lapse meteorological sequences beloved of wildlife programmes. At eleven I decide to head back to the lighthouse in preparation for leaving: with supplies down to one tea bag, I need to scrounge food off the keepers.

This is annoyingly difficult to achieve, all the men apart from the head keeper apparently having taken vows of silence in keeping with their monastic lifestyle. Even Mr MacLeod, the Eddisonian abbot, seems cautious about helping. Not that I have any real cause for complaint: lighthouse-keeping must nurture reticence, the more so in a place where an irregular straggle of long-distance walkers come begging for food and water. Besides, Mr MacLeod takes the vital photograph confirming my arrival with a hand so steady as to belie the conditions. Were it not for my screwed-up face, there could almost be no wind.

But the wind is there all right, screaming out of the southwest, dry apart from a couple of showers drenching like buckets of thrown water - yet making up for dryness in terms of ferocity. I'm seeing Cape Wrath at its wildest, its most wrathful - and, as *The Northern Times* later reports, "showing real fury".

By twelve I'm already battling, head-down, out along the road, inland from the headland. I realise if I don't cover the ground quickly, my friends may have to drive south without me: Davy, for one, I know to be working early next morning. But hurrying is impossible: Sunday's storm having found its second wind, all I can do is stagger in exaggerated drunkenness along the narrow strip of tarmac. There is no gusting, just a steady jetstream chopping at the back of knees, forcing me into roadside bogs.

The first mile is the worst: moorland gives no shelter from Atlantic blast. From here I make slightly more linearly sober progress. On first realising the need to walk, rather than be driven, out of the storm, I had been slightly peeved about the need to crank-up mind and legs again after effectively shutting them down the previous evening. Now, for one last time, energy surges back - as into a fading torch shining brightly, if briefly, after having been switched off to recharge overnight. Revitalising too is the knowledge it doesn't matter how tired I feel come evening. I might be done-in, but I will also be done.

As the road enters the military danger area, signs warn of potentially lethal objects flying through the air or lying on the ground. All the buildings from the Kearvaig River to the kyleside cottages of Daill and Achiemore are derelict, boarded with steel plates, adding to the day's general animosity. Inspired, perhaps, by all this militaria, I organise my route-march on an old army principle: five minutes off every hour, on the hour. This eventually takes me over the peninsula's own mini-watershed, from where I first see the yellow sand-flats and turquoise waters of the Kyle of Durness, the village itself dotted in white squares across the hillside beyond.

Another mile brings the ferry cottage at the road-end, where a man standing looking through binoculars almost falls over in surprise when the object of his scanning speaks from right beneath his eyes! As expected, Michelle and the others have phoned the lighthouse, then here, on realising the ferry to be off. They are waiting at Grudie Bridge in Strath Dionard, the point where I will first meet the public road - but can hang on only until half-four at the latest.

It is presently just after three - I have covered ten miles quicker than hoped - so the offer of coffee and an apple is speedily accepted. These kind folk are in-laws of the genuine boat-people: away on holiday.

After being given directions as to the best route along the now trackless shore, I head out into the gale for the final three miles. Has anyone ever wished so fervently for, and cursed so vehemently the lack of, a bridge across the kyle as I do now? There is, though, nothing for it but to batter along the hummocky flank of Beinn an Amair. The wind, having slackened a little in the leeward mile before the cottage, gives full vent to its violence. Several times I'm toppled, thrown against the slope, and it is a relief to improvise a handrail from a wire fence.

The gale has greater force than anything I have ever known. For all my wonder at its power - I had been similarly in awe of the Kinloch Hourn rain - I never want to see its like again. The only mitigating circumstances both stem from the absence of water: the wind is, mercifully, a dry wind, while I'm able to cut across the head of the kyle due to the tide being out.

This said, fusionless sand combines with wind to make the crossing more cakewalk than piece of cake. I'm aware of walking at twenty-or-so degrees off the vertical, and of this feeling perfectly stable!

Just after four, I reach a grassy promontory holding the sanctuary of the Grudie Land Rover track. There, ahead, is the road, and a few minutes more brings sight of a car in a layby. At first I'm not sure - there is no sign of Michelle, Davy or Craig - then three figures emerge and I'm hurrying, waving to the first glimpse of friends. They wave back.

I'm running now, running past the ruins of a broch, down across a plank bridge to the road, running toward the welcome of shouts and a tune played on a mandolin, running from weeks of tiredness, elations, frustrations, running from the disorientation of a world alternately tent-sized and sky-wide. Running from the narrow tunnel of ambition into the spacious hall of a high summer holiday, running from an unsteady, ever-changing world to one filled with familiarity. Running from a world of places to one of people, running from a means to an end.

Running home.

Watershed hills / index

Hills in italics lie on the watershed, but were omitted for reasons detailed in the excuse list on p239. Various non-watershed hills climbed are given in a separate table. Total numbers of Munros etc *strictly on the watershed* are as follows: Munros (Mu) 45, Corbetts (C) 25, Donalds (D) 14, Marilyns (Ma) 105. Heights such as c530 indicate estimates to the nearest contour.

Hill	Metres	Type	Grid ref	OS map	Page(s)
Larriston Fells	512	Ma	NY569921	80	24
Peel Fell	602	Ma	NY626997	80	26
Hartshorn Pike	545		NT626015	80	26-27
Wigg Knowe	491		NT575041	80	27
Fanna Hill	514		NT569032	80	27
Leap Hill	471		NT514014	79	28
Greatmoor Hill	599	Ma	NT489007	79	28
Cauldcleuch Head	619	MaD	NT458008	79	28
Tudhope Hill	599		NY431991	79	29
¹ *Carlin Tooth*	511		NY419989	79	29
¹ *Dod Hill*	494		NT409001	79	29
Comb Hill	514		NT395004	79	30
Wisp Hill	595	Ma	NY386993	79	30
Pikethaw Hill	564	Ma	NY369978	79	30-31
White Hope Edge	475		NY337979	79	31
² *Black Burn Head*	471		NY331990	79	33
² *Stock Hill*	477		NY322030	79	33
² *Craik Cross Hill*	451		NT303048	79	33
² *Black Knowe*	451		NT287078	79	33
² *Quickningair Hill*	488		NT271074	79	33
Cross Hill	442		NT253080	79	33
² *Bloodhope Head*	c530		NT225098	79	33
Ettrick Pen	692	MaD	NT199077	79	33-34
Hopetoun Craig	632		NT188068	79	34
Wind Fell	665	D	NT179061	79	34

—————————— Ettrick Head ——————————

Hill	Metres	Type	Grid ref	OS map	Page(s)
Capel Fell	678	MaD	NT164069	79	35
Bodesbeck Law	662	D	NT169103	79	35
Bell Craig	624	D	NT187129	79	35
Andrewhinney Hill	677	MaD	NT198139	79	35
Herman Law	614	D	NT214157	79	35
Watch Knowe	606		NT184160	79	36
Lochcraig Head	800	D	NT167176	79	38
Firthybrig Head	763		NT158172	79	38
Raven Craig	685		NT141140	78	38
Hart Fell	808	MaCD	NT114136	78	39
Whitehope Heights	637	D	NT095139	78	39
Chalk Rig Edge	499		NT076135	78	39
Great Hill	466		NT068132	78	39
Annanhead Hill	478		NT058132	78	39
Flecket Hill	463		NT049138	78	39
Clyde Law	546		NT027170	78	42
Black Dod	547		NT032197	78	42
Whitecamp Brae	545		NT040213	72	42

Hill	Metres	Type	Grid ref	OS map	Page(s)
Coomb Dod	635		NT046238	72	42
Hillshaw Head	653	D	NT048246	72	42
Glenwhappen Rig	688	MaD	NT059257	72	43
Culter Fell	748	MaD	NT053291	72	43
Scawdmans Hill	573		NT054320	72	43-44
White Hill	399		NT055338	72	45
Goseland Hill	435	Ma	NT071351	72	45

────────── *Southern Upland Fault* ──────────

Hill	Metres	Type	Grid ref	OS map	Page(s)
Gallow Law	355		NT083402	72	46
[3] Broomy Law	426	Ma	NT085429	72	46
Black Mount	516	Ma	NT080459	72	46
Mendick Hill	451	Ma	NT121505	72/65	48
North Muir	358		NT104511	72/65	48
Catstone	448		NT097527	72/65	48
Fadden	465		NT097539	72/65	48
Craigengar	518		NT090551	72/65	48
Henshaw Hill	417		NT061545	72/65	48
[4] Hendry's Corse	c360		NS973578	72/65	49
[4] Leven Seat	356		NS946576	72/65	53
[4] Hare Hill	314		NS910537	72/65	53
[4] Auchterhead Muir	290		NS893553	72/65	53
[4] Cant Hills	301		NS852619	65	53
[3] Duntilland Hill	290		NS832640	65	53
[3] Black Hill	285		NS828650	65	53
Stanrigg	219		NS799690	64	55
Palacerigg	171		NS786732	64	55-58
[5] Unnamed Point	156		NS754761	64	59

────────── *Forth and Clyde Canal* ──────────

Hill	Metres	Type	Grid ref	OS map	Page(s)
Cowden Hill	c140		NS768802	64	59
Tomtain	453		NS721814	64	60
Garrel Hill	458		NS704811	64	60
Black Hill	c460		NS672811	64	60
Lecket Hill	546		NS644812	64	60
Holehead	551		NS617826	64/57	61
Dungoil	426		NS634845	64/57	61
Gartcarron Hill	321		NS651847	64/57	61-62
Cairnoch Hill	413		NS697857	57	63-64
Hart Hill	436		NS696883	57	64
Carleatheran	485	Ma	NS687918	57	64
Stronend	511	Ma	NS629895	57	64-65
Buchlyvie Muir	175		NS580916	57	66
[3] Bat a'Charchel	229		NS495923	57	68
Green Hill	271		NS483928	57	70

────────── *Highland Boundary Fault* ──────────

Hill	Metres	Type	Grid ref	OS map	Page(s)
Gualann	461		NS458944	57	70
Binnean nan Gobhar	586	Ma	NS419968	56	70-71
[6] Beinn Uird	597	Ma	NS339985	56	72
Ben Lomond	974	MaMu	NN367029	56	76-80
Cruinn a'Bheinn	633	Ma	NN365052	56	80
Cruachan	537		NN351077	56	80
Maol a'Chapuill	513		NN366077	56	80

Hill	Metres	Type	Grid ref	OS map	Page(s)
Beinn Uamha	598	Ma	NN386069	56	80-81
Maol Mor	686		NN380116	56/50	83
Beinn a'Choin	770	MaC	NN354130	56/50	83
Stob nan Eighrach	613		NN343144	56/50	83
Ben Ducteach	589		NN347154	56/50	83
Parlan Hill	663		NN353170	56/50	83
Beinn Chabhair	933	MaMu	NN367179	56/50	84-85
An Caisteal, S Top	c910		NN379190	56/50	85
Beinn a'Chroin, W Top	938		NN386185	56/50	85
Beinn a'Chroin	940	Mu	NN394186	56/50	85
[7] Stob Glas	815		NN404200	56/50	85
Cruach Ardrain	1046	MaMu	NN409211	56/51	85-86
Craw Knowe	464		NN355241	50	87
Creagan Soilleir	646		NN340253	50	87
Cruachan Cruinn	586		NN325234	50	87
Beinn Dubhchraig	978	MaMu	NN308255	50	87-88
Ben Oss	1029	MaMu	NN287253	50	88
Beinn Laoigh	1130	MaMu	NN266263	50	88-89
Beinn Chuirn	880	MaC	NN281292	50	90
Meall Odhar	656	Ma	NN298298	50	90
Sron nan Colan	590		NN312302	50	90
Beinn Bheag	655		NN316325	50	91
Beinn Odhar	901	MaC	NN338338	50	93
Beinn Chaorach	818	MaC	NN359328	50	93-94
Cam Chreag	884	MaC	NN375346	50	94
Beinn a'Chaisteil	886	MaC	NN348364	50	94
Beinn nam Fuaran	806	MaC	NN361382	50	94
Beinn Mhanach	953	MaMu	NN373412	50	96
Beinn a'Chuirn	923		NN360409	50	96-100
Beinn Achaladair	1038	MaMu	NN344432	50	101-102
Beinn a'Chreachain	1081	MaMu	NN373441	50	102
[8] Guala Mhor	798		NN403458	51	103
[8] Meall na Feith' Faide	c830		NN413454	51	103
[8] Meall Buidhe	910	MaC	NN426449	51	103
[8] Meall a'Ghortain	502		NN378492	50	103
[8] Glas Bheinn	501	Ma	NN327473	50	103
Meall Mor	492	Ma	NN304471	50	106
[9] Meall Beag	475		NN295475	50	106
Beinn Toaig	834		NN262455	50	106
Stob a'Choire Odhair	947	MaMu	NN257460	50	107
Stob Ghabhar	1090	MaMu	NN230455	50	107
Clach Leathad	1098		NN240493	50	107
Meall a'Bhuiridh	1108	MaMu	NN251503	41	107
Meall nan Ruadhag	646		NN298577	41	109
Stob na Cruaiche	739	Ma	NN363571	41	110
Meall Liath na Doire	c580		NN400585	41	110
Carn Dearg	941	MaMu	NN418661	42	112
Sgor Gaibhre	955	MaMu	NN444674	42	112
Sgor Choinnich	929		NN443683	42	112
Meall a'Bhealaich	865		NN453695	42	112
Beinn a'Chumhainn	901		NN462710	42	112
Ben Alder	1148	MaMu	NN496718	42	114-116
Sron Coire na h-Iolaire	955		NN513704	42	117
Beinn Bheoil	1019	MaMu	NN517717	42	117

Hill	Metres	Type	Grid ref	OS map	Page(s)
[9] Meall Mor	527		NN539765	42	118
[9] Meall Beag	516		NN555779	42	118
Meall Leac na Sguabaich	850		NN570809	42	118-119
Beinn Eilde	674		NN564851	42	119
Creag Ruadh	622	Ma	NN558914	35	121
Meall Ghoirleig	526		NN515907	35	121
Stob Coire Dhuibh	916		NN496917	34	121
Carn Liath	1006	Mu	NN472903	34	122
Stob Poite Coire Ardair, E Top	1050		NN437892	34	122
Meall Ptarmigan	815		NN426903	34	122
Creag a'Bhanain	849		NN432911	34	122
Creag a'Chail	760		NN403959	34	123
Carn Leac	884		NN407977	34	123
Poll-gormack Hill	806		NN391980	34	123
Leac nan Uan	693		NN372966	34	123
Carn Dearg	817	MaC	NN349967	34	123
Carn na Larach	745		NN334965	34	124
Beinn Bhan	712		NN326966	34	124

——————————— *Great Glen* ———————————

Hill	Metres	Type	Grid ref	OS map	Page(s)
Ben Tee	904	MaC	NN241972	34	127-128
Meall a'Choire Ghlais	900		NN220957	34	128
Sron a'Choire Ghairbh	937	MaMu	NN222945	34	128
Meall an Tagraidh	761		NN195940	34	133
Meall na h-Eilde	838	MaC	NN185946	34	133-134
Meall Coire nan Saobhaidh	826		NN175951	34	134
Geal Charn	804	MaC	NN156943	34	134
Carn Dubh	604		NN140945	34	134
Sgurr Choinich	749	Ma	NN128949	34	134-135
Meall Lochan nan Dubh Lochan	567		NN088945	33	135
Meall Blair	656	Ma	NN077951	33	135
Mam an Doire Dhuinn	564		NN043956	33	135
Sgurr Mhurlagain	880	MaC	NN012945	33	135-136
Fraoch Bheinn	858	MaC	NM986941	40/33	137-138
Druim a'Chuirn	815		NM962950	40/33	138
Sgurr Cos na Breachd-laoidh	835	MaC	NM948946	40/33	138
An Eag	873		NM943959	40/33	138-140
Sgurr nan Coireachan	953	MaMu	NM933958	40/33	140
Garbh Chioch Bheag	968		NM918959	40/33	141
Garbh Chioch Mhor	1013	MaMu	NM909961	40/33	141
Sgurr na Ciche	1040	MaMu	NM902966	40/33	141-143
Meall a'Choire Dhuibh	740		NM919981	40/33	143
Sgurr Airigh na Beinne	776		NG924007	33	144
Sgurr a'Choire-bheithe, E Top	c860		NG900013	33	144-145
Slat Bheinn	700	Ma	NG910028	33	145
Sgurr a'Chlaidheimh, NW Top	c830		NG942035	33	146-147
Sgurr a'Chlaidheimh	841		NG952031	33	146-147
Sgurr a'Mhaoraich	1027	MaMu	NG984065	33	150-152
Sgurr Thionail	906		NG985089	33	152
Sgurr a'Bhac Chaolais	885	MaC	NG958110	33	152-153
Creag nan Damh	918	MaMu	NG983112	33	155
Sgurr Beag	896		NG997110	33	155
Sgurr an Lochain	1004	Mu	NH005104	33	155

Hill	Metres	Type	Grid ref	OS map	Page(s)
Sgurr an Doire Leathain	1010	MaMu	NH015099	33	156
Sgurr Coire na Feinne	902		NH027093	33	156
Sgurr a'Bhealaich Dheirg	1036	MaMu	NH035143	33	157-158
Sgurr a'Dubh Doire	963		NH035185	33	158-159
Beinn Fhada	1032	MaMu	NH018192	33	158-159
Sgurr Gaorsaic	839	MaC	NH036219	33/25	170
Beinn an t-Socaich	910		NH051218	33/25	170
Sgurr nan Ceathreamhnan, W Top	1143		NH057228	33/25	170-171
Stuc Bheag	1075		NH053237	33/25	171
Stuc Mor	1041		NH054243	33/25	171
Creag Ghlas	856		NH046264	33/25	171
Sgurr na h-Eige	657		NH052276	33/25	171
Carn na Breabaig	678	Ma	NH067301	25	172
An Socach	1069	MaMu	NH100332	25	172-173
An Cruachan	706	Ma	NH094359	25	173
Beinn Dronaig	797	MaC	NH037382	25	174
Sail Riabhach	771		NH037405	25	174-175
Bidein a'Choire Sheasgaich	945	MaMu	NH049412	25	174-175
Beinn Tharsuinn, W Top	795		NH043430	25	175-176
Beinn Tharsuinn	863	MaC	NH055433	25	176
Sgurr Choinnich	999	Mu	NH076446	25	177
Sgurr a'Chaorachain	1053	MaMu	NH087447	25	177
Sgurr nan Ceannaichean	915	MaMu	NH087480	25	178
Moruisg	928	MaMu	NH101499	25	178

─────────── *Glen Carron / Strath Bran* ───────────

Hill	Metres	Type	Grid ref	OS map	Page(s)
Carn Beag	550		NH108555	25	179-180
Beinn na Feusaige	625	Ma	NH093543	25	180
Meallan Mhic Iamhair	499		NH068543	25	180
NE ridge of Carn Breac	c600		NH052539	25	180
Carn Loisgte	446		NH035577	25	180
Bidein Clann Raonaild	466	Ma	NH054593	25	180-181
Carn a'Ghlinne	539		NH067608	19	188
Carn na Garbh Lice	517		NH088609	19	188
An Cabar	537		NH108604	19	188
Meall a'Chaorainn	705	Ma	NH136604	19	188
Fionn Bheinn	933	MaMu	NH147621	20	188-189
Beinn nan Ramh	711	Ma	NH139662	19	190
¹ An Carnan	446		NH108675	19	190
¹ Mointeach Leacaidh	422		NH093675	19	190
Groban	749	Ma	NH099709	19	190
Meallan Chuaich, N Top	697		NH116697	19	191
A'Chailleach	999	MaMu	NH136714	19	193
Toman Coinich	935		NH148714	20	194
Sgurr Breac	1000	MaMu	NH158711	20	194
Sgurr nan Clach Geala	1093	MaMu	NH184715	20	195
Carn na Criche	961		NH196725	20	196
Sgurr Mor	1110	MaMu	NH203718	20	196
Beinn Liath Mhor Fannaich	954	Mu	NH219724	20	196
Beinn Liath Bheag	665		NH243736	20	196
Meall Feith Dhiongaig	c530		NH261771	20	198
Beinn Enaiglair	889	MaC	NH225805	20	198

Hill	Metres	Type	Grid ref	OS map	Page(s)
Iorguill	872		NH239816	20	198
Beinn Dearg	1084	MaMu	NH259812	20	198
Meall nan Ceapraichean	977	Mu	NH257825	20	199
Eididh nan Clach Geala	928	MaMu	NH257842	20	199
Toman Coinich	862		NH272844	20	201
Meall a'Choire Ghlais	804		NH273859	20	201
Seana Bhraigh, SE Top	906		NH288872	20	201
Seana Bhraigh	927	MaMu	NH281878	20	201-202
Creag Dhubh	592		NH264892	20	202
Meall nam Bradhan	677		NH267903	20	202
[9] Mullach a'Bhrian Leitir	406		NH273930	20	202
Creag Ruadh	396		NH241944	20	203-204
Creag Ghrianach	410		NH229948	20	204
Meall Liath Choire	548	Ma	NH227962	20	204
Meall an Eich Ghlais	463		NH208971	20	204
Beinn Donuill	448		NH190981	20	204
Cnoc a'Choilich	415		NH180996	20	204
Na Dromannan	408		NC205010	15	204
Meall a'Bhuirich Rapaig	474		NC255026	15	205
Meall a'Chaoruinn	454		NC263043	15	205
Meall nan Imrichean	298		NC260069	15	205
Cnoc na Glas Choille	307		NC276081	15	205
[9] Cnoc Chaornaidh	285		NC307084	15	213
Unnamed Point	358		NC291108	15	213
Ruighe Chnoc	368		NC288125	15	213
Meall a'Bhraghaid	688		NC298142	15	213-214
Breabag, Creag Liath	815	MaC	NC287158	15	214
Breabag Tarsuinn	718		NC292180	15	214
Conival	987	Mu	NC303199	15	215
[10] Beinn an Fhurain	860		NC303215	15	217
Mullach an Leathaid Riabhaich	720		NC294246	15	217
A'Chailleach	431		NC295266	15	217
Unnamed Point	486		NC301269	15	217
Beinn Leoid	792	MaC	NC320295	15	217
Meallan a'Chuail	750	Ma	NC345293	15	217
[9] Meall an Fheur Loch	613	Ma	NC362310	16	217
Cnoc a'Choilich	372		NC375343	16	218
Meallan Liath Beag	567		NC368374	16	218
Unnamed Point	741		NC364389	16	219
Meallan Liath Coire Mhic Dhughaill, NE Top	761		NC361398	16	219
Meall Garbh	752		NC369403	9	219
Sabhal Beag	732	Ma	NC373429	9	219
Sabhal Mor	703		NC360440	9	219
Meall Horn	777	MaC	NC353449	9	219
Creagan Meall Horn	729		NC345457	9	219
Creag Dionard	778		NC339483	9	222-223
Foinaven, Unnamed Point	806		NC325487	9	223
Foinaven, Unnamed Point	867		NC319495	9	223-224
Foinaven, Ganu Mor	914	MaC	NC315507	9	224
Foinaven, Ceann Garbh	901		NC313515	9	224
Cnoc a'Mhadaidh	589		NC325525	9	224
Meall na Moine	316		NC293567	9	225

Hill	Metres	Type	Grid ref	OS map	Page(s)
Farrmheall	521	Ma	NC308588	9	225
Meall na Moine	464		NC284620	9	226
Creag Riabhach	485	Ma	NC279638	9	226
Beinn Dearg	423		NC279658	9	226
Cnoc an Daimh	270		NC271689	9	226
Cnoc a'Ghiubhais	297		NC266701	9	226
Cnoc nan Tri-mile	c130		NC276713	9	226
Dunan Mor	163		NC261740	9	226

—————————————— Cape Wrath ——————————————

Excuses:

1 Diversion for water

2 Forestry

3 Farmland

4 Old mineworkings

5 Took direct line through Cumbernauld

6 Missed summit - poor navigation

7 Diverted slightly to avoid crags

8 Omitted following fall on Beinn a'Chuirn

9 Small hill omitted at start / finish of big day

10 Diverted to spend night at Inchnadamph

The following summits were also visited, either as off-route additions or because the watershed passed very close by. Additional ascents were also made of Ben Lomond (NN367029 - OS56) and An Eag (NM943959 - OS40/33).

Hill	Metres	Type	Grid ref	OS map	Page(s)
Dod Fell	463		NY327968	79	31
White Coomb	822	MaCD	NT163151	79	38
Cardon Hill	676		NT065315	72	44
Chapelgill Hill	696	D	NT068304	72	44
An Caisteal	995	MaMu	NN379193	56/50	85
Beinn Tulaichean	946	Mu	NN416196	56/51	85
Fiarach	652	Ma	NN345262	50	87
Creise	1100	MaMu	NN238507	41	107
Stob Poite Coire Ardair	1054	Mu	NN429888	34	122
Gleouraich	1035	MaMu	NH039054	33	131
Spidean Mialach	996	MaMu	NH066043	33	131
Sgurr Beag	890		NM959971	40/33	139
Sgurr Mor	1003	MaMu	NM965980	40/33	139
Sgurr an Fhuarain	901	MaC	NM987980	40/33	139
Sgurr a'Choire-bheithe	913	MaC	NG895015	33	144-145
Sgurr nan Eugallt	894	MaC	NG931045	33	146
Sgurr a'Chuilinn	c750		NG982121	33	155
Maol Chinn-dearg	981	Mu	NH032088	33	156
Sgurr Mhic Bharraich	781	MaC	NG917174	33	164-165
Sgurr nan Ceathreamhnan	1151	MaMu	NH057228	33/25	170-171
Carn Breac	678	Ma	NH045530	25	180
Creag Rainich	807	MaC	NH097751	19	192
Sgurr nan Each	923	Mu	NH184697	20	195
Meall Glac an Ruighe	859		NH265862	20	199-200
Glas Bheinn	776	MaC	NC255265	15	216-217
Beinn Uidhe	740		NC281251	15	217
Carn Dearg	796		NC377389	16	218
Meallan Liath Coire Mhic Dhughaill	801	MaC	NC357392	15	219

CAPE WRATH

slowly

MUNRO'S RETURN

reel time

Cape Wrath by Rachel Smillie ·· Munro's Return by Craig Smillie   © 1987